Outcome-Based Evaluation

Outcome-Based Evaluation

Robert L. Schalock
Hastings College
Hastings, Nebraska

Plenum Press • New York and London

361.0068
S298o
1995

Library of Congress Cataloging-in-Publication Data

Schalock, Robert L.
    Outcome-based evaluation / Robert L. Schalock.
        p.   cm.
    Includes bibliographical references and index.
    ISBN 0-306-45051-8
    1. Human services--Evaluation--Methodology.   2. Evaluation
research (Social action programs)   3. Present value analysis.
I. Title.
HV11.S36   1995
361'.0068--dc20   95-33352
                                                            CIP

ISBN 0-306-45051-8

© 1995 Plenum Press, New York
A Division of Plenum Publishing Corporation
233 Spring Street, New York, N. Y. 10013

10 9 8 7 6 5 4 3 2

Printed in the United States of America

To my students, program adminisitrator friends, colleagues, and my wife Susan, who have been receptive and supportive of my ideas and efforts throughout my career.

My thanks also to Sharon Enga and Lori Christy for their expert technical assistance provided to me in writing this book.

Preface

This book is the product of 30 years of experience with program evaluation. During this time, both service recipients and educational and social programs have experienced major cultural and political shifts in service delivery philosophy, including a focus on quality, mainstreaming, deinstitutionalization, community inclusion, and an emphasis on measurable outcomes. Recently stakeholders of these programs have demanded more than just the provision of service, forcing program administrators to evaluate their programs' effectiveness and efficiency. The "era of accountability" is here, and my major goal in writing this book is to help current and future program administrators understand that they need to look beyond simply the provision of service. Indeed, they need to be competent in *outcome-based evaluation*, which I define as a type of program evaluation that uses valued and objective person-referenced outcomes to analyze a program's effectiveness, impact or benefit–cost.

By design, this book can be read from the perspective of a consumer or producer of outcome-based evaluation. As a consumer, the reader will be introduced to the various techniques used in outcome-based evaluation and how to interpret data from outcome-based evaluation analyses. As a producer, the reader will be instructed in how to do outcome-based evaluation analyses, along with how to use and act on their results. For both the consumer and producer, two questions should guide the use of outcome-based evaluation. For what purpose will I use the outcome-based evaluation data? What information will I need for the intended use? Numerous examples of outcome-based evaluations that reflect answers to these two questions will be provided throughout the text.

The reader will encounter a number of key terms throughout the text. Chief among these are the following:

- Valued, person-referenced outcomes that reflect both the results of the intervention provided and an enhanced quality of life for the service recipient.

- Performance-based assessment that involves using objective indicators to evaluate a person's adaptive behavior level and role status.
- Outcome-based analyses that include effectiveness, impact, or benefit–cost. These analyses are used respectively to determine whether the program is meeting its goals, whether the program makes a significant difference, or whether the program represents a reasonable return on investment.
- Data-based management systems that are used to provide the information necessary for both outcome-based analysis and formative feedback that can be used by program administrators to increase their programs' effectiveness and efficiency.

I have attempted to make the book as "user friendly" as possible. I realize that most of the readers are neither program evaluators nor statisticians. As a teacher and program evaluator for these 30 years, I have discovered that outcome-based evaluation requires primarily logical thinking and being clear in the questions asked. Once one knows where he/she is going and the basic road map to get there, then the journey is much easier. Thus, I have attempted throughout the text to provide the reader with easily read and followed tables, graphs, and exhibits that should facilitate both our tasks. For those readers who like to count and keep track, there are 16 figures, 33 tables, 34 exhibits, and 20 guiding principles that summarize key points. For those readers who want to go into greater detail, I have provided study questions and a list of additional readings for each chapter.

Whether the book is read from cover to cover or by topical area, my goal has been to make your journey easier by stressing the critical need for thinking clearly and asking specific questions that can then be answered via one or more of the outcome-based evaluation analytic techniques discussed in the text's 13 chapters. The book is divided into five sections, beginning with an overview and concluding with the future of outcome-based evaluation.

Working with program administrators for the last 30 years has made me sensitive to the challenging job they face. Their task is probably best exemplified in a recent book by Hammer and Champy (1993) entitled, *Reengineering the Corporation: A Manifesto for Business Revolution*. In the book, the authors discuss the "three Cs" of current service delivery: consumers, competition, and change. Consumers are asking more from education and social programs; fiscal restraints are forging new, competitive service delivery mechanisms; and change is constant. Thus, any program evaluation effort must be designed and implemented within the current zeitgeist that demands accountability within the context of the "three Cs."

My hope and anticipation is that this text will assist present and future program administrators to understand and use outcome-based evaluation to demonstrate their programs' effectiveness, impact, or benefit–cost. If this is the case, the journey has been both beneficial and rewarding.

Contents

I. AN OVERVIEW OF OUTCOME-BASED EVALUATION

II. OUTCOME-BASED EVALUATION ANALYSES

III. OUTCOME-BASED EVALUATION DATA

IV. REPORTING AND ACTING
ON OUTCOME-BASED EVALUATION RESULTS

Outcome-Based Evaluation

I

An Overview of Outcome-Based Evaluation

*If you don't know where you are going,
you will wind up somewhere else.*
YOGI BERRA

My wife has an excellent corollary to this quotation: "And you might not go anywhere." As a teacher and program evaluator, I do not want either of these scenarios to be true of the readers of this book. Whether you are a consumer or a producer of evaluation, it is essential to know where you are going as you either read about or do outcome-based evaluation (OBE), and that is the purpose of the first part of this text.

Chapter 1 introduces you to the "Whats" and "Whys" of OBE and discusses a number of interrogatories that are essential to understanding OBE: its definition, performance-based assessment, the selection of person-referenced outcomes, the uses of OBE data, and an OBE model that will guide our odyssey. The chapter also discusses a number of reasons why an outcome-based approach to program evaluation is the better way to address the major current trends impacting educational and social programs: the quality revolution with its emphasis on quality-of-life outcomes; consumer empowerment; increasing accountability demands; and the emerging supports and pragmatic program evaluation paradigms that are challenging us to look differently at the way we think about and do program evaluation.

Chapter 2 addresses an issue that I am sure you are already thinking about: "Where do I begin and how do I proceed?" In this chapter I answer that question by suggesting that you (1) develop the program's mission and goals statement; (2) provide interventions or services that are consistent with your mission and goals; (3) select and measure valued, person-referenced outcomes; and (4) implement a data management system. Probably the most important part of Chapter 2 centers on a number of valued, person-referenced outcomes that meet five criteria: outcomes valued by

1

the person, approach is multidimensional, data are objective and measurable, outcome is connected logically to one's program or services, and outcome may be evaluated longitudinally.

Throughout these two chapters the reader will want to keep the definition of *outcome-based evaluation* clearly in mind: *Outcome based evaluation is a type of program evaluation that uses valued and objective person-referenced outcomes to analyze a program's effectiveness, impact, or benefit–cost.*

1

The Whats and Whys of Outcome-Based Evaluation

Overview

Welcome to the 1990s! In case you haven't noticed, things have changed significantly in the world of service delivery and program evaluation over the last few years. The term that is used most frequently to reflect this change is *paradigm*, which refers to how we approach or think about something. Indeed, both human service programs and the techniques we use to evaluate their efforts and outcomes are currently undergoing a "paradigm

3

shift" characterized by terms such as *empowerment, equity, supports, inclusion, accountability,* and *pragmatic evaluation.* This paradigm shift, occurring at the same time that we are seeing an increased competition among service providers and constant social–cultural change, has resulted in new ways of thinking about program evaluation and the techniques we use to evaluate a program's effectiveness, impact, or benefit–cost.

My major purpose in writing this book is to familiarize you with this changed thinking, and to acquaint you with the rapidly emerging outcome approach to program evaluation. My goal is to make you a more knowledgeable and effective evaluation consumer and producer. As a consumer of program evaluation, you need to understand what OBE is, along with its proper use. As a producer of OBE, you need to know how to use its techniques so that you are accurate, credible, and communicative.

Our odyssey begins by discussing what program evaluation is, and why it is necessary in today's world to focus more on measurable, person-referenced outcomes. By the end of the chapter, you will know what OBE is and why it is emerging rapidly as an essential approach to program evaluation. Along the way, we will compare outcome-based evaluation with other conceptual approaches to evaluation. Additionally, I will introduce two models that will guide our work throughout the text. The first is a model of outcome-based evaluation that shows the relation among a program's mission, processes, outcomes, and uses of OBE analyses. The second model outlines an approach to understanding and using the concept of *quality of life* to select valued, person-referenced outcomes that form the basis of outcome-based evaluation.

Definitions of Program Evaluation

Program evaluation is not new. Its origins can be traced back to at least the 1960's, when we first began to see a major increase in social programs and requests to "evaluate" them. Throughout the ensuing years, definitions of program evaluation have remained fairly consistent as reflected in the following exemplary definitions.

> Evaluation is the collection and use of information to make decisions about [an education] program. (Cronbach, 1963, p. 672)

> The purpose of evaluation research is to measure the effects of a program against the goals it sets out to accomplish as a means of contributing to subsequent decision making about the program and improving future programming. (Weiss, 1972, p. 4)

> Evaluation research is the systematic application of social research procedures for assessing the conceptualization, design, implementation, and utility of social intervention programs. (Rossi & Freeman, 1989, p. 18)

> Program evaluation is the systematic collection of information about the activities, characteristics, and outcomes of programs for use by specific people to reduce uncertainties, improve effectiveness, and make decisions with regard to what those programs are doing and effecting. (Patton, 1986, p. 14)

Note the two communalities in these definitions:

1. Using research procedures to systematically collect information about the activities, characteristics, and outcomes of social programs.
2. Using program evaluation data for decision making and/or program improvement.

It is important to point out at the outset that program evaluation is not the same as basic research. As discussed by Cronbach and Suppes (1969), basic research is undertaken to discover new knowlege and to test hypotheses and theories. In this sense, basic research is *conclusion oriented*. In contrast, program evaluation is undertaken to inform decision makers, clarify options, reduce uncertainties, and provide feedback to decision makers and stakeholders about the program in question. Thus, program evaluation is more *decision oriented*. A key point made throughout this book is that outcome-based evaluations permit better decisions about a program's effectiveness and efficiency. With that point clearly in mind, let's look now at the "Whats" of outcome-based evaluation.

The Whats of Outcome-Based Evaluation

Definition

Outcome-based evaluation encompasses the central question of what education and social programs ought to achieve for persons receiving them: valued, person-referenced outcomes. This notion provides the basis for the definition of OBE, which is *a type of program evaluation that uses valued and objective person-referenced outcomes to analyze a program's effectiveness, impact, or benefit–cost*.

A number of terms are important in one's understanding of the definition. Chief among these are the following:

- Program evaluation: a process that leads to judgments about the effectiveness, impact, or benefits–costs of a program.
- Programs: a set of operations, actions, or activities designed to produce certain desired outcomes. In these programs, *habilitation* refers to acquiring ability not possessed previously; *rehabilitation* to

reacquiring lost ability. For ease of communication, I will frequently use *(re)habilitation* to refer to these two processes.

- Objective: observable and measurable data.
- Person-referenced: related to the individual's adaptive behavior and role status. *Adaptive behavior* refers to those behaviors that are required by different major life-activity areas such as home and community living, school or work, and health and wellness. *Role status* is a set of valued activities that are considered normative for a specific age group. Examples include school, independent living, employment, and recreation/leisure pursuits.
- Outcomes: changes in adaptive behavior(s) and role status that are logical consequences of the (re)habilitation service(s).
- Effectiveness: the extent to which a program meets its stated goals and objectives.
- Impact: whether the program made a difference compared to either no program or an alternate program.
- Benefit–Cost: whether the program's benefits outweigh the costs.

Performance-Based Assessment

Outcome-based evaluation requires *performance-based assessment*, which is a concept that has captured the attention of policy makers, practitioners, researchers, and program evaluators alike (Baker, O'Neil, & Linn, 1993; Clark & Friedman, 1993; Schalock & Kiernan, 1990). The term is attractive because it calls for demonstrating what is obtained from an education or social program. In this text, I will use the term to refer to using objective indicators to evaluate a person's adaptive behavior level and role status.

Adaptive Behavior

The term *adaptive behavior* refers to those behaviors that are required for successful adaptation to or functioning in different major life-activity areas such as home and community living, school or work, and health and wellness. The more important of these include self-care, receptive and expressive language, learning, mobility, self-direction, and capacity for independent living and economic self-sufficiency. One's present functioning on these adaptive behaviors is the focus of assessment, and reducing limitations of them is the primary focus of the educational or social program. The focus of performance-based assessment is to determine specific changes that have occurred in the major life-activity areas as a function of the intervention or services received.

Role Status

The term *role status* refers to a set of valued activities that are considered normative for a specific age group. Examples include one's living arrangement, employment setting, education level, community participation, recreation–leisure patterns, and health status. For youth, attending school is a valued, age-specific activity, whereas for high school graduates and adults, living and working in the community are valued activities. Note the importance in Exhibit 1-1, for example, of the status outcomes of graduates from a special education program.

Selection of Person-Referenced Outcomes

Person-referenced outcomes should encompass either adaptive behaviors or role status (as described earlier). In thinking about which person-referenced outcomes to use in OBE, five criteria need to be met: (1) outcome is valued by the person, (2) approach is multidimensional, (3) data are objective and measurable, (4) outcome is connected logically to the program, and (5) outcome may be evaluated longitudinally. After discussing each of these, I will present a number of valued and objective person-referenced outcomes that meet the five criteria.

Outcome Is Valued by the Person

As discussed later in the chapter, education and social programs are currently changing the way one thinks about and approaches individuals receiving services. No longer are these individuals considered "patients" or "clients" who are passive service recipients; rather, they are considered "customers" or "consumers" who are expecting to be treated as anyone else and are demanding quality and outcome-oriented interventions (Eisen, Grob, & Dill, 1991). For example, under the 1992 Amendments to the Vocational Rehabilitation Act (P.L. 101–452) the process for determining consumer eligibility has been greatly expanded and streamlined. First and foremost, all people with disabilities are presumed to be able to benefit from an employment outcome (i.e., a job) and no longer have to prove their "potential" for such an opportunity and outcome.

This shift toward consumer equity and empowerment is truly revolutionizing education and social programs. Specifically, assessment is beginning to focus much more on those functional behaviors that will result in enhanced role statuses; person-centered planning is now the *modus operandi*, and outcome-based evaluation efforts are increasingly directed at

---

Exhibit 1-1
**Example of a Longitudinal Follow-up of Graduates
from a Special Education Program**

The purpose of the study (Schalock, Holl, Elliott, & Ross, 1992) was to summarize the current employment and living status of 298 students verified as either specific learning disabled (SLD) or mentally handicapped (MH), who graduated between 1979 and 1988 from a rural special education program. Each graduate and/or parent was contacted by phone for the purpose of collecting five sets of outcome data on each graduate: (a) current employment status; (b) employment outcomes (number of weeks employed during the last year, hours worked per week, and wages per hour); (c) work-related benefits; (d) current living arrangement; and (e) primary source of income. Data were also collected on 12 predictor (of outcomes) variables, including student/family characteristics, school variables, and the 1989 unemployment rate for the student's county of residence.

Results indicated that (1) 77% of the sample were working either full- or part-time in jobs related to services, agriculture/farm, or construction/manufacturing and that most persons had never changed or lost their jobs during the survey period; (2) most former students were living semi-independently with parents or roommates, or in supported living arrangements; (3) across all outcome measures, students verified as SLD did better than students verified as MH; and (4) significant predictors of the outcomes included tested IQ, gender, verified handicap, hours in vocational programs, school enrollment, and years taught by the resource teacher.

---

analyzing outcomes related to changes that have occurred in the person's adaptive behaviors and role status. It is critical to point out, however, that valued, person-referenced outcomes don't just happen. They are the result of committed, competent personnel and quality services. Thus, education and social programs must continue to stress quality processes as well as quality outcomes.

Multidimensional Approach

Current thinking about evaluating the effects of education and social programs is that the outcome assessment should encompass a wide range of valued, person-referenced outcomes. Note, for example, the number of "predictor variables" used in the evaluation study summarized in Exhibit

Exhibit 1-2
Factors Affecting the Posthospital Status
of Persons with Mental Illness

The longitudinal study (Schalock et al., in press) involved two phases: Phase I (1988–1990) involved 309 adults with mental illness; Phase II (1991–1992), which constituted the cross-validation phase, included 78 adults. During each phase, data were collected either on admission, discharge, 12–15 months following discharge, or upon readmission to a mental health facility. Thirty-two predictor variables, reflecting recipient characteristics, treatment interventions, and posthospital living and work status and community use patterns, were considered the independent variables. The outcome (dependent) variable was *recidivism*, defined as returning to the facility (or any other state-administered psychiatric facility) within 12–15 months after discharge.

The primary diagnosis for the 387 persons included organic brain syndrome (8.6%), schizophrenic disorders (37.6%), affective disorders (34%), and adjustment disorders (10.1%). The sample averaged 2.9 previous admissions to the facility. Marital status included 42.7% single, 22.4% married, 25% divorced, 4.8% separated, and 4.7% widowed/widowered.

The procedure involved selecting every second person admitted to the facility, excluding transfers from other state facilities. Interview/record review data were obtained at three points, including admission, discharge, and 12–15 months following discharge or upon readmission. Trained interviewers obtained the follow-up information preferably in face-to-face interviews; however, if this was not possible due to physical location, then the interview could be done by phone, by mail, or by proxy (parent or spouse).

During the 5-year study period, 28.5% of the sample had returned within the 12- to 15-month follow-up period, and 3.9% were in another state facility upon follow-up contact. For the remaining 67.6%, 42.9% were interviewed face to face, 39.4% by telephone, 14.4% by proxy, and 3.3% by mail.

Results of the study indicated that (1) those who returned had more previous admissions, were less likely to be employed on admission, rated themselves on discharge as less improved on physical health and ability to cope, had used more community resources, reported more physical health problems, and performed on their own fewer instrumental activities of daily living; and (2) significant predictor variables included number of previous admissions, number of reported health problems, employment status, and the person's performance level on the instrumental activities of daily living.

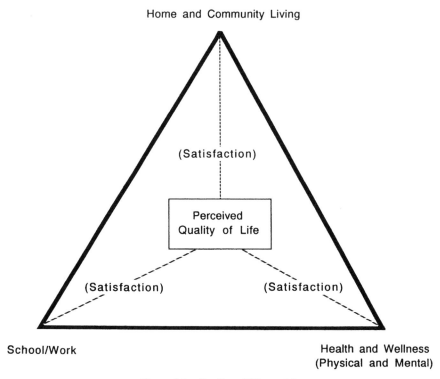

Home and Community Living

(Satisfaction)

Perceived
Quality of Life

(Satisfaction)   (Satisfaction)

School/Work

Health and Wellness
(Physical and Mental)

Figure 1.1. Quality of life model.

1-2. My bias (which will be apparent throughout the text) is to use a multidimensional approach to outcome assessment.

A model for using a multidimensional approach is presented in Figure 1.1. This model suggests that a person's perceived quality of life (QOL) is related significantly to factors within three major life domains: home and community living, school or work, and health and wellness. The model is based on a synthesis of recent QOL models (Schalock, 1990, 1994) and is consistent with the current:

- Paradigm shift, with its emphasis on inclusion, equity, empowerment, and community-based supports.
- Quality revolution, with its emphasis on quality enhancement and quality management.
- Conception that satisfaction serves as an intervening variable between each of the three major life-activity domains and the person's perceived QOL.

- Documentation that persons can be more independent, productive, community integrated and satisfied when interventions and services are based on quality enhancement and integration principles.
- Emphasis on social validity, which is the degree to which a program addresses an issue of social importance in its implementation without creating socially unacceptable side effects.

The QOL model presented in Figure 1.1 reflects a multidimensional approach to selecting valued, person-referenced outcomes. It also provides a useful model for determining whether education and/or social programs have a positive impact on a person's perceived quality of life.

Objective and Measurable Data

The great German poet Goethe is purported to have said that "good science is predicated on good measurement." This statement has two significant implications for OBE. One is that OBE should be approached from a scientific perspective (which I will attempt to do); the other is that our basic source of data must be objective and measurable.

I devote an entire chapter to how one measures person-referenced outcomes. For the time being, keep in mind that evaluation requires data, and data must be objective and measured in order to have meaning. Thus, valued, person-referenced outcomes selected for analysis must be:

- Objective in that they are observable in the person.
- Measured in ways that meet the requirements of reliability (consistency) and validity (reflects valued, person-referenced changes in adaptive behavior and role status).

Outcome is Connected Logically to the Program

This is such a simple criterion that it is often overlooked. The criterion requires that the analyzed person-referenced outcomes logically be the product of the (re)habilitation services received. This criterion further requires that (a) the person-referenced outcomes can be attributed to the intervention or services in that one can see clearly that there is a link between the services received and the person-referenced outcomes; and (b) the outcomes are sensitive to change and intervention. For example, independent-living training should have outcomes that enhance a person's capacity for independent living, and employment-training programs should result in increased jobs for persons. Special education programs that stress increased self-care skills should result in these outcomes, and mental health programs that focus on medication compliance should have outcomes commensurate with that focus. We will discuss later a number of related issues, but for the time being, just remember that the outcomes analyzed should be connected logically to the program.

Outcomes May Be Evaluated Longitudinally

Education and social programs need to involve long-term follow-up studies and not just "intervene and place" as has been the historical pattern for many programs. Note, for example, that following persons for 15 years, as described in Exhibit 1-3, is frequently necessary to evaluate the long-term effects of a program.

This criterion of evaluated longitudinality is critical for a number of reasons:

- The effects noted immediately after intervention are not always the same as those noted over time. Indeed, some intervention effects that appear to be effective in the short run do not show sustained effects, and conversely, some interventions that produce little or no effect immediately show significant effects sometime later (Kazdin, 1993; Morell, 1979).
- One's role status changes slowly and usually not overnight. How long, for example, did it take you to obtain your current living and work position?
- Impact and benefit–cost analyses are dependent on longitudinal changes in a person's adaptive behavior and role status.
- The current emphasis on supports requires that one evaluate not just the person's adaptive behaviors and/or role status, but also his/her support network. This too emerges over time.

Table 1.1 lists a number of exemplary valued and objective person-referenced outcomes that meet these five criteria: outcome is valued by the person, approach is multidimensional, data are objective and measurable, outcome is connected logically to the program, and may be evaluated longitudinally. Note that the outcomes are grouped according to whether they represent adaptive behavior or role status. Although I will use these exemplary outcomes throughout the text for expository purposes, I do not intend to imply that they are the only ones that can be used. Indeed, Table 2.2 in Chapter 2 summarizes a number of other outcomes that might be more appropriate for your use, depending on your program's mission and goals.

Uses of OBE Data

One of the advantages of OBE is that data resulting from the procedures discussed in this text can be used for a number of purposes, includ-

---

Exhibit 1-3
Placement from a Community-Based Mental Retardation Program: A 15-Year Follow-up

This study (Schalock & Genung, 1993) was designed to evaluate the current status, quality of life, and movement patterns of 85 individuals with mental retardation placed into independent housing and competitive employment 15 years ago. Subjects were 85 individuals (42 males, 43 females) who had been placed from the program into either independent living or competitive employment environments and who had remained within that placement for a minimum of 2 years. Their average age was 39.5 years and average full-scale IQ (Wechsler Adult Intelligence Scale) was, at the time of last testing, 67.

In most cases, contact for the purpose of providing assistance or updating demographic records had been maintained between the person and the program. For the current study, local case managers were trained in survey techniques and on the specific survey instruments used. Observation, interview, and measurement data were aggregated into three major data sets: current status, quality of life, and historical descriptive data (see Exhibit 6-2 for a description of the assessment procedures used).

Results indicated that (1) 59% of the individuals were no longer receiving any services, living in their current residence for an average of 12.4 years; (2) 19% of the sample was currently receiving program services; (3) the remaining percentages were either living with family, in mental health facilities, or could not be located; (4) the nonservice group reported receiving more support from family, advocates, and neighbors; (5) the nonservice group was experiencing better desired community outcomes and more independence and productivity; (6) the two groups ("59 and 19") were quite similar in how they use their time during nonworking days; and (7) both groups were "somewhat to very satisfied," with no significant group differences obtained on an 11-item satisfaction scale. Both groups expressed less satisfaction with their health, health care, and their economic/financial situation.

---

ing the analysis of a program's effectiveness, impact, or benefit–cost. Each of these three uses are defined here, with brief examples of each presented in Exhibit 1-4:

1. *Effectiveness Analysis*: determines the extent to which the program obtains its goals and objectives.
2. *Impact Analysis*: determines whether the program made a difference compared to either no program or an alternative program.

Table 1.1. Exemplary Person-Referenced Outcomes

Adaptive behaviors	Role status
Activity of daily living	Home and community living arrangements
Instrumental activities of daily living	Ownership indicators
Communication skills	Education indicators
Social skills	Employment indicators
Job skills	Health and wellness indicators
Self-direction	
Functional academic skills	
Recreational skills	
Leisure skills	

3. *Benefit–Cost Analysis*: determines whether the program's benefits outweigh the costs. Two criteria are used to answer this question: equity and efficiency. Equitable programs contribute to balancing the needs of the various groups in society, whereas efficient programs are those that serve to increase the net value of goods and services available to society.

OBE analysis results can be used for a number of formative feedback purposes that are summarized briefly in Table 1.2 and discussed in detail in Chapter 11. The more important of these uses include reporting program outcomes, program or systems change, and policy evaluation. A key point to keep in mind is that results from these analyses provide formative feedback to program administrators, policy makers, and funding bodies so that they can use the information for program/system change resulting in increased equity, efficiency, and valued, person-referenced outcomes.

Outcome-Based Evaluation Model

By now, you should have a good feeling for the "Whats" of OBE, including its definition, performance-based assessment, the selection of valued and objective person-referenced outcomes, and the uses of OBE data. Now we need a model that will guide our work throughout the remainder of the text. Figure 1.2 provides such a model that is derived from current evaluation theory, current education and (re)habilitation service delivery systems, and the need to understand the role of OBE in light of these current phenomena. The model's major purposes are to assist the reader to conceptualize OBE, provide a broad perspective on the function of OBE, and serve as a guide in the systematic development and imple-

---

Exhibit 1-4
Examples of Outcome-Based Evaluation Analyses

Effectiveness Analysis

A number of years ago, we (Schalock, Harper, & Genung, 1981b) were interested in determining whether placement from a community-based program for persons with mental retardation fulfilled its primary goals of placing people into environments that were more independent and productive. We found that yes, persons were generally in more independent and productive environments, but that the quality of life was not as high as it might be. Thus, some of the agency's goals were achieved, but not all, for part of its mission statement referenced "enhancing the quality of lives of those persons served." This is often the case in effectiveness analysis; the results are inconsistent.

Impact Analysis

When the program referenced above was just getting into supported living and natural environments, we were interested in whether persons within the program learned more skills within an artificial training environment (the day activity center) or one's own apartment. To answer this question, we (Schalock, Gadwood, & Perry, 1984) compared behavioral skill acquisition rates in 10 matched pairs of persons with mental retardation who received individualized, prescriptive programming for 1 year in one of two training environments: one's own apartment vs. a group home adjacent to the adult developmental center. After 1 year, the two groups were compared on the number of skills gained. As might be predicted, the persons who received training in their apartments gained three times the skills of the group home participants.

Benefit–Cost Analysis

Lewis, Bruininks and Thurlow (1991) assessed the costs and outcomes of all students from 1 to 5 years after they graduated or completed educational programs in two special schools. The analysis involved comparing the costs and benefits from two perspectives: that of the student and that of the rest of society. Specific results are presented in Exhibit 5-3.

---

mentation of OBE efforts. The model's major components include the following:

1. The agency's mission statement and goals that should drive the program's efforts.
2. The intervention or services that should reflect the agency's mission statement and goals.

Table 1.2. Types of OBE Analyses and Their Most Appropriate Formative Feedback Uses

Type of analysis	Definition	Most appropriate uses
Effectiveness	Extent to which program obtains its goals and objectives	Reporting program outcomes Program change
Impact	Whether the program makes a difference compared to either no program or an alternative program	Program change Systems change Policy evaluation
Benefit–Cost	Whether the program's benefits outweigh the costs (equity and efficiency considerations)	Policy evaluation Systems change

3. Valued and objective person-referenced outcomes related to adaptive behaviors and role status.
4. Formative feedback that assures stakeholders a strong voice in the design and management of programs, links both facility evaluation and program improvement to person-referenced outcomes, allows for the systematic evaluation and improvement of services, and identifies the potential foci for program change.

Outcome-Based Evaluation Compared to Other Program Evaluation Approaches

I am indebted to a number of individuals who have over the years brought program evaluation to its current status of acceptance and utility (Shadish, Cook, & Leviton, 1991). My emphasis on outcome-based evaluation in this book will be better appreciated if viewed within the context of other conceptual approaches to program evaluation. I have attempted to

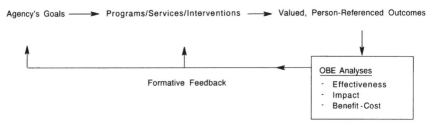

Figure 1.2. Outcome-based evaluation model.

illustrate this in Table 1.3, which summarizes key components of nine conceptual approaches to program evaluation. The right column of Table 1.3 lists the OBE term or concept that the readers will find in this volume.

What should one glean from Table 1.3? Probably at least the following commonalities should be seen among the approaches:

- Information about program promises and outcomes.
- Use of multiple approaches to gathering information.
- Importance of internal and external validity.
- Importance of program monitoring.
- Multiple interests in program evaluation.
- Use of data for decision making.
- Importance of models to guide program evaluation efforts.

The Whys of Outcome-Based Evaluation

Outcome-based evaluation is important because it encompasses the central question of what education and social programs ought to achieve for persons receiving them: valued person-referenced outcomes. Additionally, OBE is important because it is an effective response to the current zeitgeist characterized by six major trends: (1) the quality revolution, (2) consumer empowerment, (3) increased demands for accountability, (4) the supports paradigm, (5) the emerging pragmatic evaluation paradigm, and (6) the emphasis on enhanced functioning. Each of these trends represents an important "Why" of outcome-based evaluation.

The Quality Revolution

We are currently experiencing a quality revolution that focuses on quality of life, quality enhancement techniques, quality management techniques, and quality assurance. This revolution, evident in both industry and human services, stresses that quality is integral to both the processes we use in service delivery and the outcomes from those services. In reference to OBE, I will stress throughout this text that quality and quality outcomes should be guiding principles around which person-referenced outcomes are selected and interpreted.

Consumer Empowerment

Today, the customer or consumer is number one. The consumer movement is revolutionizing the way that educational and social programs operate and the outcomes that they use to evaluate their interventions or

Table 1.3. Integration of the Text's Outcome-Based Evaluation Approach with Other Conceptual Approaches to Program Evaluation

Conceptual approach	Brief explanation of approach	Text approach
1. Formative vs. summative (Chambers, 1994; Posavac & Carey, 1980; Rossi & Freeman, 1985; Scriven, 1967, 1972)	Formative = improve program planning and implementation Summative = decisions about program continuance, replication, selection	Effectiveness analysis Impact and benefit–cost analysis
2. Performance measurement	Information about the outcomes Effectiveness of program effort	Effectiveness analysis
Efficiency measurement (Suchman, 1967)	Information about costs and their outcomes	Benefit–cost analysis
3. Goal attainment scaling (Kiresuk & Lund, 1978)	Determining goal attainment level and using this information to modify future activities	Effectiveness analysis
4. Responsive evaluation	Evaluations that emphasize program goals as evaluation criteria	Effectiveness analysis
Naturalistic observation (Stake, 1978, 1980)	Use of interviews, case study, and observation	Data sources
5. Process model of the program	A program model that explicates inputs, implementation and outcomes	Focus on outcomes Program evaluation model (Figure 1.2)
Experimental methods (Weiss, 1972, 1987)	Use of research methods to assess goal achievements	Effectiveness analysis
6. Performance-oriented evaluation	Evaluation to help managers achieve high organizational outcomes	Effectiveness analysis
Rapid feedback evaluation	A quick assessment of program performance of agreed-upon objectives and indicators.	Formative feedback Critical performance indicators
Performance monitoring (Wholey, 1981, 1983)	Establishment of ongoing process and outcome program monitoring system	Management data system
7. Utilization-focused evaluation (Patton, 1986)	Utilization should be the driving force in an evaluation There are multiple and varied interests around any evaluation	Contextual analysis
8. Theory-driven program evaluation (Chen & Rossi, 1983, 1989; Finney & Moos, 1989)	Constructing models of how programs work, using the models to guide question formulation and data gathering	Program evaluation model (Figure 1.2) with inputs, processes, and outputs
9. Theory-driven approach to validity (Campbell & Stanley, 1963; Chen & Rossi, 1987)	Internal validity = the extent to which the effect of the treatment variables can be disentangled from the correlated extraneous variables External validity = the extent to which generalizations can be made to future applications of the program.	Data criteria (Part III)

services. Critical concepts in this movement include choices, inclusion, equity, supports rather than facilities, and consumer-driven evaluation. Outcome-based evaluation efforts must therefore focus on valued, person-referenced outcomes that reflect choices as to where one lives and works; decisions about what is important in one's life; inclusion in regular school–work–home environments; adaptive behaviors; and role status.

Increased Accountability

Funders, program managers, policy makers and consumers are all demanding program outcome data. The current trend is to define accountability in terms of consumer outcomes and organizational effectiveness and efficiency. For example, the Government Performance and Results Act, signed into law in 1993, requires federal agencies to specify what they will do with the money they get and will be measured against those promises. Additionally, at least 38 states currently have an accountability system that involves public reports of school performance. Even accreditation agencies, such as the Accreditation Council (1994), and the Commission on the Accreditation of Rehabilitation Facilities (CARF) (1995), are accrediting programs on the basis of outcomes rather than service delivery processes. We are also seeing an increased need for cost containment and relating costs to outcomes. OBE is consistent with this increased need for accountability.

Supports Paradigm

We are currently experiencing a change in the way people with special needs are viewed and served. This change is referred to as the *supports paradigm* (Schalock, 1995; Schwartz, 1992). This paradigm shift is to a large extent grounded in the philosophy of normalization and involves a move away from a defect orientation that focuses primarily on a person's deficits and toward an outcome or role status–based orientation that asks the question, "What supports are needed to help a particular person function in age-relevant social roles within the community?" Although still emerging, the supports paradigm extends across disciplines and (re)habilitation areas, including education (Snell, 1993), families (Roberts, Wasik, Casto, & Ramey, 1991), mental retardation (Luckasson et al., 1992) mental health (Schalock et al., in press), employment (Nisbet & Hagner, 1988; Rusch, 1990; Wehmnan & Moon, 1988), and medicine (Coulter, 1991).

The impact of the supports paradigm on OBE is considerable. Support assessment involves many disciplines working as a team, analyzing a variety of assessment findings that include both norm-referenced tests and criterion-referenced measures, observation, and interaction with the person. The anticipated levels of support are then based on the strengths and limitations of the person and his/her environment, not simply on the individual's diagnosis. With an individual's support profile at any given time, there is likely to be a varied array of support needs and intensities, making a global summary label (e.g., "educable mentally handicapped", "severely emotionally disturbed," or "severely mentally retarded") meaningless. Ongoing supports are then provided to enhance the person's adaptive behaviors and role statuses.

Within the supports paradigm, services (whether they be supported education, employment, living, or adulthood) are based on the person's strengths and limitations, along with the specific supports the person will require to achieve his/her desired life outcomes. Additionally, the type and intensity of supports are increasingly being used as the basis for reimbursement.

As we anticipate the further emergence of the supports paradigm and its use in OBE, a number of standards should guide their use, including (Schalock, 1995):

* Supports occur in regular, integrated environments.
* Support activities are performed primarily by individuals working, living, or recreating within those environments.
* Support activities are individualized and person referenced.
* Outcomes from the use of supports are evaluated against quality indicators and valued, person-referenced outcomes.
* The use of supports can fluctuate and may range from lifelong duration to fluctuating need during different stages of life.
* Supports should not be withdrawn precipitously.

Pragmatic Evaluation Paradigm

We are also experiencing changes in how we approach program evaluation (Fishman, 1991, 1992; Maltz, 1994; Meyer & Evans, 1993). Historically, the "experimental paradigm" has been used, in which the major purpose was hypothesis testing or theory building. This approach, which required experimental and control conditions, has recently been partially replaced with a pragmatic evaluation paradigm that emphasizes a practical, problem-solving orientation to program evaluation. As stated by Fishman (1991):

> In the pragmatic paradigm, a conceptually coherent program is designed to address a significant social or psychological problem within a naturalistic, real-world setting in a manner that is feasible, effective, and efficient. Quantification is used to develop performance indicators of a system's functioning. The system is monitored in terms of both baselines and changes due to identified interventions. (p. 356)

Outcome-based evaluation is consistent with this emerging pragmatic evaluation paradigm, whose impact is apparent throughout the text. As a trained scientist, I believe in the experimental method, and will argue for good experimental/control conditions whenever possible. However, based on the pragmatic paradigm, I will also offer alternative evaluation designs that can be used. But I should add a caution: When one uses these alternatives, one needs to make more assumptions, and will have less certainty and be less precise about what the results mean.

This shift toward the pragmatic program evaluation paradigm, with its emphasis on a practical, problem-solving orientation, also affects the data collection and analysis techniques that are discussed in Part III. Equally important, it changes the role of the program evaluator to one who facilitates interpretative dialog among the program's stakeholders, attains consensus among the stakeholders about the program's values and outcomes, and incorporates the concepts of internal program evaluation, formative feedback, and quality assurance into their roles. More of this will be discussed in Chapters 7 and 14.

Enhanced Functioning

Outcome-based evaluation focuses on adaptive behaviors and a person's role status that reflects his/her enhanced functioning. In this regard, we are beginning to rethink the relationship among terms such as *pathology, impairment, functional limitations,* and *disability* (Institute of Medicine, 1991). This relationship is summarized in the sequential diagram presented in Figure 1.3. In this four-stage conceptualization of the disabling process, the "pathology" is associated with an abnormality at the cellular or tissue level, such as tuberous sclerosis. The pathology then produces an "impairment" at the organ or organ system, such as brain dysfunction. The brain dysfunction then produces a "functional limitation" at the organism level, such as low intelligence. However, the functional limitation becomes a "disability" only when it impacts or interferes with the person's social role.

This four-stage conceptualization of the disabling process has a number of implications for those readers in the field of medicine and disabilities for both service delivery and outcome-based evaluation. Among the most important are the following:

- Disability is neither fixed nor dichotomized; rather it is fluid, continuous, changing, and an evolving set of characteristics depending upon the characteristics and supports available within a person's environment (Zola, 1993).
- One lessens functional limitations (and hence a person's disability)

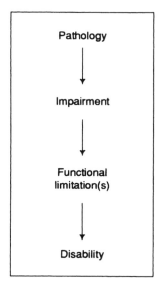

Figure 1.3. The disabling process.

by providing interventions or services and supports that focus on adaptive behaviors and role status.
- Outcome-based evaluation focuses on the extent to which the functional limitations have been reduced and the person's adaptive behavior and role status enhanced.

Summary

In summary, I have found that the first chapter of a book is usually the most important. If you like what you read, you will go on. I hope this is the case. I have attempted in this chapter to present an introduction to outcome-based evaluation that passes the "mother-in-law test," which implies that if you can communicate to your mother-in-law what you are doing, and if she understands, then you must be communicating satisfactorily.

We began by looking at the definition of program evaluation, and the five "Whats" of OBE that included its definition, performance-based assessment, the selection of person-referenced outcomes, the uses of OBE data, and an OBE model that will guide us through the text. In comparing OBE with other approaches, we found that outcome-based evaluation is both timely and appropriate because it reflects both the intent of educational and social programs and fits well the current zeitgeist's quality revolution, consumer empowerment, increased demands for accountability, supports paradigm, pragmatic evaluation paradigm, and emphasis on enhanced functioning.

It is now time to move on. If I have been successful (check me out), you should now be asking (and wanting answers to) "Where do I begin, and how do I proceed?" As we address these questions, please do not forget the major importance of outcome-based evaluation: It encompasses the central question of what educational and social programs ought to achieve for their customers: equitable and efficient services that result in valued, person-referenced outcomes.

Study Questions

1. Define outcome-based evaluation and give examples of (a) performance-based assessment; (b) valued person-referenced outcomes; and (c) its use in effectiveness, impact, and benefit–cost analyses.

2. Summarize the five criteria of person-referenced outcomes. What is the significance of each criterion in reference to the "whys of outcome-based evaluation"?

3. Compare and contrast the experimental and the pragmatic evaluation paradigms. Why does the pragmatic paradigm seem more compatible with the proposed outcome-based evaluation model (Figure 1.2)?

4. Critique the quality-of-life and the disability process models discussed in the chapter and summarized in Figures 1.1 and 1.3. Relate each model to the concepts of adaptive behavior and role status.

5. Assume the role of an evaluation producer. Outline the critical steps that you will need to perform to complete an effectiveness analysis of an education or social program. Use information found in Table 1.1 and Figure 1.2 to complete the steps.

6. Look at Table 1.1 that lists broad indicators of person-referenced outcomes. Think of some measurable examples of each. When you are done, check your answers against the more complete listing found in Table 6.1.

7. Review Table 1.2 that summarizes the types of OBE analyses and their most appropriate formative feedback use. Discuss specific information from each analysis that would be most useful to (a) program administrators, (b) policy makers, and (c) funding agencies.

8. Review Table 1.3 that integrates the text with other approaches to program

evaluation. What is unique about outcome-based evaluation and to which conceptual approach(es) is it most similar?

9. Review Exhibits 1-1 and 1-3 that summarize two different longitudinal follow-up studies. Identify the valued, person-referenced outcomes that were selected. Do these outcomes meet the criterion of (a) performance-based assessment, and (b) the five criteria of person-referenced outcomes?

10. Review Exhibit 1-2 that identifies factors that affect the posthospital status of persons with mental illness. What factors would you select if doing such an evaluation and what would be your rationale? When you have listed your factors, you might want to check Exhibit 10-1 for a listing of the actual variables used in the study.

Additional Readings

Baker, E. L., O'Neill, H. F., & Linn, R. L. (1993). Policy and validity prospects for performance-based assessment. *American Psychologist, 48*(2), 1210–1218.

Eisen, S. V., Grob, M. C., & Dill, D. L. (1991). Outcome measurement: Tapping the patient's perspective. In S. M. Mirin, J. M. Gosset & M. C. Grob (Eds.), *Recent advances in outcome research* (pp. 150–164). Washington, DC: American Psychiatric Press.

Fishman, D. B. (1992). An introduction to the experimental versus the pragmatic paradigm in evaluation. *Evaluation and Program Planning, 14,*353–363.

Meyer, L. H., & Evans, I. M. (1993). Science and practice in behavioral intervention: Meaningful outcomes, research validity, and usable knowledge. *Journal of the Association for Persons with Severe Handicaps, 18*(4), 224–234.

Mirin, S. M., & Manerow, M. J. (1991). Why study treatment outcomes? *Hospital and Community Psychiatry, 42*(10), 1007–1013.

Reichardt, C. S., & Rallis, S. F. (Eds.). (1994). *The qualitative–quantitative debate.* San Francisco: Jossey-Bass.

Shadish, W. R., Jr., Cook, T. D., & Leiviton, L. C. (1991). *Foundations of program evaluation: Theories of practice.* Newbury Park, CA: Sage.

2

Where to Begin and How to Proceed

Overview

This chapter assumes that you are an OBE producer and want to know where to begin to evaluate your program, and how to proceed in a logical way. Most of my program administrator friends either want or need to evaluate their programs, but are often lost as to what this actually means. In this regard, there are two questions that you will want to ask yourself. First, "For what purpose will I use the outcome evaluation data?" Answering this question requires that you be proactive and know where you are going with your evaluation. As we saw in Table 1.2, the three primary purposes of OBE are effectiveness, impact, and benefit–cost analysis.

Second, "What data will I need for the intended use?" Answering this question requires logical thinking. Here the tendency is to ask questions that the education or social program and data system are unable to answer. For example, many program administrators want to know whether their program is better than an alternative or is cost-beneficial, without having the capability of forming comparison conditions or having the necessary cost and outcome data required to answer the question. If, on the other hand, you want to use the data on an ongoing basis for reporting outcomes, longitudinal evaluations, program change, or policy evaluations, then you will need to be sure that your data management system has the capability for such efforts. And that is one of the primary purposes of this chapter—to familiarize you with the relationship between outcome based evaluation data use (Question 1) and data requirements (Question 2).

The chapter begins with a brief overview of what I propose as "OBE guiding principles." The chapter is then organized around the OBE model presented in Figure 1.2 with its major components of mission/goals, services, person-referenced outcomes, formative feedback, and uses of OBE data. These model components translate into four actions steps that compose the major sections of the chapter: (1) develop the program's mission and goals; (2) provide services that are consistent with the program's mission and goals; (3) select valued, person-referenced outcomes; and (4) establish a data management system.

Guiding Principles

Twenty OBE guiding principles are discussed throughout the text. The 10 core guiding principles are summarized in Table 2.1. Other principles that you will want to keep in mind as you think about where to begin and how to proceed include:

1. Be sure that the services provided are defined, operationalized, and measured, and that they logically effect the program's outcome.
2. The type of cost data collected and the complexity of the cost analysis are dependent upon the type of outcome-based evaluation analysis planned.
3. A good OBE data management system is based on collecting and organizing one's data in a 2 × 2 matrix: service recipients × core data sets.
4. Data should be collected by individuals who are trained in either standard assessment instruments, performance-based assessment techniques, and/or participant observation techniques.

Table 2.1. Outcome-Based Evaluation Core Guiding Principles

---

1. Services offered should be consistent with the program's mission and goals, and logically affect the program's outcome.
2. Person-referenced outcomes should be valued by the individual and related demonstrably to the intervention or services provided.
3. Choose your data sets carefully, because data collection is neither easy nor inexpensive.
4. Collect OBE data in four areas: recipient characteristics, core service functions, cost estimates, and valued, person-referenced outcomes.
5. The outcome-based evaluation design used depends on the questions asked, the available data, and the comparison condition available.
6. The type of outcome-based evaluation analysis conducted must be consistent with the program's capability.
7. Data should be collected by trained individuals.
8. The computerization of management data should flow from data collection format, to database management/data entry, to data manipulation and analysis.
9. The current trend is to consider generic groups with functional limitations, rather than individuals with specific diagnostic labels.
10. Contextual variables need to be included in the interpretation and application of outcome-based evaluation results.

---

5. OBE data collection should be organized around a simple matrix: service recipients × core data sets.

6. The specific statistical test that one employs depends upon (1) the level of measurement, (2) the number of persons and groups involved in the analysis, (3) the type of design that one is using, and (4) one's ability to meet the respective tests' assumptions.

7. Don't confuse the four most common statistical analyses used in OBE: descriptive statistics, exploratory correlational analysis, group comparisons, and multivariate analyses.

8. Effectiveness analysis is an absolute requirement in the 1990s.

9. Impact analysis involves comparing outcomes from two comparable conditions or groups. Statistically significant differences between these outcomes represents the program's impacts.

10. In benefit–cost analysis, the three most important analytical perspectives are social (society), participant, and the rest of society ("taxpayer").

11. In benefit–cost analysis, the comprehensive framework should include all benefits and costs, regardless of whether they can be monetized (i.e., include both tangible and intangible benefits and costs).

12. The major change indicators include consumer changes (adaptive behavior and role status) and organizational changes (resource

allocation, alignment of staff utilization patterns with agency mission, and core service functions).

Mission and Goals

The Importance of a Mission Statement

Does your program or agency have a mission statement that articulates clearly your purpose and desired outcomes? If not, you should have one before you attempt an outcome based evaluation. A statement that I find most useful to keep in mind in this regard is that "the trouble with not knowing where you are going is that you might end up somewhere else." It is no accident that the OBE model depicted in Figure 1.2 begins with one's mission and goals. It is the determination of how well the program obtains those goals that is the basis for almost all program evaluation activities and uses of OBE data, not to mention meeting the increasing demand for accountability.

If you do have a mission statement, review it. Is it filled with platitudes and "warm fuzzies" (nice, unmeasureable outcomes)? If so, I would suggest rewording it so that it meets a very basic criterion: Are your goals objective, measurable, person-referenced, and connected logically to your services? If you cannot meet this criterion, then you have a bit of work to do before proceeding as an evaluation producer. I hope that the example given in the upper portion of Exhibit 2-1 will help. Note in this exhibit on program evaluation prerequisites that the mission statement and goals lead logically to the other prerequisites, including services, outcomes, and a data system.

Public Policy Goals

One of the biggest program evaluation challenges is to ensure that specific intervention and services are consistent with the policy goals enunciated in various federal public laws and their state counterparts. Program evaluation would be much easier if such were the case.

To help this process along, let's look at four exemplary public laws and their desired outcomes, keeping in mind that they are only exemplary and that one's mission statement and goals should be consistent with the intended goals of whatever major public law or funding stream impacts your program.

The intent of Table 2.2 is to help you determine, in reference to these

---

Exhibit 2-1
Program Evaluation Prerequisites

Mission

The Mission of Agency X is to enhance the quality of life of persons with disabilities by increasing their independence, productivity, and community integration.

Services

The agency's services and staff allocation patterns are divided into three service provision components: (1) home and community living that involve supported living and community integration activities; (2) employment services that provide integrated employment opportunities with ongoing job coaching and job supports when necessary; and (3) wellness programs dealing with proper eating and exercise regimes.

Outcomes

The agency annually evaluates the person's role statuses (including living arrangement, employment status, and work environment); wellness indicators (medication level, number of hospitalizations, number of doctor appointments), and assessed quality-of-life factors (including independence, productivity, community integration, and satisfaction). Historically, this agency also evaluated functional skill acquisition ratios (Schalock & Harper, 1982), but found the process too expensive and time consuming.

Data Management System

A client demographic system has been in place for the last 15 years that has permitted the tracking of valued, person-referenced outcomes as described previously. The data system is centralized, with individual service components updating the person's outcomes at the individual's annual Individual Program Plan Review.

---

exemplary public laws, whether your program's mission and goals are consistent with the major policy and funding streams under which you operate. However, note that the desired outcomes are general, and that in reference to outcome-based evaluation, they will need to be operationalized so that they meet our criteria of being valued by the person, multidimensional, objective and measurable, connected logically to the program, and evaluated longitudinally. We will see how this is done in Chapter 6.

Table 2.2. Desired General Outcomes From Exemplary Public Laws

Public law	Desired general outcome(s)
Individuals with Disabilities Education Act (P.L. 101–476)	Free, appropriate public education Individual Education Plan Individual Family Support Plan
1992 Amendments to the Vocational Rehabilitation Act (P.L. 101–452)	An employment outcome (a job) Nondiscrimination Customer satisfaction
Americans with Disabilities Act (P.L. 101–336)	Employment Public accommodations Public services Transportation Telecommunications
Development Disabilities Act (P.L. 101–496)	Independence Productivity Community integration

Services Provided

Remember our definition of a program from Chapter 1? A *program* is a set of operations, actions or activities designed to produce certain desired outcomes. So, our next task is to think about the specific intervention or services provided that should result logically in those desired outcomes. But let's keep it simple, by asking three relevant questions:

1. Are your services consistent with your mission statement and program goals?
2. Are your services oriented toward desired person-referenced outcomes?
3. Are your staffing patterns aligned with your mission and goals?

If you answered "yes" to each of these questions, then your OBE task will be much easier; if not, you have some work to do and I hope the service description found in Exhibit 2-1 will help.

The need to have your services consistent with your mission and goal statements may sound a bit elementary. However, I have seen numerous examples of programs that have wonderfully stated mission and goal statements, but services that are not consistent with those statements. For example, I have seen special education programs with the goal of "increased community integration" for the student, but with neither Individual Education Plan-related activities nor staff allocation patterns directed at community activities. Similarly, I have seen goals in adult disability services related to integrated employment outcomes, but with staffing patterns directed at sheltered employment or center-based adult day services. And finally, I have seen mental health programs that philosophically stress community adjustment, but with little or no attention to providing the opportunities and supports necessary for this to occur.

Person-Referenced Outcomes

Table 1.1 listed a number of exemplary person-referenced outcomes related to adaptive behaviors and role status. Although these outcomes can be used as a guide in your initial thinking about outcome-based evaluation, at this point, it is necessary to expand to encompass program areas in which the reader will be working. Table 2.3 summarizes a number of potential person-referenced outcomes for such programs as vocational rehabilitation, education, mental health, chemical dependency, corrections, the homeless, senior services, child development, major life-activity areas, and health and wellness.

In thinking about which person-referenced outcomes to select as the basis for your outcome-based evaluation activities, keep the following five criteria clearly in mind:

1. Valued by the person
2. Multidimensional
3. Objective and measurable
4. Connected logically to the program
5. Evaluated longitudinally

Data-Management System

Good management requires good data. Thus, at the beginning of your evaluation planning, be sure that you have a data management system that meets the following five key criteria (these will be elaborated on in Chapter 7):

- Person referenced
- Complete (available for all program participants)
- Timely (current and covers the period of time you are interested in)
- Affordable (can obtain and analyze the data within the constraints of one's resources that include time, money, and expertise)
- Accurate (reflects actual events and characteristics).

A viable data-management system is the *sine qua non* of outcome-based evaluation. You simply cannot get along without one. Don't even

Table 2.3. Potential Person-Referenced Outcomes for Different Program Types

Vocational rehabilitation	Education	Mental health	Chemical dependency	Corrections	Homeless	Senior services
Adaptive behavior-level changes	Attendance	Living/Employment status	Functional level	Recidivism	Arrest rates	Activities of daily living
Quality-of-life indicators	Grades	Symptom reduction	Symptom reduction	Diversion programs	Physical health	Living arrangements
Labor market behavior	Adjustment ratings	Quality-of-life indicators	Recidivism	Criminal offense record	Mental health	Global life satisfaction
Living arrangements	Educational status indicators (credits; diploma)	Safety/welfare	Labor market	Prosocial behavior	Housing/living conditions	Mortality/ longevity
Community integration activities	Behavior competencies	Current and past psychopathology	Self-concept	Life domain changes	Victimization	Institutionalization
Reductions in public transfer monies	Inclusion indicators	Replacement skills and behavior	Motivation	Home	Social contacts/ stability	Health status
	Postsecondary status	Medication level		School	Income/ employment	
	Quality of student life	Perceptions of significant others		Work		
				Employment		

Child development	Teacher education	Major life activity area	Activities and instrumental activities of daily living	Health and wellness
Physical	Changes in teachers' perceptions	Self-care	Activities	Number of illnesses
Cognitive	Changes in teachers' conceptualizations	Language	Eating	Pain level
Psychosocial	Changes in student experiences	Learning	Toileting	Use of health-care system
Self-help	Changes in classroom practices	Mobility	Dressing	Stiffness/soft tissue swelling
Language–speech		Self-direction	Bathing	Medication compliance
Parent–child interaction		Capability for independent living	Transfer	Dexterity
Parental coping skills		Economic self-sufficiency	Instrumental activities:	Psychotropic utilization rate
			Meal preparation	Nutritional status
			Housekeeping	Leisure and recreational activities
			Taking medication	
			Money management	
			Telephone use	

try. Why? Because OBE requires and uses data as discussed in the following three subsections on (1) the relationship between OBE data use and data requirements, (2) formative feedback, and (3) internal program evaluation.

Relationship between Outcome-Based Evaluation Data Use and Data Requirements

Each of the three types of outcome-based evaluation analyses— effectiveness, impact, and benefit–cost—require different data sets that involve recipient characteristics, the core services received, person-referenced outcomes, cost estimates, benefit estimates, and comparison conditions. A summary of the relationship between the OBE data uses and data requirements is found in Table 2.4.

What one generally sees in Table 2.4 is that data requirements become more stringent and demanding in either impact or benefit–cost analysis, largely because of the need for more sophisticated comparison conditions and cost–benefit impact statements. We will return to this issue in considerable detail in Chapters 4 and 5. For the time being, study Table 2.4 and

Table 2.4. Relationship between Outcome-Based Evaluation Analysis and Data Requirements

OBE analysis	Data requirement
Effectiveness	Recipient's characteristics (age, gender, diagnosis, adaptive skill level, role status)
	Services received (assessment training, intervention, supports, service coordination)
	Cost estimates (average cost/participant)
	Person-referenced outcomes (adaptive skill level, role status)
	Comparison condition (person as own comparison, pre–post changes, longitudinal status comparisons)
Impact	Recipient characteristics
	Services received
	Cost estimates (average cost/participant)
	Differential person-referenced outcomes (impacts)
	Comparison condition (hypothetical comparison, matched pairs, experimental/ control, program vs. alternative)
Benefit–Cost	Recipient characteristics
	Services received
	Differential costs (impacts)
	Differential person-referenced outcomes (impacts)
	Comparison condition (experimental/control; program vs. alternative)

your current data management system in reference to how you answered Questions 1 and 2 ("For what purpose will I use the OBE data?" "What data will I need for the intended use?"). The initial determination of your data needs and availability is an important step in either augmenting or changing your current data management system (more of this in Chapter 7).

Formative Feedback

Figure 1.2 (Outcome-Based Evaluation Model) noted the critical importance that feedback plays in allowing organizations to evaluate how well their person-referenced outcomes are being met. Based on this feedback, programs can then modify their services and interventions to enhance their desired outcomes.

One of the primary purposes of a data management system is to provide meaningful information (referred to as *formative feedback*) to program administrators and other key stakeholders. Such formative feedback

- Assures stakeholders a strong voice in the design and management of programs.
- Is an ongoing part of service delivery and ongoing data collection, not something that is "added on" for program evaluation purposes.
- Links both facility evaluation and program improvement to person-referenced outcomes.
- Allows for the systematic evaluation and improvement of services.
- Identifies the potential foci for programmatic or systems change.

Internal Program Evaluation

The use of formative feedback information can also be considered as internal program evaluation. Its key aspect is that it is a part of an organization's data management system and thus does not require external, duplicative monitoring and evaluation efforts. My experience has been that many program administrators feel that they need to have their programs evaluated by an outside "expert." Although this may be the case at times, by far the more reasonable approach is to establish an ongoing data management system that serves as the basis for continuous internal evaluation. To quote Clifford and Sherman (1983):

> Internal evaluation is a tool of management science as much or more than it is either a product or tool of social science. The internal program evaluator has a long-term commitment to change through enhancement of the quality of decision making within the organization. (p. 23)

In today's world of tight budgets, few programs can afford external evaluators, and thus your initial thinking needs to involve a mind-set that includes the use of outcome-based data for ongoing formative feedback and internal evaluation purposes. There are additional strengths to the concept of internal evaluation:

- It focuses on self-monitoring and self-improvement.
- It attempts to be comprehensive, correct, and credible to all stakeholders.
- It allows for a better understanding of the organization's contextual variables and the perspectives of the various stakeholders.

If a data management system is the basis for formative feedback and continuous internal evaluation, then it needs to be "user friendly," with the data collected as part of the program's ongoing activities. Such is the case of the example given in the bottom section of Exhibit 2-1. Note that the majority of the data sets analyzed are collected as part of the person's yearly Individual Program Plan review. For programs that might not have this option, then it is possible to collect such data routinely on admission, at various points during the intervention or service provision, and at discharge or follow-up. The key point to remember is that a data management system should allow for formative feedback, ongoing internal evaluation, and outcome-based evaluation.

Summary

In summary, I hope this chapter has fulfilled its promise of helping you know where to begin and how to proceed. The common theme throughout the chapter has been that outcome-based evaluation is not difficult if one asks clear questions and thinks logically. Thus, we began the chapter by asking you to answer two key questions: "For what purpose will I use the OBE data, and what data will I need for the intended use?" The chapter was built around the OBE model depicted in Figure 1.2 that translates into four action steps: (1) develop your mission statement and goals; (2) provide services consistent with one's mission and goals; (3) select valued, person-referenced outcomes; and (4) establish a data management system. Key concepts introduced included the importance of understanding the proposed OBE guiding principles, the relationship between OBE analysis and data requirements, and using data for both formative feedback and internal program evaluation purposes.

We are now ready to start on a more detailed "How to" approach to outcome-based evaluation. The next three chapters outline and discuss the three types of outcome-based evaluation analysis: effectiveness, impact, and benefit–cost. After discussing the "How to" of these three analyses in Part II of the text, we will focus in Part III on how one collects, manages, and analyzes the data required of each analysis.

Study Questions

1. Generate a mission statement and goals for your agency (or one with which you are familiar) that specifies services and delineates specific, person- referenced outcomes.

2. Delineate the intervention or services you provide that are consistent with your mission statement and goals.

3. What specific valued, person-referenced outcomes will you use in your evaluation, and how will you demonstrate that they are consistent with the criteria: valued by the person, multidimensional, objective and measurable, connected logically to the program, and evaluated longitudinally?

4. Compare and contrast the specific data requirements you will need for conducting (a) an effectiveness analysis, (b) an impact analysis, and (c) a benefit–cost analysis (see Table 2.4).

5. How could you use the analyses identified in Question 4 for formative feedback and internal program evaluation?

6. Table 2.2 summarizes four public laws under which many education and social programs operate. If you are working in an area affected by additional public laws, what are they? What are their desired general outcomes?

7. Review the "desired general outcomes" listed in the right column of Table 2.2. Note that these outcomes are pretty general. For each, develop more specific outcomes that are person-referenced, objective, and measurable.

8. Review Table 2.3 that lists a number of potential person-referenced outcomes for different program types. Select the program type with which you are currently working (or familiar with) and discuss whether that program is currently evaluating these outcomes. If so, to what degree? If not, why?

9. Outline and discuss your approach to outcome-based evaluation. Based on your understanding of the chapter, where are there still questions or perceived barriers to the evaluation?

10. Find a journal article that evaluates an education or social program. Compare its methodology with that proposed in this chapter. What are the similarities and differences?

Additional Readings

Armstrong, M. I., Huz, S., & Evans, M. E. (1992). What works for whom: The design and evaluation of children's mental health services. *Social Work Research and Abstracts, 28*(1), 35–41.

Bolton, B. (1987). Outcome analysis in vocational rehabilitation. In M. J. Fuhrer (Ed.), *Rehabilitation outcomes: Analysis and measurement* (pp. 57–69). Baltimore: Brookes.

Brown, A. C. (1993). Revitalizing "handicap" for disability research: Developing tools to assess progress in quality of life for persons with disabilities. *Journal of Disability Policy Studies, 4*(2), 57–76.

DeStefano, L. (1986). Designing and implementing program evaluation. In F. R. Rusch (Ed.), *Supported employment* (pp. 229–247). Sycamore, IL: Sycamore.

Eisen, S. V., Dill, D. L., & Grob, M. C. (1994). Reliability and validity of a brief patient-report instrument for psychiatric outcome evaluation. *Hospital and Community Psychiatry, 45*(3), 242–247.

George, M. P., George, N. L., & Grosenick, J. K. (1990). Features of program evaluation in special education. *Remedial and Special Education, 11*(5), 23–30.

II

Outcome-Based Evaluation Analyses

Don't do anything that is not consistent with your culture.
PETER DRUCKER (1988)

This section of the book focuses on the heart of outcome-based evaluation: effectiveness, impact, and benefit–cost analyses. Each of these analyses can be used to evaluate education and social programs and provide program administrators, policy makers, funding bodies, and other constituent groups with formative feedback information that can be used to determine the following:

- The extent to which the program obtained its goals and objectives (effectiveness analysis).
- Whether the program made a difference compared to either no program or an alternate program (impact analysis).
- Whether the program's benefits outweigh its costs (benefit–cost analysis).

In reading these three chapters in which each type of analysis is described with examples, there are a number of key points that you will want to keep in mind. First, any analysis involves a comparison group or condition against which you compare the significance of the results. Second, the degree of certainty, comparability, precision, and generalizability of results from any OBE analysis is dependent largely on the OBE design used. The closer one comes to a true experimental/control comparison condition, the greater is the degree of certainty, comparability, precision, and generalizability.

Third, one's capability is critical in selecting the type of OBE analysis. As we saw in Table 2.4, there is also a definite relationship between the type of OBE analysis and data requirements. The most significant points to keep in mind here are that you will need (1) general cost estimates for

39

effectiveness and impact analyses, and detailed cost estimates for benefit–cost analysis; (2) clearly defined control groups or conditions for impact or benefit–cost analyses; and (3) multiple perspectives on benefits in benefit–cost analysis as opposed to simple outcome measures. Hence, the wisdom of Drucker's advice and our first guiding principle:

> GUIDING PRINCIPLE 1: *The type of outcome based evaluation analysis conducted must be consistent with the program's capability.*

Fourth, my capability to present detailed information about each type of analysis is limited by page constraints and personal experience. Page limitations necessitate that many of the assumptions and details involved especially in benefit–cost analysis be presented summarily. However, I do present a number of specific references at the end of Chapter 5 that allow the interested reader to pursue the issues involved in benefit–cost analysis in more detail. Additionally, I have had more experience with effectiveness and impact analyses than with benefit–cost. Similarly, I have had more practical experiences in the areas of special education, mental health, and disability programs but attempt to present analytic procedures that are appropriate to any educational or social program that one wants to evaluate.

Fifth, I am probably biased toward effectiveness and impact analyses. This bias, however, does not imply that good impact and benefit–cost analyses are unimportant. Indeed they are essential in today's world of accountability. However, wishful thinking does not produce the capability of most current programs to do benefit–cost analysis. One of my primary goals in this section of the text is to present clearly what those capabilities are, so that program administrators, policy makers, and funding bodies can better match evaluation requests with program capability.

The discussion of each type of OBE analysis will be based on a six-step approach that includes:

1. Select the questions asked.
2. Select the evaluation design (person as own comparison, pre–postchange comparison, longitudinal status comparison, hypothetical comparison group, matched pairs (cohorts), or experimental/control) to answer the question. These designs are discussed fully in Chapter 8.
3. Select the core data sets (recipient characteristics, core service functions, cost estimates, and valued, person-referenced outcomes). Details are presented in Chapter 6.
4. Measure the core data sets, which requires operational definitions that are discussed more fully in Chapters 6 and 7.

5. Collect, organize, and store the data. Procedures for doing so are discussed in Chapter 7.
6. Analyze the data (see Chapter 8).

A case study approach will be used in each chapter to highlight these steps, along with critical points to keep in mind as either an evaluation producer or consumer. Six criteria were used to select the specific case studies included in the three chapters:

1. The OBE analysis used is consistent with one of those included in this text and defined at the beginning of this overview.
2. There is a clearly described evaluation design consistent with those discussed in Chapter 8.
3. The core data sets are defined clearly and operationally.
4. Person-referenced outcomes are used that meet the five criteria: valued by the person, multidimensional, objective and measurable, connected logically to the program, and evaluated longitudinally.
5. Data analysis used either elaborates on or reflects those discussed in Chapter 8.
6. The analysis was published in an edited book or journal.

The Spanish philosopher Ortega y Gasset is purported to have said that "human life is a constant preoccupation with the future." The same can be said about outcome-based evaluation analysis. Although few education or social programs are currently doing effectiveness, impact, or benefit–cost analyses, the future is clear: they will. Hence, my hope is that the following material will assist both evaluation producers and consumers to feel comfortable with their futures, and be competent in meeting the challenges of outcome-based evaluation.

3

Effectiveness Analysis

Overview

Effectiveness analysis addresses the question of whether the program met its intended goals and objectives. Its major purposes include reporting a program's results, providing the basis for data-based management (formative feedback), and providing information for programmatic changes. This type of OBE analysis is the one most commonly used today due to the shift toward pragmatic program evaluation, practical and ethical problems in establishing experimental/control conditions, and the resources (time, money, expertise) required for impact or benefit–cost analysis. Thus, effectiveness analysis is the type of OBE analysis the reader is most likely to do and read about.

As stated previously, any analysis involves making comparisons between one condition or status and another. In reference to effectiveness analysis, the most typical evaluation (comparison) designs include person-as-own comparison, pre–postchange comparison, or longitudinal status comparisons. Although these are the easiest comparison conditions to generate, the number of assumptions that one makes in using them limits the analysis's precision, certainty, comparability, and generalizability. However, these limitations should not discourage the reader from doing good effectiveness analysis that can provide essential information to all interested stakeholders regarding the program's results, which in turn can be used for data-based management, reporting, and program change purposes. As stated by Morell (1979):

> An important purpose of outcome evaluation is to help form theories concerning the operation and effectiveness of social programs. Although evaluation which follows the experimental prescription may well be the most useful tool for such an endeavor, it is by no means the only tool. The development of theory is far removed from a one-to-one correspondence with experimental results, and factors such as plausibility and reasonableness play an important role in theory development. Those concepts emerge from an intimate understanding of the program or treatment under study, and one must give serious consideration to any research which may help increase such understanding. (p. 7)

Steps Involved in Effectiveness Analysis

Effectiveness analysis involves eight critical steps summarized in Table 3.1. The process begins by identifying the purpose of the analysis and then progresses to establishing and describing a comparison condition; describing the core data sets, their measurement, and how the data were analyzed; summarizing the major results and discussing them in reference to formative feedback uses; and outlining the implications of the results for programmatic change. Each of these steps can be seen clearly in the following two case studies whose general purpose was to evaluate the respective programs' goals of enhancing either the posttraining or postgraduation status of service recipients.

Study 1: Longitudinal Status Analysis

Purpose/Questions Asked

The three purposes of this analysis (Schalock & Lilley, 1986) included (1) evaluating the clients' current living and employment status; (2) determining the relationship of client characteristics and training variables to

Table 3.1. Steps Involved in Effectiveness Analysis

---

1. Identify clearly the purpose. For effectiveness analysis, it is to determine the extent to which the program obtained its goals and objectives.
2. Establish a comparison condition by using one or more of the following evaluation designs: person as own comparison, pre–post change comparisons, or longitudinal status comparisons.
3. Describe how the comparison conditions were established and how service recipients entered the condition.
4. Describe the core data sets (recipient characteristics, core service functions, cost estimates, and person-referenced outcomes) and how they were operationalized and measured.
5. Describe how the data were analyzed, including specific statistical tests and tests of significance.
6. Summarize the major results in reference to the purpose of the effectiveness analysis.
7. Discuss the major results in regard to formative feedback uses.
8. Outline the implications of the results for programmatic changes.

---

successful placement; and (3) evaluating each client's quality of life through personal interviews and objective measurement.

Evaluation Design

A longitudinal status-comparison design was used. Contact had been maintained during the 8 to 10 years with each client for the purpose of either providing assistance or updating client demographic files. During the (then) current analysis, personal contact was maintained with each client.

Core Data Sets and Their Measurement

1. *Recipient characteristics.* Persons involved in the analysis were 85 (42 males, 43 females) service recipients who had been placed 8 to 10 years prior into either independent living or competitive employment environments and who had remained within that placement for a minimum of 2 years. The average age was 30 (range = 26 to 67), SD = 10.4 and average full-scale IQ (Wechsler Adult Intelligence Scale) was 67 (range = 40 to 91, SD = 12). All persons had been assessed during their initial program involvement on the Basic Skills Screening Test, which is a standardized criterion-referenced instrument containing 107 behavioral skills that comprise seven skill domains: (1) sensorimotor functioning, (2) visual processing, (3) auditory processing, (4) language, (5) symbolic operations, (6) social–emotional behavior, and (7) work skills. Additionally, the level of

family involvement was determined for each person by having two staff members who best knew the person and his/her family rate the family's involvement on the following 3-point scale:

1 = Either not involved or not supportive of client movement or placement.

2 = Moderately involved with assisting the client's community placement and adjustment.

3 = Strongly supportive of the client's community placement and successful adjustment.

2. *Core service functions.* During their program involvement, each person had received a number of units of service that were computed based on staff functions and time parameters. Specific types included training, assistance, case management, supervision, support, and transportation.

3. *Cost estimates.* Average costs per year were computed for each person by dividing the agency's total yearly cost by the number of persons receiving services during the fiscal year. These historical costs were not used as part of the effectiveness analysis.

4. *Person-referenced outcomes.* Four outcomes were used in the effectiveness analysis: current programmatic status, current living/work placement, current financial status, and quality of life.

a. *Current program status.* Each person's programmatic status was rated as active, if receiving programmatic employment and community-living training that involved five or more written prescriptive programs; active/enabler assistance, if the person was in one of the two training components, but receiving follow-up in the other component; or terminated, if not receiving any of these service functions.

b. *Current living/work placement.* Each person's community-living environment-placement status was classified as supervised living, if a natural home, group home of five or more individuals, or Intermediate Care Facility for the Mentally Retarded; semi-independent living, if extended family, certified foster home, group home of four or fewer individuals, transitional living unit, or supervised/supported apartment; or independent living, if an independent apartment, home, or a cooperative client-owned living arrangement. Similarly, the person's employment status was classified as sheltered work, if sheltered workshop, center industry, or prime manufacturing; semicompetitive employment, if work stations in industry, on-the-job training, or sheltered enclaves; or competitive employment, if employed competitively either full- or part-time.

c. *Current financial status.* The person's current source of income and monthly amount were tabulated for the previous 12 months. Income categories were either wages or entitlement monies, including Social Security

Insurance (SSI), Social Security Disability Insurance (SSDI), Social Security Assistance (SSA), or Aid to the Aged, Blind, and Disabled (AABD).

d. *Quality of life*. Each person completed (on his/her own or with assistance in reading and interpreting the question) the 30-item Quality of Life Questionnaire (Schalock & Keith, 1993) that used a 3-point rating scale to assess three quality-of-life factors: environmental control, social interactions, and community integration.

Results

Three groups emerged on the basis of participants' current programmatic status, living–work placement, and financial status: 29% maintained their living and work placements or moved into comparable environments; 47% had changed their placement categories with current statuses including living independently but unemployed or employed only part-time, being in a mental health facility, or living with family and unemployed; and 24% returned to the training program. A number of variables were found to discriminate between successful and unsuccessful living and work outcomes, including family involvement, social–emotional behavior, number of disabilities, sensorimotor functioning, symbolic operations, and auditory–visual processing. For assessed quality of life, significant correlates included family involvement, income, number of disabilities, and age. Those who were successful had a higher assessed Quality-of-Life Index than those who were unsuccessful. A summary of the major results are presented in Exhibit 3-1.

Discussion of Results and Their Implications

There were a number of implications from the analysis that were used for programmatic reporting and change purposes. First, the three groups can be viewed as reflective of students transitioning into adult services from special education programs. One group requires "no special services," one requires "time-limited services," and one requires "ongoing services." Second, there is a need to be concerned about the quality of life of persons placed from community-based programs, especially those who are living independently but are either unemployed or working only part-time. Personal interviews revealed that most were lonely and had very fragile support systems. The lucky ones had strong family support or an advocate. The third implication regards the criteria against which the effectiveness and efficiency of community-based programs are judged. If competitive employment is the criterion, then only 29% of the program's service recipients could be judged "successful." If independent living is

Exhibit 3-1
Summary of Major Community Placement Results

Results of Multiple Discriminant Analysis
on Living and Work Outcomes

	Standardized discriminant coefficients	
Predictor variable	Living Outcome	Work Outcome
Age	.19	.14
IQ	−.05	.11
Gender	−.17	.13
Number of disabilities	−.27*	−.30*
Sensorimotor	.04	.62**
Visual processing	.38**	.64**
Auditory processing	.14	.36**
Language	−.04	.03
Symbolic operations	.34**	.27*
Social–emotional	.31**	−.25*
Work skills	.14	.00
Family involvement	.87**	.61**

Total Sample Comparison on Outcome Variables

		Work	
Living	Number	Successful	Unsuccessful
Successful	69	37	32
Unsuccessful	16	1	15

Total Sample Comparison on Average Quality of Life Indices

	Outcome	
Environment	Successful	Unsuccessful
Living	67.4	53.8
Work	69.1	62.1

*p < .05
**p < .01

the criterion, then 64% of the persons were successful. If becoming a "taxpayer instead of a tax-taker" is the criterion, then 46% of the clientele were successfully (re)habilitated.

Thus, our first case study illustrates a common finding in most effectiveness analyses: unequivocal results. But that is not bad news. The critical thing is that the program was evaluated as to how well it had met its goals and objectives. As with most people's goals, the picture is often mixed.

This first study reflects the components of an effectiveness analysis and indicates how the resulting data can be used for reporting the program's results and providing formative feedback to program administrators and other stakeholders that can be used for programmatic evaluation and proposed changes. This use of effectiveness-analysis data is also reflected in our second case study.

Study 2: Postsecondary Status Analysis

Purpose/Questions Asked

The two purposes of this analysis (Schalock et al., 1986) were to evaluate the postgraduation living and work status of special education students who had participated in a community-based job exploration and training program during a 5-year period prior to the analysis, and determine the relationship between their status and 19 predictor variables, including student characteristics, school variables, and environmental characteristics.

Evaluation Design

A longitudinal status comparison design was used. Data on four major outcome categories (present employment status, current living environment, current source of income, and employment data) were collected by phone yearly following the students' graduation. These data were collected through personal interviews with the graduates and/or their family member(s). The 19 predictor variables used in the analysis included the three major categories of (1) student characteristics (age, IQ, verified handicap, gender, total days absent, and family involvement); (2) school variables (number of months in special education, percent of time in resource room, school enrollment, days absent, number of vocational programs offered by the school, number of semester hours enrolled in one or more vocational programs, total years teaching by the resource teacher, and number of endorsements held by the resource teacher); and (3) county characteristics (population, per capita income, number of businesses, labor force, and average unemployment rate for the 5 years of the follow-up period).

Core Data Sets and Their Measurement

1. *Recipient characteristics.* The 108 students who graduated from high school between 1979 and 1983 had been classified according to the State Department of Education's definitions as either specific learning disabled (SLD), educable mentally handicapped (EMH), or mentally retarded (MR). The sample included 65 students diagnosed as SLD, 31 as EMH, and 12 as MR. Average characteristics of SLD students included the following: 17.9 years of age; 92.1 IQ (Wechsler Intelligence Scale for Children); 50 males and 15 females; and 16 months in special education. For EMH students: 18.5 years; 68.1 IQ; 24 males and 7 females; and 17.1 months in special education. For MR students: 19.5 years; 44.7 IQ; 8 males and 4 females; and 17.6 months in special education.

2. *Core service functions.* The job exploration and training model used contained four essential features: (a) an extensive survey of employers concerning desired skills and behaviors for entry-level employees; (b) a student competency checklist consisting of a prioritized sequence of desired employee skills and behaviors; (c) development of training modules incorporating the desired job-related skills and behaviors; and (d) monthly training for resource teachers in job analysis, job development, and on-the-job support activities. Students were placed in a job-exploration training site based on their stated job interests plus congruence between the students' skills and the essential entry-level skills identified through the employer survey. Resource teachers provided one or more of the following training-assistance activities: skills training, maintenance training, supervision, or assistance.

3. *Cost estimates.* These were not available for the period covered by the analysis. However, if necessary, historical costs could have been estimated based on the program's yearly budget.

4. *Person-referenced outcomes.* The four major outcome categories and data sets included: (a) present employment status (employed, unemployed, school, community-based mental retardation program, prison or mental health facility); (b) current living environment (supervised [home or group home], semi-independent [staffed apartment, dormitory], or independent); (c) current primary source of income (parents/relatives, public, personal); and (d) employment data (hours/week, hourly wage, weeks employed per year, number of jobs since graduation, total months employed since graduation, and total earnings since graduation).

Results

The effectiveness analysis revealed five significant results. First, 61% of the graduates were working competitively. Second, 22% were living independently. Third, students diagnosed as SLD were more likely to be employed, live independently, and be self-sufficient than those diagnosed as EMH or MR. Fourth, students whose families were moderately to highly involved with the students' programs were more successful on the employment-related outcome measures. And fifth, significant predictors included both student characteristics and environmental variables. A summary of the stepwise multiple regression of predictor variables on the outcome measures is presented in Exhibit 3-2.

Discussion of Results and Their Implications

The finding that 61% of the graduates were employed at least 1 year following graduation supports the job-training/placement model used, because this percentage was slightly higher than rates reported at that time by other investigators. Second, three variables were consistently significant predictors of person-referenced outcomes: (1) number of semester hours in vocational programs; (2) the level of family involvement; and (3) type of handicapping condition (students verified as SLD or EMH consistently did better on the outcome measures). And third, the high percentage (78) of students who were still living in supervised arrangements (generally at home) suggested the need for special education programs to also focus on teaching community-living skills and procuring community-living support systems.

The analysis also had a number of weaknesses that were reported. First, complete data were available on only 81% of the total number of graduates during this period because a conservative decision ruled that only students with complete data sets would be used in the analysis. A second weakness relates to predictive validity and the failure of any multiple R squared (see Exhibit 3-2) to exceed 52%. Hence, considerable variance among the outcome scores cannot be predicted exclusively on the basis of the 19 predictor variables analyzed. Third, there was a small sample size, especially among students diagnosed as mentally retarded.

This study reflects the reality of many effectiveness analyses: Results are often unequivocal and cost estimates for the given period frequently are unavailable. In such situations, these factors need to be pointed out so that the reader is informed and the analyst is credible. Such shortcomings generally do not reduce the importance of the effectiveness analysis, but may limit its precision, certainty, comparability, and generalizability.

Exhibit 3-2
Stepwise Multiple Regression:
Predictor Variables on Outcome Measures

	Outcome Variables*		
Predictor Variables	Present status	Current living	Primary income source
Verified handicap	16.1**	22.1	26.5
Family involvement	20.6	25.5	7.8
Total days absent		11.7	
Gender		18.2	
Semester hours in vocational			17.6
programs			13.8
			21.8

	Number of jobs	Months employed	Total earnings
IQ	8.6		
Family involvement	15.2	29.6	42.5
Per capita income		9.4	22.4
Total years teaching		19.2	31.5
Verified handicap		28.9	39.1
Total days absent		32.7	45.7
Number of businesses		35.3	48.1
Labor force		39.2	51.5
Semester hours in vocational program			16.4

	Hours per week	Hourly wages	Weeks employed a year
IQ	16.6	10.1	
Gender	23.0	20.6	23.4
Family involvement	26.3	17.7	13.2
Semester hours in vocational program	29.2	27.5	17.2
School enrollment	32.9	24.0	20.2
Verified handicap	34.9		8.0

*Only those predictor variables are listed for which the multiple R squared was maximized and the overall F-score was significant at $p < .01$.
**Percent of variance explained by R squared.

Exhibit 3-3
Suggestions for Evaluating Service Demonstration Programs

Service demonstration programs/projects frequently lack some of the following prerequisite program evaluation requirements discussed in this chapter: control or comparison groups, common intervention or protocols, common data sets, and/or common data-collection procedures. If such is the case, one might consider completing the following two-phase outcome based evaluation strategy:

PHASE 1: Identify from generally comparable program models a subset representing promising models. This can be done through evaluating either
  1. Their degree of implementation (Brekke, 1987), or
  2. Their initial results on valued, person-referenced outcomes (Mowbray, Cohen, & Bybee, 1993).

PHASE 2: Develop a detailed description of each of the promising models identified in Phase 1. This can be done through either
  1. Developing a matrix of model by critical data set: recipient characteristics, service functions, costs, and person-referenced outcomes.
  2. Using process analysis that describes the critical interrogatories of each identified model (Perry, Hoff, & Gaither, 1994; Scheier, 1994).

Before completing this chapter on effectiveness analysis, it is important to discuss how one should approach evaluating service demonstration programs such as those found frequently in the areas of substance abuse, crime reduction, diversion programs, programs for the homeless, or for training programs. These demonstration services or programs generally do not have control or comparison groups, common interventions or protocols, common data sets, or common data procedures (Schlenger et al., 1994). When this is the case, one should consider the two-phase approach outlined in Exhibit 3-3. Note that the two phases include (1) identifying from generally comparable program models a subset representing promising models; and (2) developing a detailed description of each of the promising programs or services.

Summary

In summary, this chapter has focused on effectiveness analysis, the major purpose of which is to determine the extent to which the program obtained its goals and objectives. Data resulting from effectiveness analyses are used primarily for reporting program results, and as a basis for data-based management (formative feedback), programmatic change, and improvement. The two case studies presented in this chapter show the critical steps involved in either conducting or understanding effectiveness analysis, along with how the results, implications, and potential weaknesses of the analysis should be reported.

In today's world of increasing accountability requirements, it is essential that program managers do effectiveness analysis. Although the extent and complexity of these analyses will depend upon the program's capability (such as we saw in Exhibit 3-3), no program in the 1990s should be without this type of outcome-based analysis. All stakeholders are concerned about the degree to which a program meets its goals and objectives; and all program administrators need to have the results from their effectiveness analyses for reporting and program improvement purposes. Chapters 10 and 11 discuss additional points about reporting and acting on the results of one's effectiveness analysis. For the time being, you might want to keep our second guiding principle clearly in mind.

GUIDING PRINCIPLE 2: *Effectiveness analysis is an absolute requirement of program management in the 1990s.*

Study Questions

1. Summarize the basic components, uses, and weaknesses of effectiveness analysis. Why is it the most commonly used type of outcome-based evaluation analysis?

2. Assume that you are an administrator of an educational program and plan to do an effectiveness analysis of your program. Outline the specific steps and procedures of your analysis, following the eight steps summarized in Table 3.1.

3. Assume that you are an administrator of a mental health program for either children or adults and plan to do an effectiveness analysis of your program. Outline the specific steps and procedures of your analysis, following the eight steps summarized in Table 3.1.

4. Assume that you are an administrator of a disability program and plan to do an effectiveness analysis of your program. Outline the specific steps and procedures of your analysis, following the eight steps summarized in Table 3.1.

5. Compare the effectiveness analyses you have just completed with what would be required in order to do an impact or benefit–cost analysis of each of the three programs. What are the major differences among the three types of analysis?

(*Note*: You may want to refer back to Table 2.4 for the data requirements involved in impact and benefit–cost analysis.)

6. Assume that you are an administrator for a service demonstration program and are required to evaluate your initial results. Use the two-phase procedure suggested in Exhibit 3-3 to outline specific evaluation activities that you will need to accomplish.

7. After you have outlined the evaluation activities in Question 6, answer each of the following: (a) How would you evaluate the degree of implementation? and (b) What person-referenced outcomes would you use and how would you measure them objectively?

8. If you could interview a program director for 60 minutes, what questions would you ask that would provide the most valid indicators of the administrator's program's ability to do an effectiveness analysis?

9. Review a journal article on effectiveness analysis. How do the methods compare with those outlined in this chapter?

10. What obstacles do you see within educational or social programs to do effectiveness analysis? What do you feel is the basis for the obstacles, and how would you overcome them?

Additional Readings

Anthony, W. A., Cohen, M., & Kennard, W. (1990). Understanding the current facts and principles of mental health systems planning. *American Psychologist, 45*(11), 1249–1252.

Borich, G. D., & Nance, D. D. (1987). Evaluating special education programs: Shifting the professional mandate from process to outcome. *Remedial and Special Education, 8*(3), 7–16.

Brown, A. C. (1993). Revitalizing "handicap" for disability research: Developing tools to assess progress in quality of life for persons with disabilities. *Journal of Disability Policy Studies, 4*(2), 57–76.

Judge, W. Q. (1994). Correlates of organizational effectiveness: A multilevel analysis of a multidimensional outcome. *Journal of Business Ethics, 13*(1), 1–10.

Meyer, L. H., & Evans, I. M. (1993). Meaningful outcomes in behavioral intervention: Evaluating positive approaches to the remediation of challenging behaviors. In J. Reichle & D. P. Wacher (Eds.), *Communicative approaches to the management of challenging behavior*, (pp. 407–428). Baltimore: Brookes.

4

Impact Analysis

Overview

Impact analysis is not easy, but it is an essential outcome-based analysis to complete if you want to determine whether a given program made a difference compared to either no program or an alternative program. Thus, an absolute requirement in impact analysis is that you have a comparison group or condition against which you compare the significance of your results. For example, you might be interested in determining the impact of job training program "A" by comparing the posttraining job status of its graduates with graduates of job training program "B", or with persons not involved in a job training program.

It has been my experience that program administrators seldom look

57

at a comparison group of similar persons not in the program and ask, "What would have happened to my service recipients had they not entered the program?" My experience has also been that funding bodies and policy makers are very interested in impact analysis, for they want to know whether a particular education or social program made a difference, and whether some programs do better than others.

Impact analysis involves data collection, following people over time, and thinking about what actually happens to the service recipients and what would have happened had they not been served or had they served in a comparable program. Its specific purposes include the following:

1. Focusing on the program's impacts.
2. Determining whether these impacts can be attributed with reasonable certainty to the intervention or services being evaluated.
3. Providing formative feedback to program managers, policy makers, and funding bodies regarding the impact of the specific program or public policy being evaluated.

The Difference between Outcomes and Impacts

Doing an impact analysis is facilitated if you understand the difference between outcomes and impacts. This difference is diagrammed in Figure 4.1. The critical point to remember from this diagram is that program impacts represent the statistically significant differences in outcomes between the comparison conditions.

The data requirements for conducting an impact analysis are similar to those required for effectiveness analysis. They include recipient characteristics, services received, cost estimates, and person-referenced outcomes. However, there are two important differences: (1) cost estimates become more important in impact analysis because they are frequently used for equating program intensities; and (2) estimated impacts are made based on the statistically significant mean differences (if any) between the outcomes (see Figure 4.1).

However, one needs to think beyond a simple comparison of mean differences. For example, calculating group differences simply in terms of the mean values of outcome variables may produce biased estimates of intervention or treatment effect, especially if there are differences among preassigment characteristics. Hence, regression or analysis of covariance techniques are frequently used. These techniques are advantageous because they control for initial sample differences and can be expected to produce unbiased estimates of intervention effects. Regression techniques also offer two additional advantages over simple comparison of mean

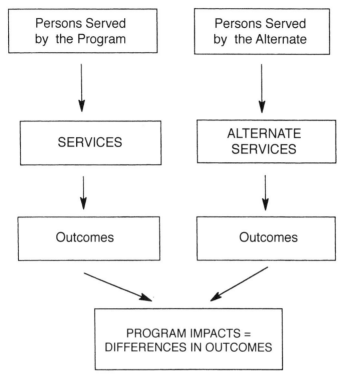

Figure 4.1 Distinction between outcome and impacts.

values: (1) they provide more powerful tests of the program's potential effects because they control statistically for the influence of other explanatory variables; and (2) by including the explanatory variables in the regression model, one can directly assess their individual net influences on the outcome variable(s).

The three typical evaluation designs used to construct the comparison condition include a hypothetical comparison group, matched pairs (cohorts), or experimental/control (see Chapter 8 for specific details about each design). Although these designs are more difficult to form, compared to those we discussed under effectiveness analysis, their use results in greater precision, certainty, comparability, and generalizability of your results. As discussed in Chapter 8, the methods of classical experiments generally provide the most accurate and statistically valid means of identifying a comparison group, because these methods randomly assign program applicants or participants to either experimental or control conditions. The advantage of this design is that if the number of persons assigned is moderately large, the analyst can be reasonably sure of the comparability of the two groups. In particular, the comparability of the groups in terms of unmeasurable characteristics is important, since it is very difficult to control for the influence of such characteristics using statistical methods. Furthermore, results based on data generated from an experimental design tend to be stable with respect to change in the specific details of the estimation process.

Although experimental/control designs have been used for some social programs, they are not always feasible. For example, it may not be possible to conduct random assignment in an entitlement program that guarantees services to all members of a specific target group. However, if all applicants cannot be served or if the intervention is a new one in which there is still doubt about its impact, then random assignment can be a fair way of deciding who should get the program services. Another alternative is to use matched pairs (cohorts) in which one member of each pair receives one type of intervention or (re)habilitation service, and the other member the other (comparison).

When it is infeasible to use either the experimental/control or matched pair OBE design, then a third approach to identifying a comparison group is to use conjecture in which a hypothetical comparison group is generated (see Exhibit 8-4). By relying on a general knowledge about the average outcomes of nonparticipants or on a knowledge of preenrollment status, the analyst may estimate what would have happened to participants had they not enrolled in the program. Some researchers of supported work programs, for example, have estimated impacts under the assumption that had participants not enrolled in the program they would have continued in the activities they had prior to enrollment. This evaluation design clearly represents inexact estimation procedures, and therefore results in less precision, certainty, comparability, and generalizability (Noble & Conley, 1987).

Steps Involved in Impact Analysis

The steps involved in conducting an impact analysis are summarized in Table 4.1. They begin by stating the purpose of the analysis, continue with establishing and describing the comparison conditions, describe the core data sets and how they were collected and analyzed, summarize the major results, discuss these results in reference to formative feedback, and outline the analysis's implications for programmatic changes.

As with the previous chapter, a case study approach will be used to discuss the critical components and process steps involved in conducting

Table 4.1. Steps Involved in Impact Analysis

1. Identify clearly the purpose. For impact analysis, the purpose is to determine whether the program made a difference compared to either no program or an alternative program.
2. Establish a comparison condition by using one or more of the following evaluation designs: hypothetical comparison group, matched pairs (cohorts), or experimental/ control.
3. Describe how the comparison conditions were established and how service recipients entered the program.
4. Describe the core-data sets (recipient characteristics, core service functions, cost estimates, and valued, person-referenced outcomes) and how they were operationalized and measured.
5. Describe how the data were analyzed, including specific statistical tests and tests of significance.
6. Make impact statements (based on significant mean differences) and indicate their level of statistical significance. Summarize other major results based on the statistical analyses used.
7. Discuss the major results in reference to policy development and evaluation.
8. Outline the implications of the results for programmatic changes and/or policy development and evaluation.

(or understanding) impact analysis. Two studies will be reviewed—one reasonably simple, and the other much more involved. These studies were selected on the basis of their meeting the following six criteria:

1. The definition and approach to impact analysis is consistent with that presented in the text.
2. There is a clearly described evaluation design.
3. There are clear operational definitions of the core data sets.
4. Person-referenced outcomes were used that meet the five criteria (valued by the person, multidimensional, objective and measurable, connected logically to the program, and evaluated longitudinally).
5. Data analysis reflects an elaboration on the statistical analyses discussed in Chapter 8.
6. The analysis was published in an edited journal or book.

Study 1: The Impact of Different Training Environments

Purpose/Questions Asked

The purpose of this analysis (Schalock, Gadwood, & Perry, 1984) was to determine the impact on behavioral-skill acquisition rates of 10 matched pairs of persons with mental retardation who received individualized, prescriptive programming for 1 year in one of two training environments: their own apartments or a group home.

Evaluation Design

Ten matched pairs were selected from among the 40 clients within two community-living skills-training programs. These two training programs had equivalent programmatic philosophy, assessment techniques, prescriptive programming techniques, staff–client ratios, and staff competencies. Ten community-living skills instructors with BA degrees in social science were involved. Five instructors provided training in staffed apartments and five within the center-based program. All staff had demonstrated 22 prescriptive programming competencies at the end of their initial 2-day in-service training, and again on a competency probe conducted just before the study. The 14 program-writing competencies involved writing measurable behavioral objectives, demonstrating content and process task analyses, utilizing appropriate reinforcement and correction procedures, and specifying client data to be recorded. The 8 program-conducting competencies involved following the prescribed strategies as outlined on the written program sheet, actively prompting and correcting if necessary, and recording training data during the training session. Each staff was rated (5-point Likert Scale) on each competency during the competency probe.

Clients were matched on gender, age, IQ (Wechsler Full-Scale), duration of prior community-living skills training, skill level on the Community Living Skills Screening Test, medication history, and number of recorded negative behavior incidents. Clients and staff within the two training programs were essentially equivalent before the analysis began.

Core Data Sets and Their Measurement

1. *Recipient characteristics.* The analysis involved 20 adult clients currently enrolled in the two training programs described already. The 10 females and 10 males averaged 31 years of age with an average IQ (Wechsler Full-Scale) of 51, and had been enrolled in the community-living training program for 23 months. Each client was assessed independently by two instructional staff prior to the study on the criterion-referenced Community Living Skills Screening Test. Across the 10 behavioral domains assessed by the test, interobserver reliability coefficients averaged .85, generalizability coefficients .84, and test–retest reliabilities .87.

2. *Core service functions.* Clients lived in either a group home or a staffed apartment during the 1-year study. A staffed apartment was a

residential quadplex with three clients and one part-time staff who provided general supervision in the evenings and on weekends. Group homes were renovated family homes that provided room, board, and live-in staff supervision for 8 to 10 clients. They were not used for systematic training. During the study, training occurred within either a current-living or center-based training environment. Training in the current-living environment involved 1:1 instruction by community living instructors in the client's individual apartment within the staffed apartment quadplex; center-based training occurred in a large group home adjacent to the adult developmental center that provided the facilities for 1:1 instructing in the same programmatic areas.

Data from the criterion-referenced Community Living Skills Screening Test were used to develop the client's annual Individual Program Plan (IPP). The IPP specified the specific behavioral skills within each of the IQ behavioral domains on which the person was to receive prescriptive programming the next year. These prescriptive programs were carried out within the respective environments (current-living or center-based) for 1 year. The pass criterion for each prescriptive program was that stated in the criterion-referenced test.

Training in both settings averaged 6 hours per day. There was a 20% turnover in instructional staff during the year. All replacement staff received in-service training and demonstrated the required prescriptive program-writing and program-conducting competencies before their involvement with the clients.

3. *Cost estimates.* Cost estimates were made on the basis of the number of training units received by the participants. The costs were the same for all participants regardless of the training location.

4. *Person-referenced outcomes.* The major outcome variable was the number of behavioral skills acquired that met the pass criterion. Skill maintenance was evaluated by reassessing each person on the Community Living Skills Screening Test 1 year after the beginning of the analysis period.

Results

Persons receiving training in their staffed apartments gained significantly more ($p < .05$ in all comparisons) community-living skills in 7 of the 10 skill-training areas than the center-based group. These differences are summarized in Exhibit 4-1 (top portion). The point biserial correlation between skills gained and dichotomized training location was .70 ($df = 18$, $p < .01$).

The next step in the data analysis involved determining the relative

---

Exhibit 4-1
Results of Impact Analysis of Different Training Environments

---

Impact on Number of Community-Living Skills Gained

Behavioral domain	Training environment means		Estimated impact
	Apartment	Center	
Personal maintenance	2.4	0.7	1.7*
Dressing/clothing care	1.6	0.5	1.1*
Eating/food management	1.4	0.3	1.1*
Social behavior	0.5	0.4	0.1
Expressive skills	0.7	0.8	0.1
Home living	2.2	0.5	1.7*
Money skills	0.6	0.2	0.4
Time awareness and utilization	1.9	0.3	1.6*
Recreation and leisure skills	0.6	0.1	0.5*
Community awareness and utilization	1.5	0.7	0.8*
Total	13.4	4.5	8.9*

Multiple Discriminant Analysis Results

Multiple discriminate variable	Wilks's Lambda	Standardized discriminant coefficient
Task analysis steps	.30	0.46
Social behavior skills	.23	−0.76
Age	.20	−0.43
Program frequency	.18	1.04

Multiple Regression Results

Multiple regression variable	Beta	Multiple R	F
Task analysis steps	−.89	.78	15.21**
Program frequency	−.68	.82	6.71**
Social behavior skills	−.47	.87	3.62*
Age	−.08	.88	1.02

*$p < .05$ (matched pairs sample t test)

---

contribution of 32 predictor variables to the behavioral skill (outcome) data. This involved a three-step process. First, the outcome measure (number of skills) was converted to a dichotomized variable by ranking the number of skills gained, determining the median, and assigning each person a 1 or a 0, based on whether he/she was above or below the median. Second, a multiple discriminant analysis was conducted to determine predictors for the dichotomized variables. Given the small sample size and large number of predictor variables, the variables entered into the equation were limited to those 19 that were significantly ($p < .05$, two-tailed) related to the outcome variable. Thus, each variable was considered independently in relation to the outcome variable, which improves prediction. The standardized discriminant coefficients and Wilks's Lamda for the four discriminant variables are summarized in the middle portion of Exhibit 4-1. Two significant discriminating variables were the client characteristics of age and number of social behavior skills; and two were the training variables of average number of steps per task analysis and average number of times per week the prescriptive program was run.

Third, a stepwise multiple regression was run against the outcome variable to determine the relative contribution of the four discriminating variables. Exhibit 4-1 (bottom) lists those predictor variables up to which the multiple R squared was maximized and the overall F-score was significant. The three significant predictor variables were number of task-analysis steps, programming frequency, and assessed number of social behavioral skills.

Discussion of Results and Their Implications

This impact analysis found that significantly more community-living skills were acquired when skills training occurred in the client's living environment than when in a center-based training facility. Indeed, clients acquired more than three times as many behavioral skills when instructed in their own apartments. Equally important, the skills were maintained, as reflected in skill-profile stability. These findings demonstrate that transfer of stimulus control is increased when an intervention brings appropriate responding under control of training stimuli similar to those found in the transfer setting. With training in the natural environment, skill generalization is enhanced, in part because the training stimulus conditions are the same as those encountered in the natural environment.

Results also support the notion that transfer of a response from one stimulus to another will be increased under two conditions: (1) when the response under stimulus control is not overly precise; and (2) when the transfer and training stimuli are along relevant dimensions. In reference to the first condition, less precise stimulus control might be associated with fewer steps in the task analyses, with more verbal rather than tangible reinforcement, and with more modeling and cueing than physical prompts. In reference to the second condition, staff apartment instructors noted the intrinsic reward value of a person's performing the skill in the natural environment.

There are at least two methodological problems with this impact analysis. One relates to using gain scores as the major outcome variable. Potential weaknesses include the presence of artifacts, a possible regression to the mean, or a potential plateau effect. We attempted to overcome these weaknesses by using multiple outcomes (skill acquisition and stability), independent evaluators, and an assessment instrument with demonstrated reliability and predictive validity.

The second problem related to the lack of random assignment to the two training environments. This problem raises the possibility of regression toward different means, thereby destroying any representativeness of the original group. The analysis represents a common circumstance associated with outcome-based analyses in which the analyst is not in a position to implement a truly randomized design. As discussed in Chapter 8, governmental regulations and political, community, financial, and practical considerations all affect decision making concerning sample selection. Under such circumstances, what are the choices? They appear to be either to make no attempt at empirical evaluation or to find a method that without randomization provides a reasonably sound basis for interference about effects. In this analysis, a three-step multivariate matching technique was used: (1) identifying distinct subgroups within the larger group that consisted of individuals with similar responses to particular sets of stimuli; (2) matching service recipients on a pairwise basis by an interdisciplinary team; and (3) applying a variety of tests to the matched pairs to demonstrate equivalence of the matching. At this point,

> the same selection procedure is completed, and from then on the assumption is that it has produced equivalent experimental and control groups; and the testing for impact of an intervention proceeds along the same lines as it would in studies in which the sample members had been randomly assigned to the experimental and control groups. (C. Sherwood, Morris, & S. Sherwood, 1975, p. 195)

Study 2: The Impact of Transitional Employment Programs

Purpose/Questions Asked

The purpose of this analysis (Kerachsky, Thornton, Bloomenthal, Maynard, & Stephens, 1985) was to evaluate the impact of transitional employment programs in enhancing the economic and social independence of young adults with mental retardation. The Structured Training and Employment Transmittal Services (STETS) analysis was designed to address five basic questions:

1. Does STETS improve the labor-market performance of participants?
2. Does STETS participation help individuals lead more normal lifestyles?
3. In what ways do the characteristics and experiences of participants influence the effectiveness of STETS?
4. Does STETS affect the use of alternative programs by participants?
5. Do the benefits of STETS exceed the costs?

Evaluation Design

An experimental/control design was used, in which individuals were assigned randomly into STETS/non-STETS groups. Eligibility criteria were established for two purposes: (1) to limit program participation to those who could benefit potentially from program services, and (2) to encourage projects to recruit and enroll a broad range of clients in order to provide an adequate information base for examining the suitability of STETS for a diverse population. Each client met the following criteria: (1) between 18 and 24 years of age, inclusive; (2) mental retardation in the moderate, mild, or lower borderline ranges; (3) no unsubsidized full-time employment of 6 or more months in the 2 years preceding intake, and no unsubsidized employment of more than 10 hours per week at the time of intake into the program; and (4) no secondary disability that would make on-the-job training for competitive employment impractical.

Core Data Sets and Their Measurement

1. *Recipient characteristics.* The sample consisted of 437 individuals: 226 experimentals and 211 controls. Of the sample, 59% were male, 50% were minority ethnic/social groups, 60% of the measured IQs were in the mild range and 12% in the moderate range of mental retardation, 80% lived with parents and 10% in supervised settings, fewer than 30% could manage their own finances, 67% were using some form of public assistance with prior vocational experiences limited primarily to workshops and activity centers, and 33% had no work experience the 2 years prior to enrollment.

2. *Core service functions.* STETS involved the following three sequential phases. Phase I involved assessment and work-readiness training. This phase combined training and support services in a low-stress environment, the goal of which was to help participants begin to develop the basic work habits, skills, and attitudes necessary for placement into more demanding work settings. This preliminary stage, which was limited to 500

hours of paid employment, occurred in either a sheltered workshop or nonsheltered work setting; in all cases, the participants' wages were paid by the project.

Phase II involved a period of on-the-job training in local firms and agencies. During this stage, participants were placed in nonsheltered positions that required at least 30 hours of work per week, and in which, over time, the levels of stress and responsibility were to approach those found in competitive jobs. Wages were paid by either the project or the employers, or some combination of the two. The STETS program provided workers in Phase II with counseling and other support services, and it helped the line supervisors at the host company conduct the training and necessary monitoring activities.

Phase III, which included postplacement support services, began after participants had completed Phase II training and were performing their jobs independently. The purpose of this phase of program services was to ensure an orderly transition to work by tracking the progress of participants, by providing up to 6 months of postplacement support services, and, if necessary, by developing linkages with other local service agencies.

3. *Cost estimates.* The cost accounting framework (see Chapter 5 for a detailed discussion of this concept) disaggregated costs into three components: the operating costs of the projects, compensation paid to participants while they were in Phase I or II activities, and central administrative costs. The average STETS service package cost an average of $6,200 per participant. Estimated cost figures are summarized in reference to the benefit–cost analysis example found in Chapter 5 (see Exhibit 5-2).

4. *Person-referenced outcomes.* The STETS impact analysis focused on 3 general outcome categories and 11 specific variables. These included (a) employment (percent employed in regular job or any paid job; average weekly earnings in regular job; and average weekly earnings in any paid job); (b) training and schooling (percent in any training or any schooling); and (c) income sources (percent receiving SSI or SSDI; average monthly income from SSA or SSDI; percent receiving any cash transfers; average monthly income from case transfers; and average weekly personal income). These person-referenced outcomes were collected at months 6, 15 and 22 of the project.

Results

The estimated program impacts on the key outcome measures are summarized in Exhibit 4-2. Note that the significance of the impacts (denoted by asterisks in the table) depend upon the evaluation period. Employment in regular jobs was significantly greater for experimental-group members than for control-group members, and by month 22, experimentals were an average of 62% more likely than controls to be employed in a regular job. A significant increase in average weekly earnings was also seen in the experimental group, as was a significant decrease in the percentage of experimental group members in training.

Discussion of Results and Their Implications

An interesting finding of the impact analysis was that the significant impacts related to school and some transfer uses disappeared by the end of the demonstration period, which reinforces the need in impact analysis to collect data longitudinally. Because of these significant impacts on the incidence of job holdings, hours worked, and earnings, it might be expected that the STETS demonstration would also have impacts on other areas of participants' lives—especially their overall economic status, their independence in financial management and living arrangement, their use of formal and informal services, and their general level of involvement in regular, productive activities.

The expected direction and duration of the effects of the program on economic status, measures of independence, and lifestyle were not always clear. Several factors in particular cloud the results of the evaluation of these impacts. First, the increased earnings observed for experimentals appear to be partially offset by decreases in transfer benefits and other sources of income, thereby diluting the overall financial impacts of the program. Second, although STETS may have had impacts on financial management skills and independent living arrangements, those impacts may follow others with a considerable time delay, in which case the 22-month observation period was too short to observe them. Third, although the program generated increased earnings for sample members, those increases might not have been enough to enable them to live independent lifestyles, especially in larger cities. Finally, parents and counselors might have wished to see more concrete and stable earnings gains before they were willing to give the sample members greater independence.

Despite these limitations in the ability to detect long-term effects, the analysis evaluated the impacts due to the strong policy interest in understanding the effects of transitional employment programs on the lifestyles of participants. In general, some relatively small program effects were observed on such measures of independence, overall economic status, services received from community agencies, and involvement in activities oriented toward employment. However, these effects generally declined to a great extent in the postprogram period, seemingly due to two factors. First, in the later observation periods, either the direct effects of STETS

Exhibit 4-2

Estimated Program Impacts on Key Outcome Measures

Outcome measures	Month 6			Month 15			Month 22		
	Experimental group mean	Control group mean	Estimated impact	Experimental group mean	Control group mean	Estimated impact	Experimental group mean	Control group mean	Estimated impact
Employment									
Employed in regular job (%)[a]	11.8	10.7	1.1	26.2	16.8	9.4**	31.0	19.1	11.9**
Employed in any paid job (%)	67.8	45.2	22.6*	44.8	43.6	1.2	44.7	43.7	1.0
Average weekly earnings in regular job	$11.81	$9.81	$2.00	$26.90	$16.31	$10.59**	$36.36	$20.55	$15.81**
Average weekly earning in any paid job	$52.39	$25.93	$26.46**	$37.91	$26.48	$11.43**	$40.79	$28.41	$12.38**
Training and schooling									
In any training (%)	61.7	40.6	21.1**	20.60	28.4	-7.8*	16.6	29.1	-12.5**
In any schooling (%)	7.5	15.7	-8.2**	6.2	10.1	-3.9	8.0	11.4	-3.4

Income sources									
Receiving SSI or SSDI (%)	26.3	31.0	−4.7	33.1	40.7	−7.6**	34.9	40.2	−5.3
Average monthly income from SSI or SSDI	$66.41	$74.59	−8.18	$91.35	$109.65	−$18.30	$99.27	$120.03	−$20.76
Receiving any cash transfers (%)	31.7	43.1	−11.4*	44.5	51.5	−7.0*	49.6	52.0	−2.4
Average monthly income from cash transfers	$80.23	$99.98	−$19.75	$114.78	$138.72	−23.94	$126.53	$136.08	−$9.55
Average weekly personal income[b]	$71.72	$50.94	$20.78**	$67.22	$59.67	$7.55	$71.59	$62.39	$9.20

Note: These results were estimated through ordinary least squares techniques.
Source: Reprinted by permission from S. Kerachsky, C. Thornton, A. Bloomenthal, R. Maynard, and S. Stephens, 1985, *Impacts of Transitional Employment for Mentally Retarded Young Adults: Results of the STETS Demonstration,* Mathematica Policy Research, P.O. Box 2393, Princeton, NJ 08543-2393.
[a]Regular jobs are those that are neither training/work–study nor workshop/activity center jobs.
[b]Personal income includes earnings, cash transfer benefits (Aid for Families with Dependent Children [AFDC], general assistance, Supplemental Security Income, and Social Security Disability Insurance), and other regular sources of income.
*Statistically significant at the 10% level, two-tailed test.
**Statistically significant at the 5% level, two-tailed test.

participation on such outcomes as total income, service utilization, and level of inactivity were no longer evident; or, where they were evident (as with personal income), the estimated effects were not statistically significant. Second, whereas the STETS experience provided a head start toward independence for many sample members, those who did not participate in the program (controls) also began to achieve similar levels soon afterward. Additionally, although certain subgroups (e.g., those with a moderate level of retardation) did seem to continue to benefit from the program, even those who were more likely to achieve and maintain positive effects from their experience in STETS exhibited relatively low levels of independence by the end of the observation period. Thus, given the short postprogram period for which data were available, one cannot tell whether a more economically and socially independent lifestyle would eventually be achieved by the participants, or whether the effects of participating in a transitional employment program would become more evident at a later period.

This last statement reflects the reality frequently found in even a large, well-funded impact analysis such as STETS: Despite rigorous experimental methodology, there can still be uncertainly in the impact measures obtained. As is also frequently the case in such analyses, the comparison between experimental and control participants is weakened because some members of the control group obtained assistance in finding employment from other sources. Consequently, the difference in outcomes between the experimental and control groups underestimates the full impact of the STETS demonstration on earnings.

Summary

In summary, impact analysis focuses on a program's impacts and is used to determine whether these impacts can be attributed with reasonable certainty to the intervention being studied. Impact analysis asks a very basic question: whether the program's impacts make a difference compared to either no program or an alternative program. You should remember the following guiding principle in conducting (or reading about) an impact analysis:

GUIDING PRINCIPLE 3: *Impact analysis involves comparing outcomes from two comparable conditions or groups. Statistically significant differences between these outcomes represent the program's impacts.*

There are a number of additional key points to remember about impact analysis. First, it is best to use an experimental/control evaluation design if at all possible, for that will increase the analysis's certainty, precision, comparability, and generalizability. Second, the data requirements for an impact analysis are stringent, with special emphasis on person-referenced outcomes (from which impacts will be determined) and core-service functions (for establishing the comparison conditions and cost estimates). And third, outcomes are not the same as impacts. At their simplest level, impacts represent the significant differences between the mean scores on person-referenced outcomes for the two comparison conditions (see Figure 4.1).

The two studies summarized in this chapter should help you appreciate the complexity of impact analysis, but more important, should facilitate your understanding of—and competency in doing—impact analysis. Impact analysis is important not just in its own right, but also as the basis for the third type of outcome-based analysis (benefit–cost) discussed in the following chapter. As we will see, benefit–cost analysis involves impact statements to which benefits and costs are assigned.

Study Questions

1. What is the difference between outcomes and impacts (see Figure 4.1)? Relate this difference to the concept of a comparison condition and the three OBE evaluation designs most probably used in impact analysis to constitute the comparison condition.

2. Assume that you are a special-education policy maker and plan to do an impact analysis of your state's special education programs. Outline the specific steps and procedures involved in such an impact analysis, following the eight steps summarized in Table 4.1.

3. Assume that you are a State Director of Mental Health who plans to do an impact analysis of your state's aftercare program. Outline the specific steps and procedures involved in such an impact analysis, following the eight steps summarized in Table 4.1.

4. Assume that you are a State Director of Vocational Rehabilitation who plans to do an impact analysis of your state's supported employment program. Outline the specific steps and procedures involved in the analysis, following the eight steps summarized in Table 4.1.

5. Compare the steps and procedures involved in your impact analyses with those listed for your effectiveness analyses (see Chapter 3 Study Questions 2, 3, and 4). What additional questions are you able to answer on the basis of your effectiveness analysis? Generally speaking, what did these additional answers "cost you"?

6. Review Figure 4.1. Select an alternative program to yours and compare the persons served and the services provided by the alternate. Why does this exercise result in a realistic hesitancy to compare program outcomes?

7. What do you do if there is no alternate program and you still need (or want) to complete an impact analysis?

8. Review Exhibit 4-1. What is meant by "estimated impact," and how are these impacts determined?

9. Review Exhibit 4-2. What general trend across time do you see for the program's impacts? What are the implications for demonstrating the program's accountability?

10. Why is it that impact analysis results are often equivocal? Despite this, why are impact analyses so important?

Additional Readings

Folz, D. H., Gaddis, L., Lyons, W., & Scheb, J. M. II. (1993). Saturn comes to Tennessee: Citizen perceptions of project impacts. *Social Science Quarterly, 74*(4), 793–802.

Frey, S. J., & Dougherty, D. (1993). An inconsistent picture: A compilation of analyses of economic impact of competing approaches to health care reform by experts and stakeholders. *Journal of The American Medical Association, 270*(17), 2030–2042.

Mirin, S. M., Gossett, J. M., & Grob, M. C. (Eds.). (1991). *Recent advances in outcome research.* Washington, DC: American Psychiatric Press.

Seltzer, G. B., Begun, A., Mailick-Seltzer, R., & Wyngaarden-Krauss, M. (1991). Adults with mental retardation and their aging mothers: Impacts of siblings. *Family Relations, 40*(3), 310–324.

Zador, P. L., & Ciccone, M. A. (1993). Automobile driver fatalities in frontal impacts: Airbags compared with manual belts. *American Journal of Public Health, 83*(5), 661–670.

5

Benefit–Cost Analysis

Overview

Benefit–cost analysis represents the "granddaddy" of outcome-based analysis. Although complex, its purpose is to answer a simple, straightforward question that program administrators, funding bodies, policy makers, and taxpayers are most interested in: Does a program's benefits outweigh its costs? Although a simple question to ask, we will see in this chapter that a simple answer is most difficult and typically given with a number of cautions.

The primary issue addressed by benefit–cost analysis is whether the impacts of the program are big enough to justify the costs needed to produce them. As a type of outcome-based analysis that weighs a program's benefits and costs, it relies heavily upon the clear delineation and measurement of impacts and the costs involved in generating them. Indeed, one cannot do benefit–cost analysis without detailed information about impacts, which you'll remember from Chapter 4, are the statistically significant differences between program mean scores and those from properly constituted comparison conditions. Hence, a comparison group is essential in benefit–cost analysis, and the preferred OBE design is the experimental/control in which program or service recipients are assigned randomly to the two comparison conditions. My advice is to not attempt benefit–cost analysis unless you can use an experimental/control design, or have two programs that you wish to compare that are truly equal except for core-service functions.

Because of its major focus, benefit–cost analysis is used frequently for policy evaluation. Current public policy is based on two fundamental principles: equity and efficiency. Equitable programs contribute to balancing the needs and desires of the various groups in society, whereas efficient programs are those that serve to increase the net value of goods and services available to society. Benefit–cost analysis is a tool developed to determine whether a program produces effects that justify the costs incurred to operate the program.

Historical Approaches to Benefit–Cost Analysis

Early approaches to benefit–cost analysis focused almost exclusively on efficiency issues, attempting to measure in dollars all program inputs and resulting effects. As a result, benefit–cost analysis has been adopted slowly by persons evaluating human service programs, whose major goals typically include achieving important social and (re)habilitation outcomes, which are largely unmeasurable in monetary terms (Lewis et al., 1991).

Because of its historical overreliance on efficiency issues and its corresponding perceived inappropriateness to evaluate human service programs, one can find alternatives to the benefit–cost analysis model presented in this chapter. One such alternative is effectiveness–cost analysis in which the costs and outcomes of alternative programs with similar goals are used to assess the relative efficiency of the two programs. To quote Lewis et al. (1991) regarding effectiveness–cost analysis:

> In the use of this technique, it is assumed that only programs with similar goals can be compared and that a common measure of effectiveness can be used to assess them. This common measure of outcome data then can be combined with costs in order to provide an effective-cost ratio that will enable the analyst to judge which of the alternatives provides the maximum outcome per level of cost or which program requires the least cost per level of effectiveness. (p. 133)

More recently, approaches to benefit–cost analysis have emerged that address both efficiency and equity issues (Conley & Noble, 1990; Kerachsky et al., 1985; Noble & Conley, 1987; Rusch, 1990; Rusch, Conley, & McCaughlin, 1993; Schalock & Thornton, 1988; Thornton, 1984; Thornton & Maynard, 1989). These newer approaches stress that one does not have to monetize all of the benefits accruing to the particular program. As stated by Noble and Conley (1987) in reference to the benefit–cost analysis of supported employment programs:

> There are many other benefits of supported and transitional employment programs. A return to work frequently will cause expenditures in day care and other treatment programs to decline—a cost savings that may be as great or greater than the cost of a supported or transitional employment program. A return to gainful work may increase savings and thereby contribute to capital formation. It may make it possible for siblings to attend college, which will subsequently raise their earnings. Integrated employment in regular work sites is not only normalizing but has the potential to reduce the maladaptive behavior of some persons with disabilities, particularly if working alongside workers without disabilities provides role models of "normal" behavior. Integrated employment also has the potential to improve the welfare of society by increasing its acceptance and accommodation of persons with special needs. (p. 165)

Benefit–Cost Analysis Model

The benefit–cost analysis model presented in this chapter reflects this current trend toward using both monetized and nonmonetized benefits to evaluate efficiency issues. The suggested approach also allows one to examine which groups in society gain from a program and which groups pay. This examination of equity is particularly important for social programs, since a goal of many of these programs is to increase social equity by reallocating resources or equalizing opportunities. In fact, to many consumers, equity concerns dominate efficiency concerns. Additionally, the suggested approach is based on the premise that one needs to look at all benefits and costs of a program, even though one may be able to monetize only some of them.

The broader perspective on benefit–cost analysis leads to a more complete analysis, and also minimizes the tendency to reduce benefit–cost analysis to a simple ratio of benefits to cost. Thus, the suggested benefit–cost analysis model allows one to view the analysis as a process for systematically sorting through the available evidence of the multiple costs and benefits associated with (re)habilitation programs, rather than relying on any single estimate of value or benefit–cost ratio.

Even though benefit–cost analysis is a powerful tool for evaluating the benefits and costs of (re)habilitation programs, there are a number of controversial issues surrounding its use, including the following:

1. Difficulty in establishing the alternative or counterfactual comparison group(s) against which the program is being compared.
2. No consensus on the time frame for estimating benefit streams.
3. Its numerous assumptions and estimates regarding costs and impacts.
4. Considerable controversy involved in estimating dollar values for program effects.
5. Methodological problems involved in incorporating intangible effects that are often a central concern of human service programs.
6. The considerable time and resources needed to complete a thorough benefit–cost analysis.

Despite these concerns and potential problems, the current zeitgeist demands that we do benefit–cost analyses, if they are consistent with the questions we are asking and our capability to do the analysis.

The purpose of this chapter is to acquaint the reader with the various procedures involved in conducting (or understanding) a benefit–cost analysis. The chapter's format deviates from the previous two in that the two case studies will be integrated into the six procedural steps outlined. The first study is an extension of the STETS evaluation (Kerachsky et al., 1985) of transitional employment programs summarized in the previous chapter on impact analysis. The second study is a benefit–cost analysis of supported employment programs in Minnesota (Lewis, Johnson, Bruininks, Kallsen, & Guilley, 1992). In that analysis, data on costs and person-referenced outcomes were collected on 1,892 individuals being served in 11 supported employment agencies offering programs in habilitation training, on-site employment, and community-based group and individual supported employment. From these data, benefits and costs were estimated to explain possible efficiency effects resulting from the programs.

Benefit–Cost Analysis Procedural Steps

Benefit–cost analysis makes more sense if one thinks logically and sequentially. Thus, this section of the chapter discusses the six sequential steps involved in conducting (or reading about) a benefit–cost analysis. The following six procedural steps are summarized in Table 5.1:

1. Specify the structured comparison.
2. Define the analytical perspective.
3. List the expected impacts (benefits and costs).
4. Develop the accounting framework.
5. Estimate the benefits and costs.
6. Present and interpret the results.

Table 5.1. Procedural Steps Involved
in Benefit–Cost Analysis

1. Specify the structure comparisons
2. Define the analytical perspective
   a. Social
   b. Participant
   c. Rest of society
3. List the expected impacts
   a. Benefits
   b. Costs
4. Develop the accounting framework
5. Estimate benefits and costs
   a. Estimate costs
   b. Estimate program impacts
   c. Value program impacts
   d. Include intangible benefits
   e. Aggregate the value benefits and costs
6. Present and interpret the results

Specify the Structured Comparisons

This first step requires specifying the program being evaluated and the alternative (counterfactual) with which it will be compared, and defines the scope and ultimately the results of the benefit–cost analysis.

The two most common evaluation designs used in establishing the structured comparisons are the experimental/control design and the use of intact groups that are roughly equivalent. In the STETS project, for example, participants were placed randomly into the program and non-program groups. The research sample consisted of 437 individuals (226 experimentals and 211 control group members) residing in five U.S. cities. The Minnesota project, which used an intact group comparison of participants in comparable programs, was a collaborative effort among the Institute on Community Integration at the University of Minnesota, the Minnesota Division of Rehabilitation Services, and 11 cooperating service providers of supported employment sites in five Minnesota rural and urban counties. The 11 agencies varied in size and total number of persons served, varying from 35 to over 500 persons. The agencies selected represented 9% of all agencies in the state providing supported employment, which in turn included over 20% of all supported employment consumers in the state. The 11 agencies consisted of 5 day-activity centers, 4 vocational rehabilitation facilities, 1 mental health training facility, and 1 regional treatment center. Each of the agencies had from one to four program options. The structured comparison in the STETS project was program vs.

nonprogram (experimental/control) participants; in the Minnesota analysis, the structured comparison was supported vs. alternative habilitation/day-activity programs.

Specifying the structured comparison also requires that one describe two of the four core data sets: recipient characteristics and core-service functions (cost estimates and person-referenced outcomes are included in later procedural steps). In reference to STETS, these were described in Chapter 4. For the Minnesota project, the primary population consisted of people labeled as moderately to severely mentally retarded. Operationally defined core-service functions included habilitation training, on-site employment, group employment with support, individual employment with support, and competitive employment. Information on individual consumers' work activities were collected related to type and level of program participation (number of daily hours and days per year within each subprogram area) and earnings (hourly wage rates and annual earnings) within each program area.

Define the Analytical Perspective

Any public policy or program will affect many groups. For example, a special education program will clearly affect participating students and their families and may have long-run effects on agencies and employers in the community. It will also have an impact on government budgets and hence, indirectly affect taxpayers. Each of these groups has a perspective on the policy or program, and each of these perspectives will have relevancy to decision making. Thus, equity issues need to be addressed in a benefit–cost analysis through the perspectives of specific groups affected by the policy or program. The three most appropriate analytical perspectives include the social ("society as a whole") perspective, the participant perspective, and the rest of society ("taxpayer") perspective. This concept is so important in benefit–cost analysis that it represents our fourth guiding principle:

> GUIDING PRINCIPLE 4: *In benefit–cost analysis, the three most important analytical perspectives are the social (society) perspective, the participant perspective, and the rest of society ("taxpayer") perspective.*

The three perspectives included in the proposed benefit–cost model and the major foci and concerns of each are summarized in Table 5.2.

For the issue of economic *efficiency*, the social (i.e., "society as a whole") perspective is relevant. It captures the net effect of the program on the aggregate value of available goods and services by determining the change in the total resources of society caused by the program under

Table 5.2. Benefit–Cost Analytical Perspectives and Major Foci/Concerns

Benefit–cost analytical perspective	Foci/Concerns
Social ("society as a whole")	Includes participants and "rest of society" Efficiency issues: Captures net effect of the program on the aggregate value of available goods and services
Participant	Equity issues Benefits and opportunity costs
Rest of society ("taxpayer")	Includes all persons not enrolled as participants of the program Equity issues Includes taxes needed to finance the program and reductions in the expenditures for alternate programs

evaluation (relative to the alternative comparison). Because the participant and rest-of-society perspectives represent mutually exclusive groups that in total represent all of society, only those benefits (or costs) that accrue to one group within society and have no equal offsetting cost (or benefit) to the other group will remain in the social perspective. Others will net out to zero in the social perspective. Consequently, the social net present value of calculation will include only the value of outcomes that affect the total amount of resources (goods and services) available to society. The *equity* implications of the program, on the other hand, can then be assessed by examining any net shifts in resources between participants and the rest of society.

The perspective of program participants is particularly important, because it indicates the extent to which they will benefit from the (re)habilitation services. The participant perspective is important from both a benefits and cost perspective. People want to see valued, person-referenced outcomes from the (re)habilitation services received; but in some cases, there are also opportunity costs to the participant associated with program involvement. For example, when one is in school or training, wages and other benefits usually are not available; hence, the person is foregoing the opportunity to earn money until after job placement. This is equally true of college students as well as others who are in extended training programs.

It is also useful to consider the perspective of everyone else in society ("the rest of society"). This group includes all the persons not enrolled as participants in the program. This perspective will capture all effects that do not accrue to the program participant. In particular, it will capture the taxes needed to finance the program and any resulting reductions in expenditures for alternative programs. Since the focus of this analytical perspective is often the taxpayer, some benefit–cost analyses (see Exhibit 5-3 for example) refer to this perspective as "taxpayer."

Depending on the particular concerns of the analyst, other analytical perspectives may also be used. However, since the analysis will require estimates of effects on each perspective, the complexity of the analysis increases rapidly with the number of perspectives, and it is usually preferable to disaggregate society into only the two major perspectives described—participants and the rest of society ("taxpayers").

A final word regarding defining the analytical perspective. It is important that when defining or selecting perspectives for an analysis of equity, the groups chosen be mutually exclusive, yet, in total, include everyone in society. By defining perspectives in this way, the sum of the valued benefits and costs for each individual perspective will equal the net effect as seen by the perspective of society as a whole. In the benefit–cost model presented in this chapter, the sum of benefits and costs accruing to program participants and the rest of society will equal the net benefits to society as a whole. It should be noted, however, that this "adding up" property necessitates assuming that a dollar of benefit or cost to one person is equivalent to that of any other person. The perspective of society as a whole would thereby ignore all redistributional questions and focus on aggregate resource-use questions. This is a convenient but not critical assumption. The analysis could assume other distributional value systems, giving more or less weight to the resources owed by specific groups in society. However, given the difficulty of defining and using such a system, as well as its inherently controversial nature, the "equal value" system makes the better sense (Schalock & Thornton, 1988).

List the Expected Impacts (Benefits and Costs)

This third procedural step follows directly from defining the structured comparison and developing the analytical perspective. In developing this list, it is important to follow two general rules:

1. Be as comprehensive as possible when considering the expected impacts and resource uses of the program.
2. Estimate benefits and costs relative to what would have happened under the comparison situation.

The results of this step will define the specific data the analyst ultimately will need to collect and analyze in order to estimate benefits and costs. Therefore, the results of this task are important and necessary input into designing the actual benefit–cost analysis. An example from the

STETS program is presented in Exhibit 5-1. Note a number of factors associated with the expected benefits and costs. First, the three common analytical perspectives (social, participant, and rest-of-society) are listed. Second, numerous impacts are listed. These include program costs; output produced by participants; effects on other programs, including residential situation, transfer payments, and taxes; transfer administration and intangibles, such as preference for work, increased self-sufficiency, increased variation in participant income, foregone nonmarket activity, and increased independent living. And third, note that the individual components are evaluated from the perspective of being a net benefit (+), a net cost (−), or neither (0).

At first glance, completing Exhibit 5-1 appears relatively straightforward (and indeed, it generally is). However, when one actually gets involved in attempting to identify and sort out the various types of potential effects from the three analytical perspectives, the process requires careful consideration of the interactions of outcomes among these different perspectives. So, let's discuss two general rules that should help.

First, the analyst must try to be as comprehensive as possible when considering the expected impacts and resource uses of a program, even though not all expected benefits and costs will actually be valued. The analyst must attempt to identify all changes in behavior or outcomes that would lead to a real change in the use or availability of resources. For example, special-education programs may produce a change in students' use of a variety of other support service programs. Since a change in the use of such services represents a real change in the use of resources available to society, the effect of this change in behavior should also be included in the expected impacts. It is also important that the benefits and costs that cannot be valued monetarily be identified and accounted for in the framework. Frequently, these are the most important.

Second, benefit and cost impacts are measured relative to what would have happened under the comparison situation. Each of the identified benefits or costs of a program represents the difference between the expected outcomes or resources of the program or policy being evaluated and those under the specified comparison situation. For example, a vocational special-education program may generate an increase in a student's lifetime earnings over what his/her earnings would have been in the absence of the program. Similarly, this program may reduce (relative to the comparison situation) the level at which certain ancillary services have been used. The impacts to be measured as benefits in these examples are the increases in earnings or the reductions in ancillary-service use.

If a particular use of resources would be the same under either the program or the comparison situation, then it should be omitted from the

Exhibit 5-1
Expected Benefits and Costs Matrix by Analytical Perspectives

	Analytical Perspective		
Impact Categories	Social	Participant	Rest of society
I. Program costs			
Project operations	−	0	−
Payments to participants	0	+	−
Central administration	−	0	0
II. Output produced by participants			
Phase I and Phase 2 output	+	0	+
Output forgone while in STETS	−	−	0
Increased out-of-program output	+	+	0
III. Other programs			
Reduced use of:			
Sheltered workshops	+	0	+
Work-activity centers	+	0	+
School	+	0	+
Job-training programs	+	0	+
Case-management services	+	0	+
Counseling services	+	0	+
Social/recreational services	+	0	+
Transportation services	+	0	+

framework. For example, consider the resources involved in transporting participants to a vocational training program. If the alternative is to place them in a nonvocational program that would require the same amount of transportation, then the choice between alternatives would not affect transportation costs. Thus, they could be excluded from the framework, despite the fact that transportation is an expensive cost item. In this way, the framework can be simplified, and analytical resources can be devoted to the critical changes produced by the program.

In summary, the primary purpose of listing the expected impacts is to help organize and conduct the benefit–cost analysis and ensure that all the major impacts of the (re)habilitation program are captured accurately in the analysis. This process involves (1) identifying all changes in resource availability (relative to the comparison situation); (2) assessing whether

IV. Residential situation			
Reduced use of:			
Institutions	+	0	+
Group homes	+	0	+
Foster homes	+	0	+
Semi-independent residential	+	0	+
programs			
V. Transfer payments and taxes			
Reduced SSI/SSDI	0	–	+
Reduced other welfare	0	–	+
Reduced Medicaid/Medicare	0	–	+
Increased taxes	0	–	+
VI. Transfer administration			
Reduced use of SSI/SSDI	+	0	+
Reduced use of other welfare	+	0	+
Reduced use of Medicaid/Medicare	+	0	+
VII. Intangibles			
Preferences for work	+	+	+
Increased self-sufficiency	+	+	+
Increased variation in participant	–	–	–
income			
Forgone nonmarket activity	–	–	0
Increased independent living	+	+	+

Note: The individual components are characterized from the three perspectives as being a net benefit (+), a net cost (−), or neither (0).
Source: Reprinted by permission from Kerachsky et al. (1985).

those changes actually create, save, or use resources, or whether they simply redistribute resources among groups; and (3) determining how these changes will affect the various perspectives.

Develop the Accounting Framework

Developing the accounting framework is a step that is analogous to the previous step in which the expected impacts (benefits and costs) are listed. However, in this step, one becomes more specific in establishing a workable framework for assessing the direct resource requirements for the structured comparisons, along with a method for translating these requirements into cost estimates. In thinking about developing the accounting framework, please keep our fifth guiding principle in mind.

GUIDING PRINCIPLE 5: *In benefit–cost analysis, the comprehensive accounting framework includes all benefits and costs, regardless of whether they can be monetized (i.e., include both tangible and intangible benefits and costs.)*

The translation of resources into cost estimates involves one's understanding of four key concepts: (1) net present value criterion, (2) analytical perspective, (3) assigning value to change, and (4) nonmonetized benefits.

Net Present Value Criterion

As noted previously, benefit–cost analysis makes a comparison between two structured comparisons using the criteria of economic efficiency and equity. Specifically, it asks whether the decision to fund a program or policy under study will increase the aggregate value of social resources, and whether it will produce desirable effects on the distribution of those resources compared to what would have happened under the alternative program or policy. The basic technique used to determine economic efficiency is to identify all changes in resource use (including those required to operate the program and those that result from the operations) by the program and then assign dollar values to these changes. The value of these changes are then summed together to yield an estimate of the program's net present value. This criterion reflects the difference between the benefits and costs, in which the dollar values of any benefits or costs that occur in future years are adjusted (i.e., discounted) to reflect their value in a specified base period. A positive net present value indicates that the resources are being used more efficiently than they would have been under the comparison situation; a negative net present value indicates that the program's resources could have been used more efficiently elsewhere.

Analytical Perspective

The net present value criterion is also used to address equity issues. However, instead of aggregating all changes in resource use, the analysis considers the changes from the perspectives of the various groups in society that are affected by the program. As we saw in reference to the third procedural step (see Table 5.2), the three most common perspectives are social, participant and rest-of-society ("taxpayer"). For example, consider the students enrolled in a special education program. Part of the analysis of equity is to ascertain whether this group benefited from their participation in the program; similarly, the analysis will consider whether the taxpayers who fund the program obtained benefits that outweigh the costs. Although the analysis can typically identify the major benefits and costs for these groups, it has no special criteria for assessing whether net shifts in resources between these and other groups are desirable. The appropriate criteria will vary, depending on the program under study and the groups affected. Thus, the value of shifts between groups must be determined within the broader context of public policy.

Assigning Values to Change

Estimating the value of changes in resource use requires a consistent means of assigning values to changes. The proposed benefit–cost model uses an approach based on the concepts that underlie the calculation of the gross national product (GNP). The GNP is a measure of the value of the goods and services a country produces in a year. Nonproductive activities, such as shifts in funds within or between sectors of the economy with no corresponding contribution to overall production, are excluded from the GNP calculations. This measure is estimated by aggregating the dollar values of all the goods and services produced, in which the dollar values are the market prices of the various items being produced. A potential weakness of using this approach should also be kept in mind: The social value of public services such as education or welfare programs may be inadequately captured from the amount of dollars spent to provide the services, and they are therefore inadequately represented in the estimated GNP.

Nonmonetized Benefits

Social programs often generate outcomes that have no observable market value, or the value of which is not adequately reflected in the interactions of the marketplace. These outcomes include such things an increased self-concept, enhanced quality of life, and the provision of special opportunities to specific needy populations. In any of these instances, the GNP approach is likely to exclude some key benefits or costs. However, these excluded items must usually be treated as unmeasured benefits in the analysis, measuring them as will be outlined in Chapter 6. For example, in the STETS analysis, "intangible" impacts included preference for work, increased self-sufficiency, increased variation in participant income, foregone market activity and increased independent living. In the Minnesota analysis, "other benefits" included increased community integration, better quality of life, and increased self-esteem.

Estimate Benefits and Costs

Once one has listed the expected impacts (benefits and costs) and developed the accounting framework, then the fifth benefit–cost procedural step is to estimate the actual benefits and costs. This step involves five substeps: (1) estimating program costs, (2) estimating program impacts, (3) valuing the program impacts, (4) including intangible benefits, and (5) aggregating the valued benefits and costs.

Estimating Program Costs

Most cost-analysis techniques used in benefit–cost analyses use a resource-components approach to developing cost estimates. This approach requires a comprehensive listing of all the direct program and supplemental services within an agency or delivery system, the determination and measurement of the specific resources employed within each direct program and supplemental area, and the valuing of these resources in monetary terms. For example, Lewis et al. (1992) determined overall program costs on the basis of standardized cost data (obtained through the examination of program reports and budget, and audited expenditure records) and the number of consumers, consumer days, and hours of service provided by the respective programs.

Estimating Program Impacts

This substep involves the eight impact-analysis steps that we discussed in the previous chapter (see Table 4.1). There are two points to remember here. First, impact analysis involves estimating the extent to which the outcomes of program recipients differ from those persons in the comparison condition by determining the statistical significance of mean differences. Second, the usefulness of the benefit–cost analysis will be increased as more "nonmonetized" outcomes are measured and included in the analysis.

Valuing the Program Impacts

Once the impacts have been measured, the analyst must then determine the value of these effects. Two methods are useful here: dollar values and shadow prices.

DOLLAR VALUES.   This is the most direct method, in which one simply measures the person's increased earnings, changes in transfer-payment receipts, tax payments, or medicaid/medicare benefits. It is essential, however, that these values be expressed in current-year values to control or adjust for inflation.

SHADOW PRICES. These prices represent estimated dollar values that reflect the average resource value of specific activities and goods. The use of shadow prices represents a major source of uncertainty in benefit–cost analysis, because they may not capture the true resource cost of the impacts. There are resources available for making such estimates such as publications by the Social Security Administration (*Social Security Bulletin and Annual Statistical Supplement*), and the U.S. Department of Labor, Bureau of Labor Statistics. If shadow prices are used, the analyst needs to recognize their uncertainty and discuss the implications of their use.

Including Intangible Benefits

There are two methods in which intangible benefits can be incorporated into the benefit–cost analysis. One, which is true of the analyses summarized in Exhibits 5-2 and 5-3, is to reference them and then simply evaluate them as to whether they represent a net benefit (+), cost (−), or neither (0). The second method, which relies on the measurement techniques summarized in Chapter 6, is to actually refer to the mean values (and their significance) between the two structure comparisons. This second method rests on a clearer conception and measurement of valued, person-referenced outcomes than has traditionally been the case, and thus also represents the next evolutionary change in the emerging area of benefit–cost analysis.

Aggregating the Valued Benefits and Costs

If substeps 1–4 have been completed correctly, then this final substep is very straightforward. It involves producing net present values to the various components of the benefit–cost analysis. However, this substep involves more than simply summing the estimated value of the benefits, for almost all programs occur at different points in time. Thus, the analyst must do three things here: (1) adjust for inflation by denominating all values in dollars to a specified base period (through using actual dollar values or shadow prices); (2) calculate equivalent values by discounting those that occur in later years by a factor that reflects the return that these resources could have earned in the interim between the base period and the time of occurrence (the decision rules for doing so need to be stated clearly in the analyst's report); and (3) extrapolating on future impacts by deciding (and including in the analysis) which benefits (or costs) will persist over time, how long they will continue, and at what rate they will persist. Since this extrapolation involves considerable uncertainty, it is suggested that the analyst use straightforward methods that are based on relatively simple assumptions, and draw on available published evidence about long-term effects.

Present and Interpret the Results

Much of the value of a benefit–cost analysis stems from the process of organizing and aggregating the data. Therefore, the presentation of the analysis, which represents the sixth procedural step, should capture as much of the process as possible. There should be (1) discussion in the analyst's report regarding each of the aforementioned five procedural steps; (2) an indication of the level of certainty that can be attributed to the analysis; (3) a listing of those benefits and costs not included in the analysis; and (4) a summary table that captures the core of the analysis.

Exhibit 5-2 summarizes the estimated benefits and costs (in 1982 dollars) of STETS per participant during the observation period. The estimates presented in Exhibit 5-2 suggest that STETS created a net cost of $6,232 per participant to society during the 22-month observation period, whereas measured social benefits (increased output by participants and the reduced use of other training, service, residential, and transfer programs) totaled only $5,193 per participant. Thus, about 83% of the initial investment was offset during the 22-month observation period. Participants clearly benefited from their participation, receiving in-program compensation that more than offset their tax payments and their reduced use of transfers. Nonparticipant taxpayers incurred the costs both for operating STETS and for participant compensation. They received substantial benefits (primarily from the increased output produced by participants in STETS and the reduction in their use of sheltered workshops, other job-training programs, and transfer programs); but these benefits offset only two thirds of the costs incurred by nonparticipants. However, the trends are important: If the earnings and reduced alternative-program benefits continued for as little as 7 months beyond the 22-month point, social benefits would exceed social costs.

The STETS program was also intended to enhance the economic and social self-sufficiency of participants. The measured impacts indicated that STETS did affect the activities and opportunities that were expected to generate intangible benefits. The increased income and the increased job holding in the regular labor market provided participants with benefits that went beyond the measured increases in output. Indeed, increased social and employment opportunities were available to the participants.

Exhibit 5-2
Estimated Benefits and Costs of STETS (per Participant)

	Analytical perspective		
Impacts	Social	Participant	Rest of society
I. Program costs			
Project oeprations	−$6,050	$ 0	−$6,050
Payments to participants	0	3,094	−3,094
Central administration	−182	0	−182
II. Output produced by participants			
Phase 1 and Phase 2 output	3,434	0	3,434
Forgone output while in STETS	−425	−425	0
Increased out-of-program output	268	268	0
III. Other programs			
Reduced use of:			
Sheltered workshops	767	0	767
Secondary vocational school	428	0	428
Other school	112	0	112
Job-training programs	434	0	434
IV. Residential programs			
Reduced use of:			
Institutions	174	0	174
Group homes	72	0	72
Foster homes	7	0	7
Semi-independent residential programs	−114	0	−114
V. Transfer payments and taxes			
Reduced SSI/SSDI	0	−264	264
Reduced other welfare	0	−82	82
Reduced Medicaid/Medicare	0	−232	232
Increased taxes	0	−249	249
VI. Transfer adminstration			
Reduced use of SSI/SSDI	16	0	16
Reduced use of other welfare	8	0	8
Reduced use of medicaid/ medicare	12	0	12
VII. Intangibles			
Preferences for work	+	+	+
Increased self-sufficeincy	+	+	+
Increased variation in participant income	−	−	−
Forgone nonmarket activity	−	−	−
Increased independent living	+	+	+
Net present value (benefits less costs)	−$1,038	$2,111	−$3,149

Note: Benefits and costs are discounted to the time of enrollment using a 5% real annual discount rate.
Source: Reprinted by permission from Kerachsky et al. (1985).

However, the analysis found limited evidence of changes in such intangibles as self-sufficiency and independence. In part, such limited evidence reflects the inadequacies of the measures and the difficulty in measuring these concepts. It may also mean that self-sufficiency responds slowly to changes in opportunities. Finally, there was no measure of any overall increase in satisfaction, other than the fact that many participants appeared to remain voluntarily in their jobs.

Exhibit 5-3 summarizes part of the Minnesota benefit–cost study in which benefits and costs of community-based, individual-supported employment are presented. As one can see clearly, the benefits of the supported program versus on-site employment within a day-activity center were positive, including the other benefits such as increased community integration, increased quality of life, and increased self-esteem.

Summary

In summary, benefit–cost analysis represents a critical, albeit difficult, type of outcome-based analysis. Its purpose is to determine whether the program's impacts (benefits) are substantial enough to justify its costs. This focus is of prime concern to policy makers and funding bodies.

The benefit–cost model presented in this chapter reflects the current trend toward using both monetized and nonmonetized benefits to evaluate efficiency and equity issues. It also includes three analytical perspectives that allow one to examine which groups in society gain from a program and which groups will pay. The chapter outlined and discussed the six critical procedural steps involved in conducting (or reading about) a benefit–cost analysis. A key point stressed throughout the chapter was that benefit–cost analysis should be viewed as a broad process whereby one looks at all the benefits and costs of a program, which is both helpful to various stakeholders and also minimizes the tendency to view benefit–cost analysis as a simple ratio of benefits to costs, which is seldom the case in education and (re)habilitation programs.

This chapter completes our initial discussion of the three types of OBE analyses and the procedures involved in conducting either effectiveness, impact, or benefit–cost analysis. Throughout these three chapters, considerable mention was made of other methodological issues, such as evaluation design, data collection, and data analysis. It is to those issues that we now turn. In Part III of the text you will learn a lot about the "How to's" of outcome-based evaluation, including evaluation designs, data collection, data management, and data analysis.

Exhibit 5-3
Benefits and Cost of Community-Based Individual Supported Employment (SE) versus On-Site Employment at Site A within a Day-Activity Center Comparison Group

Impacts	Social	=	Consumer	+	Other Taxpayers
		Analytical Perspectives			
Benefits					
1. Increased productivity	$2,518		$2,518		$ 0
Additional earned income					
Additional fringe benefits	$ 277		277		0
2. Reduced use of alternative programs					
Costs of on-site employment	6,345		0		6,345
3. Decreased government subsidies					
Reductions in SSI/MA payments	0		810		810
4. Other benefits					
Increased community integration	+		+		+
Increased quality of life	+		+		+
Increased self-esteem	+		+		+
Total benefits	$9,140		$1,985		$7,155
Costs					
1. Costs of agency SE program					
Costs of individual SE	3,473		0		3,473
2. Targeted job tax credit	108		0		108
3. Increased taxes paid by consumer	0		353		($353)
Total costs	$3,581		353		3,228
Net benefits	$5,559		$1,632		$3,927

Source: Reprinted by permission from D. R. Lewis, D. R. Johnson, R. H. Bruininks, L. A. Kallsen, and R. P. Guilley, "Is Supported Employment Cost-Effective in Minnesota?", *Journal of Disability Policy Studies*, Vol. 3, No. 1, pp. 67–92. Copyright 1992 Journal of Disability Policy Studies.

Study Questions

1. Compare and contrast the "broad perspective" benefit–cost model presented in this chapter with earlier models, focusing your comparison on equity, efficiency, and monetization issues.

2. Assume that you are the Director of your state's Special Education programs and have a legislative mandate to evaluate the benefits and costs of those programs. Outline the specific steps and procedures involved in your benefit–cost analysis, following the six procedural steps listed in Table 5.1. Use the impact categories similar to those found in Exhibit 5-1 to summarize the expected benefits and costs.

3. Assume that you are the Director of Mental Health (or aging or human service) programs for your state and have a legislative mandate to evaluate the benefits and costs of those programs. Outline the specific steps and procedures involved in your benefit–cost analysis, following the six procedural steps listed in Table 5.1. Use impact categories similar to those found in Exhibit 5-1 to summarize the expected benefits and costs.

4. Assume that you are the Director of Developmental Disabilities for your state and have a legislative mandate to evaluate the benefits and costs of those programs. Outline the specific steps and procedures involved in your benefit–cost analysis, following the six procedural steps listed in Table 5.1. Use impact categories similar to those found in Exhibit 5-1 to summarize the expected benefits and costs.

5. After having completed the steps and procedures involved in your three benefit–cost analyses, discuss each of the six controversial issues regarding benefit–cost analysis listed at the beginning of the chapter.

6. Why are equity and effectiveness concerns so prevalent today? Compare these concerns from the three analytical perspectives summarized in Table 5.2.

7. Outline and discuss the strengths and limitations of benefit–cost analysis.

8. Conduct a brief literature review of at least five articles that have "benefit–cost" in their titles. Compare and contrast the approaches used with that presented in this chapter.

9. Survey a random sample of program administrators and ask them to define or describe their definition of benefit–cost. How would you compare their definitions with that presented in this chapter?

10. Which three or four person-referenced outcomes would you use in a benefit–cost analysis? Why?

Additional Readings

Barnett, S. W. (1993). Benefit–cost analysis of preschool education: Findings from a 25-year follow-up. *American Journal of Orthopsychiatry, 63*(4), 500–525.

Conley, R. W., & Noble, J. H. (1990). Benefit–cost analysis of supported employment. In F. Rusch (Ed.), *Supported employment: Models, methods, and issues.* (pp. 271–288). Sycamore, IL: Sycamore.

Hill, M., Banks, P. D., Handrich, R., Wehman, P., Hill, J., & Shafer, M. (1987). Benefit–cost analysis of supported competitive employment for persons with mental retardation. *Research in Developmental Disabilities, 8,* 71–89.

Noble, J. (1977). The limits of cost–benefit analysis as a guide to priority-setting in rehabilitation. *Evaluation Quarterly, 1,* 347–380.

Rusch, F. R., Conley, R. W., & McCaughlin, W. B. (1993). Benefit–cost analysis of supported employment in Illinois. *Journal of Rehabilitation,* April/May/June, 31–36.

III

Outcome-Based
Evaluation Data

*It is not so important where you are, but
the direction in which you are going.*
OLIVER WENDELL HOLMES

Outcome-based evaluation requires data, and that means that both OBE
consumers and producers need to be familiar with data-collection procedures, data management, evaluation designs, and data analysis. I realize
that these areas may not be your "cup of tea," but understanding and
using them correctly are essential to outcome-based evaluation analyses.
    The three chapters constituting Part III will need to be read together,
because outcome-based evaluation involves data collection, data management, evaluation designs, and data analysis. Throughout Part III, I will use
a formative feedback, decision-making model that shows clearly the relationship among the questions one asks, the evaluation design one uses, the
data one then collects to answer the question(s), and how those data can be
collected and managed so that the OBE analyses flow logically from the
questions asked.
    As we will see in this section, data refer not just to person-referenced
outcomes, but also to recipient characteristics, core-service functions, and
cost estimates of the intervention or services provided. I refer to these four
as "core data sets." Throughout the section I will also caution you to keep it
simple, for the processes discussed are both time consuming and expensive. Thus, I will present a number of guiding principles and examples that
will help in selecting the minimum data sets and correct evaluation design
that will allow you to be both accountable and able to answer your
evaluation questions.
    Before we begin these three chapters, it is important that you:

- Review your two basic questions: For what purpose will I use the
  OBE data? What data will I need for my intended use?
- Keep the following core data sets clearly in mind: recipient charac-

teristics, core-service functions, cost estimates, and valued, person-referenced outcomes.

- Remember that a key purpose in gathering OBE data is for formative feedback that provides important reporting and decision-making information.
- Keep it simple. My strong advice is to use a small number of reliable and valid core indicators.
- Focus on performance-based assessment, which involves using objective indicators to evaluate the person's adaptive behavior level and role status.

I agree with Oliver Wendell Holmes that the important thing is the direction in which one is going. I hope that these three chapters will point you in the right direction in terms of outcome-based evaluation data so that you can fulfill correctly the purpose of your evaluation efforts. They are also important chapters in our odyssey and cover topics that are sometimes unfamiliar or uncomfortable to many program administrators. But as friend and mentor Burton Blatt once told me, "Do not expect the world to change unless you yourself are willing to change."

6

Outcome-Based Evaluation Data Collection

Overview

Believe me, there is no lack of data floating around most education and social programs! The problem is that much of it either is not usable for meaningful outcome-based evaluation, or not retrievable. An unfortunate truism is that many programs are data rich but information poor. Part of the reason for this situation is that program administrators are bombarded with requests for data from funding, licensing, or accrediting bodies who frequently ask for different data sets; but part of the reason is also that most program's data systems have evolved over time, with little forethought given to the importance of developing an ongoing data-based management system that will provide data for multiple purposes, including outcome-based evaluation. I hope that this chapter will help that situation, but we also need to realize that data collection is neither easy nor inexpensive. Thus, our sixth guiding principle:

GUIDING PRINCIPLE 6: *Choose your data sets very carefully, because data collection is neither easy nor inexpensive.*

Choosing one's data sets very carefully is done partially by asking clear questions, but it also involves simplifying your data needs. My strong bias and recommendation is that using a small number of reliable and valid core data sets is better than using a larger number haphazardly. As we all know, there is an important distinction between nice-to-know and need-to-know data. Thus, in approaching the topic of OBE data collection, you might want to keep the following data-simplification techniques in mind (Johnston, 1987):

- Measure at the level of functional impairment and its amelioration, rather than at the level of the pathology or limitation.
- Group many separate measures into a smaller number.
- Group many categorical items (such as diagnoses) into a smaller number of groups according to an index of similarity (e.g., all persons with mental retardation).
- Convert items with market prices to dollar values (e.g., wages) rather than leaving them in terms such as number of treatments.
- Reduce several nonmonetary outcome measures into a single composite index of effectiveness using judgmental techniques (e.g., enhanced quality of life).

The process of data collection cannot be separated from the other processes involved in outcome-based evaluation, including knowing how to store and retrieve data, and what evaluation designs and data analyses to use. For example, whereas Chapter 6 discusses data collection, Chapter

7 includes the actual formats whereby data are collected. The formats are included in Chapter 7 because of the interface of actual data collection and data management. Chapter 8 then discusses how those data can be analyzed, based on the evaluation design that you have used. The discerning reader will note that logically, an evaluation design precedes data collection, because the evaluation design selected is the one that will best test your hypothesis or answer your evaluation question. However, I feel that evaluation designs go best in Chapter 8 because of the close connection between evaluation designs and data analysis.

The interrelationship among these processes is shown clearly in Figure 6.1. Note in the figure that the process begins with the questions asked and ends with outcome-based evaluation analyses. I will refer to this figure repeatedly throughout the remainder of the text.

This chapter contains six sections dealing with the interrogatories of data collection. Four sections deal with collecting information about the four core data sets (recipient characteristics, core-service functions, cost estimates, and person-referenced outcomes). The remaining two sections discuss a conceptual approach to measurement and a number of guidelines regarding data collection.

Recipient Characteristics

Think about three or four terms that describe your clientele best. Most program recipients can be described quite adequately using five major descriptors:

- Age and gender
- Diagnosis or verification status
- Adaptive behavior skill level
- Role status

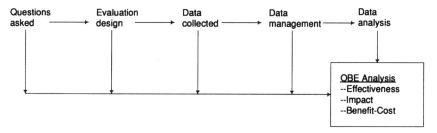

Figure 6.1.   OBE data-collection and utilization model.

Age and Gender

Age and gender are pretty straightforward recipient characteristics. They are frequently required for program-recipient description, and frequently programmatic outcomes are analyzed separately for either females or males, or for individuals of different age groupings.

Diagnosis or Verification

This is a critical characteristic to include, for one's diagnosis or verification identifies clearly the focus of your program's mission, goals, and intervention or services. Diagnosis or verification also determines eligibility for services, so from a reporting and accounting perspective, one needs to be sure that all service recipients are not just eligible for your services, but also appropriate for those services.

However, definitions of conditions do change, and you need to be kept abreast. For example, there has recently been a significant change in the definition of mental retardation, as indicated in the 1992 American Association on Mental Retardation definition, classification, and system of support (Luckasson et al., 1992, p. 1). The 1992 definition defines *mental retardation* as "substantial limitations in present functioning characterized by (1) significantly subaverage intellectual functioning (upper IQ range 70–75); (2) existing concurrently with related limitations in two or more of the following applicable adaptive skill areas: communication, self-care, home living, social skills, community use, self-direction, health and safety, functional academics, leisure and work; and (3) is manifest before age 18." This definitional change reflects the increased focus on functional behaviors related to major life-activity areas.

Similarly, there is an emerging consensus that the diagnosis of mental illness and the evaluation of mental health services should encompass both mental illness and its effects on the person's adaptive behavior and role status. For example, the new definition of *mental illness* (*Federal Register*, May 20, 1993) states that adults or children may be considered seriously mentally ill if they have a diagnosable mental illness that substantially interferes with or limits their performance on one or more major life areas. Considerations in defining a person's functioning in terms of mental illness are that (1) during the past year the person has had a diagnosable mental, behavioral or emotional disorder; (2) this disorder was of sufficient duration to meet the diagnostic criteria specified within the DSM-IV; (3) the disorder has resulted in functional impairment that substantially interferes with [the] major life-activity areas of self-care, receptive and expressive language, learning mobility, self-direction, capacity for independent living, and economic self-sufficiency.

Thus, as with the new definition of mental retardation, the new definition of mental illness also focuses on major life-activity functional behaviors. Therefore, in describing recipients' characteristics, don't overlook our seventh guiding principle:

> GUIDING PRINCIPLE 7: *The current trend is to consider generic groups with functional limitations, rather than individuals with specific diagnostic labels.*

Adaptive Behavior-Skills Level

It is increasingly necessary to consider adaptive behavior profiles as critical data sets that one can use for both the description of service recipients and as a basis for evaluating person-referenced outcomes. There is an emerging consensus on what adaptive skills data to collect in OBE. Examples that encompass the major life-activity areas are listed in Table 6.1 (left column). Approaches to measuring these adaptive skills are outlined in this chapter's fifth section on conceptual approaches to measurement.

Role Status

As discussed in Chapter 1, *role status* refers to a set of valued activities that are considered normative for a specific age group. Examples include living environment (independent, semi-independent, supervised), employment situation (employed, unemployed, employment training, sheltered work, retired), education status (grade level, graduation or dropout status), health status (independent, semi-independent, congregate care), and community inclusion and involvement. A person's statuses are very descriptive of his/her functioning level and can be used both to describe a person on enrollment and as a valued, person-referenced outcome in those programs wherein they are logically connected to the services provided. Examples are found in Table 6.1 (right column).

In summary, information about recipient characteristics is essential in OBE, and is used in all processes related to data management, data analysis, and data reporting. The description need not be overly taxing, as is seen in Exhibit 6-1. Note how a few core-recipient characteristics can give the reader a good sense of the individuals involved in the evaluation. These descriptions relate to the studies reported earlier in Exhibits 1-1, 1-2, and 1-3.

Table 6.1. Exemplary Adaptive Behaviors and Role Status Indicators

Adaptive behaviors	Role-status indicators
Activities of daily living	Home and community living
Eating	Living arrangements
Transfer/mobility	Independent
Toileting	Supported
Dressing	Congregate
Instrumental activities of daily living	Ownership indicators
Meal preparation	Own home
Housekeeping	Private telephone
Transportation/mobility	Name on rental agreement
Taking medication	Name on mailbox
Money management	Possessions
Telephone use	Education indicators
Communication skills	Grade level
Receptive skills	Classroom environment
Expressive skills	Regular
Social skills	Resource room
Receiving	Segregated
Sending	Employment indicators
Job skills	Employment status
Self-direction	Employed
Decision making	Unemployed
Self-assertion	Work environment
Functional academic skills	Integrated
Recreational skills	Segregated
Leisure skills	Health functioning indicators
	Care Status
	Self
	Supported (e.g., home health)
	Facility based
	Wellness
	Number days sick
	Number days missed work
	Number doctor appointments
	Medication level
	Number of hospitalizations
	Discomfort level

Exhibit 6-1
Exemplary Descriptions of Services Recipients

Special Education (see Exhibit 1-1)

Students participating in the study had been verified in school as either specific learning disabled (SLD) or mentally handicapped (MH) according to the diagnostic criteria used by the State Department of Education.

SLD children shall mean children of school age who have a verified disorder in one or more of the basic processes involved in understanding or using language, spoken or written. EMH children shall mean children of school age who, because of retarded intellectual development, as determined by individual psychological examination and deficiencies in social adjustment, require additional regular educational programming.

Mental Health (see Exhibit 1-2)

The primary diagnosis in the *Diagnostic and Statistical Manual of Mental Disorders*, Fourth Edition (DSM-IV) (American Psychiatric Association, 1994) for the 387 persons composing the study sample included: Attention Deficit Disorder (1.3%), Mental Retardation (2.3%), Organic Brain Syndrome (6.3%) Schizophrenic Disorders (42.8%), Paranoid Disorders (0.7%), Affective Disorders (35.%), Anxiety Disorders (0.6%), and Adjustment Disorders (10.9%). Their average age was 38.9 years; 57% were males, 43% females; 43% were voluntary admission, 8.9% were voluntary by guardian; 3.2% court order; and 33% were mental health board commitments. The sample averaged 2.9 previous admissions to the program. Marital status included 42.7% single, 22.4% married, 25% divorced 4.8% separated, and 4.7% widowed–widower. Employment status included 71.7% unemployed at the time of admission.

Disability (see Exhibit 1-3)

Subjects were 85 individuals (42 males, 43 females) who had been placed 15 years ago into either independent living or competitive employment and who had remained within that placement for a minimum of 2 years. Their average age was 39.5 years (range = 33 to 74) and their average Full-Scale IQ (Wechsler Adult Intelligence Scale) was, at the time of last testing, 67 (range = 40 to 91, *SD* = 12).

Core-Service Functions

Think for a moment about what services your program really delivers. My bet is that there are about four core functions that are provided: (1) evaluation/assessment; (2) (re)habilitation services; (3) service coordination; and (4) ongoing supports. These are the core-service functions on which you will need to collect information in OBE. In thinking about your core-service functions as they relate to outcome-based evaluation, be sure to keep our eighth guiding principle clearly in mind:

> GUIDING PRINCIPLE 8: *Be sure that the services provided are consistent with the program's mission and goals and logically affect the program's outcomes.*

Evaluation/Assessment

This information is essential for both diagnosing and intervention planning. In reference to OBE, the important thing is to approach assessment from the perspective of intervention planning so that the information can be used as baseline data against which to compare program or service-related changes.

There are a number of guidelines regarding assessment that, when followed, will result in very usable data for OBE:

- Assess in the areas in which you will provide services.
- Assess both adaptive behavioral skills levels and role status.
- Consider the assessment as baseline data against which you can later compare recipients' progress.
- Remember that there are a number of ways that you can obtain information about people, including standardized procedures, participant observation, status indicators, and performance-based assessment.

A later section of this chapter will elaborate on these guidelines. In the meantime, you might want to refer to Exhibit 6-2, which summarizes how assessment data were collected for the those recipients described in Exhibit 1-3 (p. 13).

Program Services

Program services equate usually to your (re)habilitation, intervention, training, or education program. Specifically, they are the techniques your program employs that result logically in service recipients' acquiring abili-

---

Exhibit 6-2
Example of Assessment Procedures

Procedure

In most cases, contact for the purpose of providing assistance or updating demographic records had been maintained between the person and the program. For the current study, local service staff (service coordinators) were trained in survey techniques and on the specific instruments used. Observation, interview and measurement data were aggregated into the following three major data sets.

Data Sets

CURRENT STATUS. The person's current living, employment, and legal status were determined on the basis of personal interview, observation, or record review if there was a question about the person's legal status. Coding categories for each were developed.

QUALITY OF LIFE. The comprehensive assessment of the person's QOL covered social and support networks, lifestyles and role functions, activity patterns, and satisfaction. Social networks were assessed by asking the person (or the person's proxy) to "think about the people with whom you spend your time,

and what do they do for/with you." These data were aggregated into three data sets: (1) source of support, (2) activities performed, and (3) support functions provided. Lifestyles and role functions were assessed through two standardized instruments—the Community Outcomes Scale and the QOL Questionnaire. To assess activity patterns, we asked each person (or proxy) to "think about how you spend your time on a typical day that you are at home and not at your job (or program.) How many hours (out of 24) do you spend in each of the following activities: meal preparation/eating, personal hygiene, household chores, visiting with others, sleeping, and recreation/leisure?" Satisfaction was assessed using two survey instruments: The Personal Satisfaction Survey and the satisfaction factor score from the QOL Questionnaire.

HISTORICAL DESCRIPTIVE DATA. These data were obtained by assessing all persons during their initial program involvement on the Basic Skills Screening Test, which is a standardized criterion-referenced instrument containing 107 behavioral skills that comprise 7 major life-activity areas.

Exhibit 6-3

Interrogatories Regarding Job-Placement Model

Transition component	Who	What	How	When	Where
1. Determines job interests/expectations	Resource teacher Student–parent	Parent survey Student questionnaire	Checklist Interview	16+ years Yearly at IEP/ITP	School School–Home
2. Identify work environments	Resource teacher Student–family Vocational rehabilitation	Job opportunities	Personal contact with potential employers	14+ years 11–12 grades	Community
3. Access work and work-related skills	Resource teacher School diagnostic programmers	Student Competency Checklist CAP/COP	Evaluation team	9+ years 11–12 grades	School Agency–job site
4. Conduct environmental analysis	Resource teacher Employer	Job analysis form	Observation Interview	Prior to job placement After job placement	Job site
5. Access adult service providers	Resource teacher Parents Vocational rehabilitation	Eligibility Transportation	Job coach Vocational instructor	16+ years	Community
6. Implement training/curriculum based on matching student interests with available job skills	Resource teacher Vocational teacher	Vocational materials Job exploration	Classroom instruction On-the-job training	9–12 years	School Job site
7. Provide ongoing support	Job coach Co-workers Vocational rehabilitation	Support job placement and study/family's commitment to employment	Interface Natural support systems	At job placement	Job site

ties not possessed previously or reaquiring lost ability or abilities. Consider two essential guidelines here: (l) you need to describe the specific services that are being provided (e.g., job training, training in independent living, crisis management, counseling, work release, pain reduction strategies, etc.); and (2) your description of these specific services requires a functional analysis and description of the interrogatories involved. An example (Schalock et al., 1992) is presented in Exhibit 6-3, which summarizes the interrogatories regarding a job placement model.

Service Coordination

Most service recipients receive services from a number of sources. A typical scenario for a service recipient includes state-level certification and program entry, receipt of services, and systems-level coordination of ongoing supports. Service coordination assures appropriate services and the person's acquiring maximum functioning skills and enhanced role status through three major activities: (1) working with the assessment/ intervention personnel in identifying living, work, and recreational/leisure environments, natural supports provided in those environments, and specific behavioral skills required by the specific environment; (2) interfacing with other components of the service-delivery system to obtain these opportunities; and (3) procuring the necessary supports for the individual to function well within the respective environments. The "Who" and "What" interrogatories summarized in Exhibit 6-3 show well the critical importance of service coordination as a core-service function. In reference to outcome-based evaluation, it is necessary to identify these service-coordination functions, especially if they are involved in cost estimates or OBE activities.

Ongoing Supports

The supports paradigm is increasingly impacting service provision. *Supports* can generally be considered as resources and strategies that promote the interests and causes of an individual; that enable him/her to access resources, information, and relationship within regular community environments; and that result in the person's enhanced independence, productivity, community integration, and satisfaction (Schalock, 1995).

Although the concept of supports is not new, what is new is the demonstration that the judicious use of supports results in significantly enhanced functional level and role status of persons with special needs. There has been significant work recently in identifying support functions and their intensities. This work is summarized in Tables 6.2 (support

Table 6.2. Support Functions

Supports	Description
1. Teaching	Advocating, instructing, adapting curriculum, collecting data, supervising, communicating and providing feedback
2. Befriending	Socializing, enjoying, sharing and confiding, accompanying
3. Financial planning	Advocating for benefits and coverage of services, adjusting work benefits and SSI–Medicaid, helping with money management, check cashing and budgeting, protection and legal assistance
4. Employee assistance	Provision of counseling, crisis intervention and assistance, assisting in job accommodation and redesign, enhancing job performance, supervisory training, and procurement of assistive technology devices
5. Behavioral support	Functional analysis, antecedent strategies such as the manipulation of ecological and setting events and the provision of schedule and activity choices, teaching alternate adaptive responses, building environments with effective consequences
6. In-home living assistance	Personal maintenance and care, transfers and mobility, attendant care, housekeeping and homemaker services, dressing and clothing care, home health aides, medical alert devices, communication devices, and architectural modifications
7. Community and school access and use	Carpooling and transportation programs, recreation and leisure involvement, transportation and pedestrian training, modification of vehicles, community use awareness and opportunities, and interfacing with generic agencies including schools, advocacy, and legal assistance
8. Health assistance	Medical appointments, health supervision and interventions, counseling appointments and interventions, medication taking, hazards awareness, physical therapy, and mobility assistive devices

Source: Reprinted by permission from R. Luckasson, D. L. Coulter, E. A. Polloway, S. Reiss, R. L. Schalock, M. E. Snell, D. M. Spitalnick, and J. A. Stark, *Mental Retardation: Definition, Classification, and Systems of Support*. Copyright 1982 American Association on Mental Retardation.

functions) and 6.3 (support intensities). A comprehensive OBE analysis requires that these support functions and their intensities be incorporated into a description of the services provided and their cost estimates.

Cost Estimates

After describing who is served and the core services that are provided, one needs to determine what the services cost. A cost analysis for interventions or services is one of the most important components of any outcome-based evaluation analysis. Being able to account for the resources

Table 6.3. Support Intensities: Definition and Examples

Intermittent

Supports on an "as-needed basis." Characterized by episodic nature, person not always needing the support(s), or short-term supports needed during life-span transitions (e.g., job loss or an acute medical crisis). Intermittent supports may be high or low intensity when provided.

Limited

An intensity of supports occurring on some dimensions on a regular basis for a short period of time of an intermittent nature. May require fewer staff members and less cost than more intense levels of support (e.g., time-limited employment training or transitional supports during the school to adult provided period).

Extensive

Supports characterized by ongoing regular involvement (e.g., daily) in at least some environments (such as work or home) and not time limited (e.g., long-term support and long-term home living support).

Pervasive

Supports characterized by their constancy and high intensity; supports are provided in several environments and are potentially life sustaining in nature. Pervasive supports typically are more intensive and involve more staff members and intrusiveness than do extensive or time-limited supports.

Source: Reprinted by permission from Luckasson et al. Copyright 1992 American Association on Mental Retardation.

used by a program is a crucial responsibility of any program administrator, and is an absolute accountability requirement held by funders and other critical stakeholders. Cost estimates are also important for describing the intensity of the services provided, for budgeting program replications, and for evaluating whether the impacts produced by the program are sufficiently large to justify the program. Cost estimates begin with understanding revenue and expenditures, progressing to determining total costs and average cost per program recipient.

Revenue and Expenditures

Almost all educational and social programs have multiple sources of revenue that vary from public funds to user fees. Similarly, they have numerous expenditures. The secret of developing good cost estimates is to understand fully revenue, expenditures, and other economic costs. A simple listing is presented in Table 6.4.

Table 6.4. Revenue, Expenditures, and Other Economic Cost Categories
Examined

Revenue	Expenditures	Other economic costs
Federal grants	Fixed (capital)	Start-up costs
State grants	Labor	Indirect costs
City–county grants	Patient variable (e.g., methadone,	Shared resources
Other public funds	medical supplies)	Donated capital
Client payment	Other variable (e.g., utilities,	
Private third party	office supplies)	
Public third party	Rents	
Private grants and donations		
Interest		
Other		

Source: Reprinted by permission from M. T. French, C. J. Bradley, B. Calingert, M. L. Dennis, & G. T. Karuntzos, "Cost Analysis of Training and Employment Services in Methadone Treatment," *Evaluation and Program Planning*, Vol. 11, pp. 107–120. Copyright 1994 by Elsevier Science Publishing Co., Inc.

Total Costs

Most programs have, or should have, an accounting system that will provide the basis for estimating program costs based on the expenditures and other economic costs summarized in Table 6.4. Cost estimates can be produced from this accounting system without much effort. My recommendation is that you approach the determination of cost estimates from an incremental perspective. All programs should seek to provide some basic cost information about their services that can be culled directly from their accounting systems with little work. Then, depending upon the question(s) that you are asking, programs can examine more complex analyses (such as impact or benefit–cost analysis), all of which build on the basic estimates of cost. These additional cost data provide valuable information, but require more work and more complex analyses. The extent to which it is useful to pursue these additional issues depends on the questions asked, the developmental stage of the program, the interests of the stakeholders, and the information demands of policy makers. Thus, our ninth guiding principle:

GUIDING PRINCIPLE 9: *The type of cost data collected and the complexity of the cost analysis are dependent on the type of outcome-based evaluation analysis planned.*

A detailed discussion of all the issues involved in cost analysis is beyond the scope of this book, and indeed the interested reader is referred to the suggested additional readings on cost analysis, if so inclined. For our purposes, the following guidelines should result in valid cost estimates sufficient for most outcome-based evaluations:

1. A good accounting system will generally provide adequate information to estimate the total costs of the program as seen from the perspective of its own budget.
2. The first step is to define the period over which costs will be measured. It is generally best to select the most recently completed program fiscal year.
3. Use actual recorded costs rather than basing the cost analysis on budget or planning documents.
4. If you plan to conduct benefit–cost analysis, it is essential that the period used for the cost analysis corresponds to the period for the impact or benefit analysis.
5. Once the period has been defined, the costs are totaled for that period, resulting in expenditures reflecting actual resources used. This is relatively straightforward, except for capital expenditures and when the program accounts are maintained on a cash rather than accrual basis. As discussed more fully in Schalock and Thornton (1988), the accrual system offers substantial advantages to determining cost estimates.
6. In estimating total costs, it is important to keep in mind the level of precision needed for the cost analysis. It is often unnecessary to resolve all the issues about capital costs, accruals, or other cost factors. In many cases, it is clear that such refinements will only make trivial differences in the cost estimate. A simple example of the determination of total cost is found in Exhibit 6-4 (top section).

Average Costs

Although the previous guidelines focus on total costs, determining total costs is often only an intermediate step of the cost estimate. The end goal is average costs. Total costs are determined to a great extent by the number of persons served. This means that total costs reflect program scale as much as the intensity of services provided to the typical participant.

Average costs, on the other hand, are more easily compared with estimates of program effects that will generally reflect the effect of the program on the average enrollee. Average costs also offer an important advantage when a cost analyst looks at the costs of several programs. By looking at the average costs of a program, the cost analyst can focus attention on the issues of service intensity.

Exhibit 6-4
Examples of Total and Average Cost Estimates

Expense category	Total expenses
Personnel	$518,182
Consultants	18,970
Materials and supplies	7,093
Facility costs	18,909
Other	
Travel	1,053
Communications	5,621
Training and conferences	5,649
Dues and subscriptions	2,412
Equipment	4,021
Total direct cost	581,910
Indirect costs	68,667
(For general administrative services provided to the program, such as fiscal services, accounting, purchasing, housekeeping, plant engineering, and human resources)	
Total cost	$650,577

AVERAGE COST: If the aforementioned program has had 75 persons receiving services during the last fiscal year (the year on which the above total costs would normally be determined), the average cost per service recipient would be:

$$\frac{\$650,577}{75} = \$8674.36$$

Source: Reprinted by permission from T. Criscione, T. A. Kastner, D. O'Brien, and R. Nathanson, "Replication of a Managed Health Care Initiative for People with Mental Retardation Living in the Community," *Mental Retardation*, Vol. 32, No. 1, pp. 43–52. Copyright 1994 American Association on Mental Retardation.

Average cost is generally calculated by dividing the estimate of total cost for a specific accounting period by the number of persons served during that period. Since most educational and social programs are in what one might consider a "steady state" in which movement in and out is not rapid, average cost per participant can be determined by the following formula:

$$\frac{\text{Total Cost for Time Period}}{\text{Number of Persons Enrolled during That Period}}$$

An example is shown in Exhibit 6-4 (bottom section).

Person-Referenced Outcomes

The fourth and last core data set involves valued, person-referenced outcomes that meet the five criteria: valued by the person, multidimensional, objective and measurable, connected logically to the program, and evaluated longitudinally. Examples were given in Tables 2.3 and 6.1. The core of these criteria is reflected in our tenth guiding principle:

GUIDING PRINCIPLE 10: *Person-referenced outcomes should be valued by the person and related demonstrably to the services provided.*

In summary, outcome-based evaluation requires collecting data on four core data sets including recipient characteristics, core-service functions, cost estimates, and valued, person-referenced outcomes. This requirement leads to our eleventh guiding principle:

GUIDING PRINCIPLE 11: *Outcome-based evaluation data should be collected in four key areas: recipient characteristics, core-service functions, cost estimates, and valued, person-referenced outcomes.*

How these data are collected is an issue of measurement, and that is the focus of the next section of the chapter. The section discusses conceptually how to collect data and presents a matrix showing the relationship between the four core data sets just summarized and measurement techniques.

Measurement Techniques

A framework for using one or more techniques to measure the core data sets is presented in Table 6.5. Note four aspects to the matrix. First, the core data sets are listed along the ordinate. Second, one can use potentially

Table 6.5. A Framework for Measuring Core Data Sets

	Measurement technique		
Core data sets	Standardized instruments	Performance-based assessment	Participant observation
Recipient characteristics			
Age	X		
Gender	X		
Diagnosis	X		
Adaptive behavior level	X	X	X
Role status		X	
Core Service Functions			
Evaluation/assessment	X		X
(Re)Habilitation	X		X
Service coordination	X		X
Ongoing Supports	X		X
Cost estimates	X		
Person-referenced outcomes	X	X	X

three measurement techniques (which are described later) to obtain data regarding these core data sets. Third, some data may be quantitative and some may be qualitative (e.g., satisfaction, quality of life, perceived role status) and obtained through such techniques that are described variously as ethnographic, naturalistic, or anthropological (Edgerton, 1990). The term *participant observation* is used in the matrix to refer to these qualitative methods. Fourth, the "X" denotes the suggested technique to use for the respective data set.

Standardized Instruments

Standardized instruments are used frequently to assess a number of aspects about people: their intelligence, educational level, occupational or career interests, clinical status, values, personal orientations, symptomatology, academic achievement or aptitudes. Data from standardized instruments lend themselves frequently to assessing a person's functional level and thereby are used for diagnostic, intervention, and outcome-evaluation activities.

Himmel (1984) suggests three criteria for choosing a standardized instrument: psychometric quality, a graded response format, and utility. To those, I would add the following four essential psychometric standards:

1. *Reliability.* Check the instrument's manual (or the method section of the report) about the type of reliability determined for the test or measure-

ment procedure and the magnitude of the reliability coefficient. The most common types of reliability for such procedures include test–retest, inter–intraobserver, or internal consistency. Reliability coefficients should generally be within the .80 to .85 range for the test/procedures to be "reliable" or consistent.

2. *Validity*. Again, check the manual or procedure section of the report to determine if the test/procedure's validity has been determined. Common forms of validity include content (Do the measurement items measure what the test/procedure proports to measure?), construct (Do the items measure the underlying construct being studied?), predictive (Does the person's test results actually predict anything like future living–work status or performance?), or concurrent (Are the current results consistent with a second, independent measure of the behavior/role status under consideration?). Validity coefficients should generally be within the .60 to .70 range for the test/procedure to be considered "valid."

3. *Standardization group*. Here, you want to check the manual or procedure section to determine on whom the test/procedure was developed and standardized for comparative purposes. You need to be very careful not to use norms for comparisons that were not developed on individuals similar to those on whom the measurement was made. This is an essential point in today's multi-cultural and consumer-oriented worlds.

4. *Norms*. The comparative standards—or norms—are essential to understand and should be described and presented in the manual or procedure section. Again, be sure that the normative sample is comparable to your group; otherwise, comparisons will be meaningless and fraught with practical and legal issues.

Performance-Based Assessment

The second measurement technique involves *performance-based assessment* that is defined as using objective indicators to evaluate a person's adaptive behavior level and role status. Objective measures of adaptive behavior and role status say a lot about the person, and potentially, the results of the intervention or services provided. For example, if a person can feed or dress him/herself as a result of early intervention, then the program has probably been successful. Similarly, attending regular school and being in a regular classroom potentially reflects the student's academic and social functioning. Similarly, a person's employment status reflects his/her work skills and social behavior. So, rather than measuring a large number of smaller (sometimes referred to as *splinter skills*), adaptive behavior levels and role status obtained through performance-based assessment is often the best person-referenced outcome to use in OBE. Table

6.1 listed a number of exemplary adaptive behaviors and role-status indicators that can be used in performance-based assessment. As with standardized instruments, the reliability and validity of the measurement technique used in performance-based assessment need to be demonstrated.

Participant Observation

This third measurement technique requires that the OBE data collector observe what people do, listen to what they say, and frequently participate in their daily activities. In this capacity, the data collector can study the behavior and interactions displayed in natural settings in order to describe in detail the person's behaviors, interactions, and functional level (W. Stainback & S. Stainback, 1989). To quote Edgerton (1990),

> Our ethnographic procedures required familiarity with as many aspects of a person's life as possible. Our methodological philosophy derives primarily from naturalism, rather than positivistic behavioral science. We attempt to comprehend and interpret the phenomena under study as faithfully as possible; our goal is to be true to the phenomena themselves.... To carry out ethnographic naturalism, we must have prolonged contact with people. We must become, if only relatively so, a natural part of their lives. In time, we usually gain access to more than the public domain of their lives. (p. 154)

Participant observation also lends itself to attitude surveys and other survey methods such as (1) measuring core-service functions that require a response, reaction, or opinion from the service recipient; or (2) asking open-ended consumer questions (McKillip, Moirs, & Cervenka, 1992). This method is the better one to use if your person-referenced outcomes relate to phenomena such as quality of life, consumer satisfaction, parent–child interactions, or social skills demonstrated by the individual. However, the use of participant-observation techniques does not free either the evaluation producer or the consumer from the requirements of using demonstrated reliable and valid procedures.

Guidelines For Outcome-Based Evaluation Data Collection

Chapter 7 contains actual formats for data collection. Hence, in this section, I will merely stress a number of general guidelines that are essential for valid OBE data collection. These five guidelines relate to data quantification, data-collection responsibility center, data-collection timelines, multiple perspectives on costs and outcomes, and data-management system criteria.

Data Quantification

In today's world of accountability, educational and social programs are increasingly quantifying the services that they provide and the outcomes from those services. For example, services received are usually quantified in terms of hours (of service) per day; outcomes are quantified in terms of measurable changes in adaptive skills levels, role status, satisfaction, or quality of life.

Data quantification is not as easy as it sounds. It involves (as we will see in Chapter 7) documentation that requires resources (time, money, expertise) for recording, processing, and analysis. You should keep two guidelines clearly in mind here: Core data sets should be defined both clearly and operationally.

1. *Define clearly your core data sets.* This means that you need to think clearly about specific recipient characteristics, core-service functions, cost estimates, and valued, person-referenced outcomes that you will be collecting and analyzing. Assisting you in this process was the primary purpose of the first four sections of this chapter.

2. *Define operationally your core data sets.* To *operationally define* something is to define it in reference to how it is measured. Thus, for each core data set, there needs to be clear definitions of what is being measured, so that one's data-collection efforts lead to quantifiable data that can be used for later analysis and reporting.

Quantifying recipient characteristics will probably not cause you any trouble, as long as you keep the number of characteristics reasonably small. Core-service functions and cost estimates will be a bit more difficult, but don't panic until after you've read Chapter 7. Behavioral skills level and status indicators will probably be the most difficult, and for that reason, we need to discuss briefly a number of criteria for each.

A *behavioral skills indicator* is a measure that summarizes information relevant to a particular phenomenon, or a reasonable proxy for such a measure (Jenkins, 1990). Behavioral or functional skills indicators need to meet the following criteria:

- Measure what they are supposed to measure (validity)
- Be consistent across people or raters (reliability)
- Measure change (sensitivity)
- Reflect changes only in the situation concerned (specificity)

Status indicators (Rapp Gowdy, Sullivan, & Winterstein, 1988) also need to meet certain criteria including:

- The list of statuses within a given domain, such as living, needs to be exhaustive and include all possibilities.
- Each specific status needs to be mutually exclusive.
- Statuses must be able to be hierarchically ordered from least desirable to most desirable, with a reasonable degree of consensus about the hierarchy.
- The measures need to be sensitive to change over time.

Data Collection Responsibility Center

One of the most frequently overlooked staff positions is that directed toward data collection and its management. I have a strong bias that this person is one of your most valued staff positions, and is worthy of the training and support necessary to do a job well. Remember simple statements: "GIGO—garbage in, garbage out"; and "You cannot make chicken fritters without good chicken." Thus, I would recommend the following three guidelines about who should collect data:

1. Have a person who is responsible for data collection and data management.
2. Train that person in data collection (as in this chapter) and data management (as in Chapter 7).
3. Be sure that this person works closely with your fiscal and computer personnel.

Data Collection Time Lines

When should data be collected? Answering this question requires logical thinking. One should collect a description of persons served during the enrollment process. Similarly, the measurement of the intervention or services received and their costs should occur during the persons' actual program involvement.

There are no set standards for when outcome measures should be collected, but I would recommend that they be done annually and at specified follow-up periods. If, however, you have only a short time to evaluate a program, then it is best to use short-term performance indicators, such as placement or admission rates. Usually, however, you want to look at multiple outcomes longitudinally. Thus, a quick rule of thumb is to measure outcomes annually so that individual outcomes can be aggregated into a yearly summary for all participants as part of the yearly service evaluation, performance audit, or cost summary. But don't overlook the necessity of doing longitudinal follow-up studies that include the person's adaptive behavior level, role status, and supports level.

Multiple Perspectives on Costs and Outcomes

As we saw in Chapter 5 on benefit–cost analysis, one needs to think about costs and outcomes (or benefits) from a number of perspectives. The essential question to ask in both cost and benefit analysis is, "Costs or benefits to whom?"

Any public policy or program typically affects many groups, including participants, their families, other services, employees, governments, and taxpayers. Each group has a perspective on the program and each of these perspectives will have some relevancy to decision making. Typical perspectives that are involved in outcome-based evaluation include the participant, the taxpayer, and society at large (which is composed of everyone else). You might want to refer back to Table 5.2 for a quick review.

Data Management System Criteria

We need now to make the transition between data collection in a general sense (which is what we did in this chapter) and the specific formats and procedures that one will use to actually "get the data in hand" (which is the focus of Chapter 7). The guideline to remember is that in selecting your core data sets, the data collected must both fit into and be part of your data-management system. If not, your data will sit around in piles on the floor, in a file cabinet, or in someone's trunk (I've seen examples of each). Thus, don't forget these five data-management system criteria:

1. Person-referenced
2. Complete (available for all program participants)
3. Timely (current and covers the period of time you are interested in)
4. Affordable (time, money, expertise)
5. Accurate (reflects actual events and characteristics)

Summary

In summary, this chapter has focused on a key issue in outcome-based evaluation—data collection. Throughout the chapter it was stressed that one needs to think about core data sets involving the persons served, the services received, the costs of those services, and the outcomes from them. A model was presented (Figure 6.2) that provides both the conceptual and procedural guidelines as to which measurement technique (standardized procedures, performance-based assessment, or participant observation) can be used to measure each of the core data sets. It was also stressed that regardless of the measurement technique used, both evaluation consumers and producers need to be aware of the essential psychometric standards for measurement, including reliability, validity, standardization group, and norms. Guidelines were also suggested that, if followed, will assist in one's accurate and efficient data collection efforts.

It is also important to realize that there is a definite relationship among inputs (mission/goals), process (services), and outcomes. This interrelationship points out the importance of the contextual setting in which the program functions and the critical role that contextual variables (discussed more fully in Chapter 9) play in understanding outcome-based analyses and their uses. But before considering those uses, we need to understand data-management principles (Chapter 7) and evaluation designs and data analysis (Chapter 8).

Study Questions

1. Why is it so important to simplify the data one collects for outcome-based evaluation?

2. Give specific examples of how one can simplify (by choosing key indicators) data sets regarding client characteristics, core-service functions, cost estimates, and valued, person-referenced outcomes.

3. Review the outcome-based evaluation data-collection and utilization model presented in Figure 6.1. Begin an effectiveness analysis by specifying (a) the questions asked; (b) the data you will collect to answer the question; and (c) the purpose(s) for which you will use the data.

4. If you had to choose only one indicator each of client characteristics, core-service function, cost estimate, and valued, person-referenced outcome as the basis for an impact analysis, which ones (total = 4) would you select? Why? What measurement technique would you use for each? (See Table 6.5)

5. Compare and contrast the three measurement techniques composing the proposed conceptual approach to measurement (Table 6.5).

6. Why are reliability, validity, standardization group, and norms so critical in the use of any measurement technique, including standardized procedures, performance-based assessment, or participant observation? (Hint: Even participant observation requires a reference point.)

7. Outline how you would incorporate the person's level of needed support (Table 6.3) into your approach to outcome-based evaluation.

8. Review the exemplary adaptive behaviors and role-status indicators listed in Table 6.1. Matrix those indicators against the following program types: delinquency, homelessness, substance abuse, the elderly, the medically fragile. Can you add any more indicators (check Table 2.3)?

9. Review an agency or program budget. Provide a brief summary of the program's revenues, expenditures, total costs, and average costs. What assumptions are involved in cost estimates?

10. Develop an approach to incorporating supports into the evaluation of a program. What methods do you suggest to determine their costs and benefits?

Additional Readings

Burnstein, L., Freeman, H., Sirotnik, K. Delanshere, G., & Hollis, M. (1985). Data collection: The Achilles of evaluation research. *Sociological Methods and Research, 14,* 65–80.

Kaplan, R. M. (1990). Behavior as the central outcome in health care. *American Psychologist, 45*(11), 1211–1220.

Killaugh, L. N., & Leininger, W. E. (1987). *Cost accounting: Concepts and techniques for management* (2nd ed.). New York: West.

Martin, P., & Bateson, P. (1993). *Measuring behavior: An introductory guide* (2nd ed.). Cambridge, UK: Cambridge University Press.

McGrew, K. S., & Bruininks, R. H. (1992). A multidimensional approach to the measurement of community adjustment. In M. Hayden & B. Avery (Eds.), *Community living for persons with mental retardation and related conditions* (pp. 124–142). Baltimore: Brookes.

7

Outcome-Based Evaluation Data Management

Overview

If I was successful in Chapter 6, you should now know which core data sets (recipient characteristics, core-service functions, cost estimates, and valued, person-referenced outcomes) you plan to use in your outcome-based evaluation. Now the task is to determine how best to collect and organize the data physically so that it can be used effectively in one or more of the OBE analyses described in Chapters 3–5. I refer to this process as *data management*, the result of which is the development of a viable and useful data-management system.

All program administrators have multiple data needs. They are constantly being requested by numerous stakeholders, funding bodies, researchers, and policy makers to provide information about their service recipients, the intervention or services provided, the costs of those services, and the outcomes from the services. My experiences over the years with program managers has led to two conclusions: First, data collection and management is highly frustrating to most administrators, because it requires considerable resources (time, money, expertise) that are seldom budgeted or available; and second, few program managers are trained adequately in data collection and its analysis, let alone evaluation designs and statistics. I have also found, however, that most administrators are very receptive to data, if they can be collected and analyzed in ways that are nonobtrusive, easy to understand, and useful.

Trends Impacting Data Utilization

To begin the process of developing a viable data management system, let's look briefly at three major trends impacting data utilization. First, information systems are increasingly being viewed as strategic and valuable assets to an organization. For example, Alvin Toffler (1990), in his recent book *Powershift*, suggests that we are currently seeing a shift from violence and wealth as sources of power toward a knowledge base. Similarly, the current rapid social and political changes necessitate a data collection and analysis process that is responsive to the rebirth of social activism and constituent groups and can answer questions about a program's effectiveness, impact, and/or benefit–cost. As stated by Rocheleau (1993),

> The situation has changed dramatically over the last decade.... The development of the concept of a decision support system created the basis for a strategically important information system. More important, the growth of microcomputers and end-user computing has increased access to computers so that they are no longer viewed as remote systems. Indeed, it is clear that many view information systems as strategic factors in obtaining competitive advantage. (p. 119)

Second, data are being used for formative feedback and internal decision making and evaluation. Although we discussed this concept in Chapter 2, its importance is most apparent here. A good data management system will provide critical information to program administrators about service recipients, core-service functions, costs, and outcomes. Such a system will also provide the administrator with the information required to meet the increasing need for program accountability, the data upon which to base program change and improvement, and the data required for doing effectiveness, impact, or benefit–cost analyses.

Third, the following criteria for a viable data-management system are well understood and accepted:

1. Person-referenced
2. Complete (available for all program participants)

3. Timely (current and cover the period of time you are interested in)
4. Affordable (time, money, expertise)
5. Accurate (reflect actual events and characteristics)

This chapter is organized around a very simple two-dimensional data-management model that can be used to guide both data collection and its analysis. It contains three sections that include this model, data-collection principles, and data-management issues. My goal is to assist you in establishing a data-management system that meets the five criteria listed earlier. In so doing, each of us has a responsibility. Yours is to think logically about data collection and data analysis. (It is not all that difficult, but logical thinking really helps.) My responsibility is to share both my data-management experiences and my biases. In reference to my biases, I like *table shells* (a fancy term for data-collection formats), matrices, and tabulations ("cross-tabs"). I also like to keep it simple. Thus, I may appear too simplistic in what is presented, but I have always found that it is easier to make things more difficult than to make them simple. And finally, I don't like hassles. Thus, I hope that the information presented about data-management systems will reduce your "hassle index."

Data Management Model

Program administrators frequently ask me two questions about data and its management: "How do I physically collect it?" and "How do I organize and store it for later analysis?" At that point, I draw them the data-management model depicted in Figure 7.1. Note its simplicity: Its two dimensions include service recipients (along the side) and core data sets (along the top). It then suggests that data-collection formats be designed around this model and that microcomputer-based file makers be developed to organize and store the information. Once that is done, one can conceptualize the ways in which the data can be used. For example, by summing across any one row that contains all the core data sets for any one service recipient, one can get a printout of the information for that service recipient. By summing down any one column, one can get either a simple summary or an average value for the respective core datum (such as a particular recipient characteristic, core-service function, average-cost estimate, or one or more person-referenced outcomes). At a more complex level, one can also ask for cross-tabs that show the relationship between particular subject characteristics (e.g., age, gender, diagnosis) and any program outcome (e.g., graduation, living, or employment status). Furthermore, we can analyze the data statistically, answering such questions

Core Data Sets

Service recipient I.D. number	Recipient characteristics	Core service functions	Cost estimates	Person-referenced outcomes	
				Role status	Adaptive behavior
1.					
2.					
3.					
4.					
5.					

Figure 7.1.   Data management model.

as whether there are significant differences between recipient characteristics (or groups) and specific outcomes.

Obviously, there are more complex uses of data, but for the most part, the complexity is in the statistical software packages, not in the way in which one collects and organizes the data. A guiding principle comes into play here:

GUIDING PRINCIPLE 12: *A good OBE data-management system is based on collecting and organizing one's data in a 2 × 2 matrix: service recipients by core data sets.*

Data Collection Principles

Valid data collection involves four principles. First, one needs to be very clear about how each data set is defined operationally. As discussed in the previous chapter, each data set must be defined in reference to how it is measured, with clear and unequivocal definitions. Second, the measures used must have demonstrated reliability and validity, so that one can be sure that they capture the construct being evaluated. Third, the data must be collected by individuals who are trained in data collection. Whether one uses standardized procedures, performance-based assessment, or participant observation (see Table 6.5), data collection requires a number of skills that insure reliability, validity, completeness, and accuracy. Please don't overlook our next guiding principle:

GUIDING PRINCIPLE 13: *Data should be collected by individuals who are trained in either standardized assessment instruments, performance-based assessment techniques, and/or participant-observation techniques.*

The fourth principle of valid data collection is the use of a standardized data-collection format. An example is shown in Figure 7.2. It is readily apparent that this data-collection format is consistent with the data-management model shown in Figure 7.1. Its two major dimensions are service recipients (listed sequentially down the side) and core OBE data sets (listed across the top). The task of data collection is to give an identification (ID) number to each service recipient, identify the core data sets that will be measured (being sure that they are operationally defined clearly and measured with demonstrated reliability), and then to fill in all of the cells.

Recipient Characteristics

					Role status		
I.D. no.	Age	Gender	Adaptive behavior skills (level)	Living	Employment	Education	Health and wellness

Core Service Functions (Hours)

				Cost/Funding Source Data	
I.D. no.	Assessment	Re(habilitation)	Service coordination	Ongoing supports	Average costs	Funding source(s)

Person-Referenced Outcomes

		Role status			
I.D. no.	Adaptive behavior skills (level)	Living	Employment	Education	Health and wellness

Figure 7.2.   Exemplary data-collection format.

For ease of communication, I have simply listed across the top the core data sets that we have discussed thus far. Obviously, others can be added depending upon your two questions: "For what purpose(s) will I use the outcome-based evaluation data?", and "What data will I need for the intended use?" For example, if you are doing longitudinal evaluations or multiple observations on the same person, it will be necessary to add columns that reflect level of functioning or role status at various postprogram times. The essential point to keep in mind, however, is that the table shell depicted in Figure 7.2 should serve as your model. Hence, our next guiding principle:

GUIDING PRINCIPLE 14: *OBE data collection should be organized around a simple matrix: service recipients by core data sets.*

I have found that a number of relatively simple procedures enhance the correct use of data-collection forms. One is to write a procedures manual in which I define each of the measures and provide formats for their collection. Second, I define operationally each of the major variables ("core data sets") as shown in Table 7.1. This procedure ensures clear communication and "clean" data collection. Third, I always train my data collectors in data-collection procedures, and build into the training session an opportunity to demonstrate the reliability of their measurements. Fourth, I insist that at least 10% of the data collection forms be verified for the accuracy of the data being collected. And fifth, I share the data (and its analysis) with the data collectors.

At this point you may be saying to yourself, "Yes, but what about the specifics?" It's true that the data-collection format presented in Figure 7.2 is a summary format, completed after you have actually collected the data on the individual in whatever service/intervention setting the person is in. Since it is a summary, let me share with you in Figure 7.3 an exemplary consumer-referenced intervention and support log that is filled out during the actual receipt of services. Although this data-collection form (which is actually used in an integrated employment training program) is labor intensive, it does have a number of characteristics that I hope will generalize to your efforts and thereby give you some good ideas. For example, note that the core-service functions are identified and defined clearly (see Table 7.1). In this case, minutes of service/support are being collected, and they may be beyond your capability. If so, think about hours or days. Second, note that it is recipient referenced. Hence, the data can be entered by recipient number and easily aggregated by the microcomputer into the format depicted in Figure 7.2. And third, note that it is "portable" and can travel easily with the staff member who is providing the support services.

Before leaving Figure 7.3, think logically about a number of ways the

Table 7.1. Consumer Intervention and Support Log: Operational Definitions

Week Ending: For the purpose of this form, Saturday is considered the last day of the week.

      Date: Include the month, day, and year. Record only on days you provide service.

1. *Direct job-skill training and support at the worksite*: Time spent working with a consumer at the job site, including observation. Anything actively done to train the individual on work skills or to provide emotional support or crisis intervention.

2. *Personal-Care Assistance at the Job Site*: Time spent providing personal care to the consumer at the job site.

3. *Inactive Time at the Job Site*: Time spent on the job site between periods of active intervention. Any time when you have removed yourself from active involvement and/ or observation of the individual; when you must be on-site and the time is not spent providing other types of intervention for any consumer.

4. *Consumer Training and Support*: Time spent providing support or training other than direct job-skill training. This may occur on or off the job site. It may include counseling, support groups, job-seeking skills training, assistance with money management, or grooming, etc.

5. *Screening and Evaluation*: Time spent screening referrals to determine eligibility, evaluating eligible individuals, and in career/vocational-planning activities. Includes gathering and analyzing information relevant to a consumer's employment potential. Examples: reviewing records, individual interviews, career planning, observation of individual for the purposes of evaluation.

6. *Instructional Planning and Monitoring*: Time spent developing appropriate instructional plans, including staff planning and discussion. Examples: doing progress notes or other training-related record keeping; writing task analyses; developing behavioral programs, modifications, or adaptations. Does not include job development.

7. *Employment Advocacy*:
   a. Consumer-specific job development
   b. Time spent advocating with worksite personnel for purposes directly related to employment. Examples: collecting supervisor feedback, postplacement advocacy, planning or meetings involving job site personnel.

8. *Case Management and Nonemployment Advocacy*:
   a. Time spent advocating with persons not directly related to the employment site, such as parents, bus drivers, adult service-agency personnel, etc.
   b. Time spent performing case-management tasks, such as Individual Service Plans (ISPs), phone calls, dealing with transportation, assisting with social security benefits, etc.

9. *Travel Training/transporting*: Transporting a consumer anywhere, or travel training.

10. *Travel without consumer*: Time spent traveling to a job site, meeting, consumer's home, etc., without the consumer.

11. *Miles traveled*: Miles traveled while providing services to this consumer.

Source: Reprinted by permission from Institute for Community Inclusion, Boston Children's Hospital, 300 Longwood Ave., Boston, MA 02115.

Consumer: _____

I.D. no.: _____

Program: _____

Staff: _____

Week ending: _____
(Should always be a Saturday)

DATE (Month/Day/Year)

DAY	Sunday	Monday	Tuesday	Wednesday	Thursday	Friday	Saturday	Total
1. Direct job skill training at the job site								
2. Personal care assistance at the job site								
3. Inactive time at the job site								
4. Consumer training and support								
5. Screening and evaluation (includes career planning and related assessment)								
6. Instructional planning and monitoring								
7a. Consumer-specific job development								
7b. Employment-related consumer advocacy								
8. Case management and nonemployment advocacy								
9. Travel training and transporting								
10. Travel without consumer								

Figure 7.3. Consumer intervention and support log.

data collected could be reported and analyzed. Although this is the topic of the following chapter, it is important that you see clearly the relationship between data-collection formats and your ability to answer specific questions and report specific outcomes. An obvious way that the data could be analyzed is to report simple totals for each service recipient for each of the core-service functions listed. In reference to our model (Figure 7.1) this would amount to summing across each of the columns. Second, we could group the service recipients according to some variable (i.e., age, gender, diagnosis) and summarize the hours of service received by core-service function for each of the groups. Third, we could report average hours received by support function for the entire group, and if costs were associated with those service hours, we would be in a good position to do subsequent cost analysis. We could also analyze the data for each staff person, since that data set is also included. Doing so simply requires adding one more column to the data-collection format shown in Figure 7.2. And finally, we could graph the data, develop tables, and run additional statistical analyses on the data. We will see examples of such in Chapter 8.

Data Management Issues

Wouldn't it be wonderful if data management were as logical and easy as I have thus far made it out to be? Unfortunately, for many readers, data management is a source of both frustration and potential threat. Why? Part of the answer relates to my earlier comments about logical thinking and previous training in data collection, management, and analysis. But part of the answer also lies with the computer capability of one's program, along with some what I will refer to later in this subsection as "system problems."

Computer Capability

How old is your computer or computer system and what software data-management/analysis programs does your program currently have? And maybe there is a more basic question: "Do you have someone on staff who is knowledgeable about computers and data analysis?" If not, then my strong recommendation is that you either hire or contract for such a person, for data management is not possible without a competent person who is well versed in current software packages and data analysis.

Let me draw you a picture that shows clearly the relationships among data collection, data entry, data organization, and eventual data analysis. The picture is shown as the "data flow model" depicted in Figure 7.4. Note the three-step process: data-collection format, database management/data

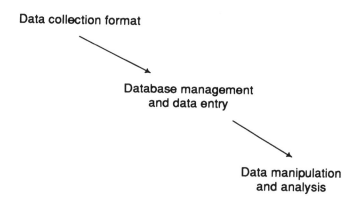

Figure 7.4.   Data-flow model.

entry, and data manipulation/analysis. The data collection form can be similar to what we just discussed (see Figure 7.2). The next component is critical: Use a database-management software program to input your data, so that it is consistent with the data-collection format, or a close proximity. Next, you will need to organize your data, which generally means labeling your variables and giving them values (which should already be done *vis à vis* your data-collection form). Remember, that most software programs (such as the Statistical Procedures for the Social Sciences packages) read numbers; hence, you need to tell it what to read. And finally, you will then ask for particular data analyses, which vary from simple cross-tabs to quite complex analyses, such as analysis of variance, multiple regression, or pattern analyses. An example of the results of the "data flow model" is presented in Exhibit 7-1.

Depending on the analysis, you may need to do some additional "massaging of the data" to get it into the correct format for the analysis, but fortunately, the software program and your computer/data analyst can work that out for you. In the meantime, don't forget our next guiding principle:

GUIDING PRINCIPLE 15: *The computerization of management data should flow from data-collection format, to database management/data entry, to data manipulation and analysis.*

Systems Problems

Many programs have trouble with data management, and the problems of data management are not unique to you or me. Recent reviews

Exhibit 7-1
Example of Data-Flow Model

Data Collection Format

This study involved measuring the perceived living-environment satisfaction of a group of 122 adults with mental illness. Individuals were in one of three types of living arrangements: independent, semi-independent, or supervised. The questionnaire was a 5-point Likert scale that asked, "Overall, please indicate how satisfied you are with your current living environment." Respondents were asked to indicate their degree of satisfaction on a 5-point scale: 5 = very satisfied; 4 = somewhat satisfied; 3 = neutral; 2 = somewhat dissatisfied; 1 = very dissatisfied.

Database Management and Entry

Data were entered so that cross-tabs and average score per living environment could be analyzed.

		Living environment		
Cross-tabs:		Semi-		
Degree of satisfaction	Supervised	independent	Independent	Total
Very satisfied (5)	0	11	5	16
Somewhat satisfied (4)	1	10	11	22
Neutral (3)	4	20	15	39
Somewhat dissatisfied (2)	4	9	11	24
Very dissatisfied (1)	4	10	7	21

AVERAGE SCORES

Supervised: mean = 2.2 (Standard error = 0.2)
Semi-Independent: mean = 3.1 (0.3)
Independent: mean = 2.9 (0.3)

Data Manipulation and Analysis

A SPSS computer program was used to analyze the cross-tabs and mean data. A chi-square analysis of the cross-tab (frequency) data indicated no significant differences (x^2 (8) = 6.57, $p > .05$). A one-way analysis of variance on the means resulted in the following summary table:

Source	DF	Sum of squares	Mean squares	F ratio	F probability
Between groups	2	8.6039	4.3019	2.7790	.0661
Within groups	119	184.2158	1.5480		
Total	121	192.8197			

(Freedland & Carey, 1992; Rocheleau, 1993; Schalock, Kiernan, Mc-Gaughey, Lynch, & McNally, 1993) of data-management systems have found a number of difficulties:

1. Ineffective communication between the user community and the developer.
2. Lack of knowledgeable end users.
3. Overoptimism about development time, development cost, and/or operational cost of the system.
4. Lack of user access, technical assistance, and output provision to end users.
5. Hardware selection and purchases based on budget criteria rather than database volume, transaction volumes, or statistical needs.
6. Inability to perform interdatabase synthesis.
7. Inadequate training on form completion and data entry.
8. Insufficient technical support.

These eight systems problems are serious, and how one overcomes them can make the difference between a viable and valid (not to mention "friendly") data-management system and one that is either ineffective or inoperable. Table 7.2 suggests a number of possible solutions based on my experience with data-management computer systems. Although these possible solutions are no panacea, I would suggest strongly that you address them, bringing in a good data-management consultant if necessary.

Summary

In summary, although a short chapter in this text, the issue of data management is probably one of the most important issues discussed thus far. By design, I wanted to keep the chapter "neat and clean" so that the critical points one needs to keep in mind about an OBE data-management system would not be lost. Those points are represented well in the four guiding principles introduced in this chapter:

1. A good OBE data-management system is based on collecting and organizing one's data in a 2 × 2 matrix: service recipients by core data sets.
2. Data should be collected by individuals who are trained in either standardized assessment instruments, performance-based assessment techniques, and/or participant observation techniques.
3. OBE data collection should be organized around a simple matrix: service recipients by core data sets.

Table 7.2. Suggestions for Overcoming Data Management Systems Problems

Problem	Suggested solution(s)
Ineffective communication between user and developer	Joint development/implementation/review groups
Lack of knowledgeable end users	In-service training
Overoptimism about development time and costs and operational costs	Use historical costs Cost studies based on actuarial data
Lack of user access, technical assistance, and output provision to end user	Shared system On-line systems
Fiscal-based hardware selection	Multiple-year acquisition/funding
Inability to perform interdatabase synthesis	Common ID numbers Knowledgeable manipulation Time-relational databases
Inadequate training on form completion and data entry	In-service training
Insufficient technical support	Interagency support teams: University/college technical-support teams/consultants

4. The computerization of data should flow from data-collection format, to database management/data entry, to manipulation and analysis.

This chapter also introduced and discussed a simple model for data collection (Figure 7.1) and the logical connection among data collection, organization/storage, and analysis. It also listed the five criteria that should guide the development and use of any data-management system: that it be person-referenced, complete, timely, affordable, and accurate.

Collectively, Chapters 6 and 7 have prepared us for our next task: understanding evaluation designs and data analysis. Once one knows the data that will be used to answer the questions asked, how those data will be operationalized and measured, how they will be collected, and how they will be organized and stored, then the next logical question is "How should OBE data be analyzed?" What we will see in Chapter 8 is that the specific analyses that one does on OBE data depend upon the evaluation design that one has used in answering one's questions, and the type of data that are available.

Study Questions

1. Summarize the three trends currently impacting data utilization. In your judgment, what is the impact of each trend on outcome-based evaluation? How

might these trends be viewed differently by a program administrator versus a service recipient?

2. Assume that you are the administrator of either an education or social program. Develop a prototype of an OBE data-management system by providing core data sets for the five service recipients listed in Figure 7.1.

3. Continue the process begun in Question 2 by expanding these data sets as reflected in Figure 7.2.

4. Assume that you are a job coach in a supported employment program. Use Figure 7.3 to collect data (on one of your classmates) who is "receiving" your job training services.

5. Assume that you are a computer systems design consultant who is helping a (re)habilitation agency to overcome their data-management problems. Outline a specific action program that would overcome the data-management system's problems, such as those listed in Table 7.2.

6. Critique the four data-collection principles discussed in this chapter. Why are they important?

7. Review a journal article that addresses the issues of data management. Compare their suggestions with the two data-management issues discussed in this chapter.

8. Draft a procedures manual that could be used to improve an agency's data-management system. What is in your manual that was not in this chapter?

9. How can the costs (in terms of person power and computerization) of data management be reduced? How can data management be made more effective?

10. Ask one or more program managers what they mean by a "data-management system." Are its components similar to those discussed in this chapter? How do they differ?

Additional Readings

Fishman, D. B. (1992). Postmodernism comes to program evaluation. *Evaluation and Program Planning, 15*, 263–270.

Freedland, K. E., & Carney, R. M. (1992). Data management and accountability in behavioral and biomedical research. *American Psychologist, 47*(5), 640–645.

Keen, P. G. W., & Morton, S. S. (1978). *Decision support systems: An organizational perspective.* Reading, MA: Addison-Wesley.

Rocheleau, B. (1993). Evaluating public section information systems. *Evaluation and Program Planning, 16*, 119–129.

Torres, R. T. (1992). Improving the quality of internal evaluation: The evaluator as consultant–mediator. *Evaluation and Program Planning, 14*, 189–198.

8

Outcome-Based Evaluation Designs and Data Analysis

Overview

Chapters 6 and 7 prepared the way for our work in this chapter on outcome-based evaluation designs and data analysis. By now, the reader should be clear about what data to collect and how to organize and manage them. The next question is, "What do I do now?"

In reality, you have probably already begun answering the question, for sequentially you would select the outcome-based evaluation design after you have decided on the evaluation question (see Figure 6.1). However, I have withheld discussion of evaluation designs until now, because they conceptually and pragmatically fit better with the various data (statistical) analyses presented in this chapter.

There are a number of key points that you will want to keep in mind as you read this chapter. First, I will summarize six outcome-based evaluation designs that one can use as the basis for effectiveness, impact, or benefit–cost analysis:

1. Person as own comparison
2. Pre–postchange comparison
3. Longitudinal status comparison
4. Hypothetical comparison group
5. Matched pairs (cohorts)
6. Experimental/control groups

Second, the specific OBE design selected will impact the number of assumptions that you need to make in analyzing the data, the degree of certainty regarding the results that you obtain, the degree of precision regarding statements made about whether the program really produced the observed outcomes, and the generalizability of your results to similar programs and their outcomes. These relationships are shown in Figure 8.1, in which the experimental/control evaluation design results in the highest certainty, precision, comparability, and generalizability because of the few assumptions that need to be made. Conversely, if you use either the person as own comparison or pre–postchange comparisons, the certainty, precision, comparability, and generalizability are low because of the large number of assumptions that you need to make about the representativeness of the small sample or the relative simplicity of a pre–postmeasure.

Third, any OBE analysis involves making a comparison of results (person or program) with another condition. Evaluation designs are used

Certainty	Precision	Evaluation Design	Comparability	Generalizability
▲ High	▲ High	Experimental/control	▲ Few assumptions	▲ High
		Matched pairs (cohorts)		
		Hypothetical comparison group		
		Longitudinal status comparisons		
		Pre-post change comparisons		
▼ Low	▼ Low	Person as own comparison	▼ Many assumptions	▼ Low

Figure 8.1   Relationships among evaluation design, certainty, precision, assumptions regarding comparability, and generalizability of results.

to provide these comparison conditions. Some comparisons are relatively easy; others are quite complex. Generally speaking, the comparison conditions used in effectiveness analysis are simpler and easier to generate than those used in impact or benefit–cost analysis.

Fourth, data analysis is used for a number purposes. The more important of these include summarizing information on the core data sets for service recipients; reporting data on core data sets to funding and legislative bodies, boards, and other stakeholders; managing information for formative feedback or internal-evaluation purposes; and serving as a basis for the three outcome-based evaluation analyses discussed in Chapters 3–5.

Each of these four points will be discussed in considerable detail in this chapter. Whether you are an evaluation producer or consumer, my goal is that you become more knowledgeable in OBE designs and see the relationship between these designs and specific data-analytic and statistical tests. I will probably not make you a statistician; but I hope you will have more confidence and competency in OBE designs and statistical techniques. The chapter contains three major sections: outcome-based evaluation designs, general principles regarding statistics, and common OBE statistical analyses.

Outcome-Based Evaluation Designs

In his book *Designing Evaluations of Education and Social Programs*, Cronbach (1982) states:

> Designing an evaluative investigation is an art. The design must be chosen afresh in each new undertaking, and the choices to be made are almost innumerable. Each feature of a design offers particular advantages and entails particular sacrifices (p. 1).

It is appropriate that we begin our discussion of OBE designs by returning to the concept of the pragmatic approach to program evaluation, looking at some of the reasons why program evaluation is moving so quickly to that concept. As discussed in Chapter 1, the current shift toward a pragmatic evaluation paradigm emphasizes operational definitions of real-world phenomena and measurement of certain quantitative program outcomes (Fishman, 1991, 1992; Guba & Lincoln, 1989). This pragmatic orientation helps describe and monitor change in a particular social program and includes criteria related to practicality, feasibility, acceptance by constituents, cost–benefits, and replication in real-world conditions. The pragmatic approach also represents a significant paradigm shift away from the experimental/control design that emphasizes the testing of hypotheses derived from theory that postulates universal principles or laws of individuals and social behavior within general types of social programs.

Consistent with the movement toward the pragmatic-evaluation approach is the fact that there are practical and ethical problems involved in establishing valid experimental/control comparison conditions. How, for example, how does one obtain a comparison group when both legal statutes and social values preclude withholding such services for controlled evaluation purposes? Similarly, legal and ethical constraints almost always prevent assigning randomly treatment applicants to no-treatment or control conditions. These difficulties can sometimes be overcome, as we will see in later examples, but they also point out the importance of basing one's program on sound theory, documented successful services, and replicated pilot programs.

In reading about the six suggested evaluation designs, you will want to keep the following guidelines clearly in mind:

1. The evaluation strategy used depends upon the questions asked and the program's capability in reference to available data sets and comparison group(s). For example, don't try to use an experimental/control evaluation design if you cannot assign participants randomly into different comparison conditions.
2. A clear evaluation focus saves valuable time and resources and reduces unnecessary frustration. Remember that OBE requires time, resources, and valid data.
3. Evaluation plans that are developed mutually by all stakeholders increase the probability that the results will be accepted and acted on to improve the program or meet accountability demands.
4. Definitive (rather than extensive) evaluation plans and activities reflect the commitment on the part of management to look critically at the program and evaluate significant outcomes. A good rule of thumb is: A well-developed and feasible evaluation plan that is small is much better than a poorly developed and unfeasible evaluation plan that is large.
5. The evaluation design used is influenced frequently by factors such as the developmental status of the program, the standardized data sets available, and the number of assumptions one is willing to make.
6. Multiple outcomes are frequently only available from established, stable programs. Thus, for new programs, one might want to scale down the magnitude of the evaluation efforts, focusing on whether the initial postintervention changes are in line with expectations.

7. There is no such thing as the "best" evaluation design independent of the questions asked. Thus, ask yourself again the two fundamental evaluation questions: "For what purpose will I use the OBE data?" and "What data will I need for the intended use?"

Person as Own Comparison

I am sure that many readers have had the same experience that I have had regarding testifying before an appropriation committee, presenting at a conference, or talking with a group of stakeholders. We have all shared success stories. Person-as-own-comparison evaluation designs allow one to do so, and at the same time, demonstrate a bit about the program's effectiveness. But before you rush out and start doing this type of OBE analysis, keep in mind the following critical point: Good single-subject research requires considerable skills at research methodology, because "controls" must be built into the design in order to demonstrate certainty and generalizability.

Examples of single-subject evaluation designs can be found in Baker and Curbow (1991), Campbell (1992), Campbell and Stanley, (1963), Cook and Campbell (1979), Hersen and Barlow (1984), and Kazdin and Tuma (1982). The essence of these designs is that you establish a baseline for the individual against which you then evaluate the effects of your intervention through one or more of the following person-as-own control designs:

Reversal (ABAB): Measure baseline (A); apply procedure (B); return to baseline (A); repeat procedure(B).

Multiple baseline across behaviors: Apply procedure to different behaviors one at a time with the same individual.

Multiple baseline across situations: Apply procedure to behaviors and at different times.

Within clinical settings, however, frequently one cannot meet the more rigorous requirements of the reversal (ABAB) design. Therefore, one will most generally use the multiple-baseline design across behaviors and situations. Although this design is less precise and therefore limits one's certainty, comparability, and generalizability, it does identify and describe promising intervention approaches. This is certainly the case with Ivan, whose characteristics, core-service functions (intervention), and person-referenced outcomes are described in Exhibit 8-1. Note also how well the person-as-own-comparison design allows one to integrate qualitative and quantitative evaluation methods (Dennis, Fetterman, & Sechrest, 1994; Reichardt & Rallis, 1994).

Exhibit 8-1
Example of Person as Own Comparison
"Ivan"

Recipient Characteristics

Ivan's behavioral concerns continued even after he moved into his new residential program; foremost among them was his severe aggression and property destruction. These occurred most often when he was denied requested items, usually coffee, leading to several incidents each day. This pattern had persisted for several years, despite a number of efforts at amelioration. His residential and day-program staff joined together in a team effort at comprehensive behavioral-support planning during a recently completed training project.

In planning for Ivan, the team faced constraints that derived from staff training and attitudes, history, and program models. These constraints had shaped the services that Ivan was receiving; unfortunately, no one was happy. Staff members had lost time due to work-related injuries resulting from his aggression, and many expressed fear of him. Because Ivan was considered dangerous to himself and others, he received high levels of staff supervision, which he did not particularly enjoy. Ivan did not use a formal communi-

cation system, although he could make some needs known. Even this was problematic, in that he often wanted items (e.g., coffee, food) or activities (e.g., going for a walk) that were not readily available, or were felt to be inappropriate for the time he requested them.

Core-Service Functions

The training-project activities followed a number of steps in developing and carrying out an individualized behavioral-support plan. First, the team conducted a functional analysis, which assisted in determination of the maintaining variables related to the behaviors of concern. The second step was to assess Ivan's preferences. Third, the team developed an initial behavioral-support plan that emphasized his participation in meaningful activities. The final aspect was to set up an instructional plan for the acquisition of alternative, adaptive behaviors. These steps were intended to maximize the likelihood of increased independence, productivity, and integration into the community, as well as improved quality of life for Ivan.

Ivan's behavioral-support plan was developed over the course of 2 months and carried out with periodic modifications for a year. Initial efforts centered on functional analysis and testing the effects of different environmental changes (e.g., increased access to coffee), which then led to changes in his daily routine to center around the activity of coffee drinking. For example, a formal means of requesting coffee was developed through the use of a tanible cue system. Later in the year, Ivan was responsible for making his own instant coffee at his residence and assisting in brewing coffee at the day program. By the end of the year, Ivan also assisted staff members in making fresh coffee during the day for others' consumption. The rationale for these changes was to increase the number of social interactions related to activities that appeared to be meaningful to Ivan. In this way, Ivan's behavioral-support plan led to developing competencies in communication, self-help, and working with others. Other changes for Ivan were an increase in the number of opportunities he had during the day to choose activities, for example, going for walks was made an available choice several times a day. The staff also continued to survey new activities that Ivan might enjoy.

Person-Referenced Outcomes

There were a number of positive outcomes attributed to the behavioral-support plan. Incidents of aggression and property destruction decreased from an average of more than five times a day to less than one every other day. When incidents did occur, they were viewed as less intense or of shorter duration. Ivan was reported to get along better with both staff and the people with whom he lived, and a broader range of staff members felt comfortable spending time with him. He began to request coffee and walks using a communication system. Although Ivan's coffee consumption did increase to about 6 cups per day, this was not viewed as problematic. As Ivan became responsible for the routines of making coffee, he came to tolerate the necessary delay in getting his coffee. A final outcome was that there were increased efforts at involving him in community activities because of the reduced threat of behavioral outbursts.

Pre–Postchange Comparisons

The requirement in this OBE design is that you have comparable measures on persons before intervention and sequentially thereafter. An example would be the employment status of service recipients after a job-training program. This technique is used frequently when there is no experimental or comparison group, and therefore it represents a low level of certainty in one's analysis. An example of organizational changes following an outcome-based staff-training program is presented in Exhibit 8-2.

Longitudinal Status Comparisons

This is a good OBE design since it allows one to look at change in service recipients over time, and determine their living, work, educational, or health/wellness status at some point following program involvement. It is also a weak design, because generally there is no control or comparison group, and therefore one is limited in the degree of certainty in precision (internal validity), comparability, and generalizability (external validity).

Longitudinal status comparisons require that (1) multiple measures are taken at regular time intervals, (2) persons are followed for extended periods after program involvement, and (3) the measures taken before or during intervention are compared with those obtained during the follow-up periods. An example is shown in Exhibit 8-3.

Hypothetical Comparison Group

This OBE design is used frequently in program-evaluation studies. What is required is that the evaluator form a hypothetical comparison group based on one's general knowledge of average outcomes from other, closely related programs; preenrollment status; archival data (e.g., published indices, such as Medicare costs); and current status data (e.g., national studies of day and employment outcomes or Bureau of Economic Research reports) that can be used as benchmarks against which to compare. By relying on a general knowledge of the average outcomes of nonparticipants or on a knowledge of preenrollment status, the analyst may estimate what would have happened to participants had they not enrolled in the program.

An example of a hypothetical comparison group is presented in Exhibit 8-4. Note the careful detail given to the assumptions made in forming the hypothetical comparison group, and the potential impact of these

Exhibit 8-2
Example of Pre–Postchange Comparison

This study (Van Gelder, Gold, & Schalock, in press) involved evaluating organizational changes resulting from an outcome-based staff-training program (see Exhibit 11-1 for a further description of the program). Administrators of each of the 33 participating programs completed on a pre–postbasis the Enhancing Employment Opportunities Program Planning-Conversion Guide (Calkins, Schalock, Griggs, Kiernan, & Gibson, 1990). The nine critical agency change functions evaluated included: philosophy, program and resources, program practices, program evaluation, person–job match, employer expectations, systems inter-face, natural environment–supports, and quality of work life. The "pre" evaluation was done the first day of the training sessions, and the "post" evaluation, 5 months later. The evaluation was done by the same person (program manager) each time.

The results of the evaluation are summarized here. The change ratio was computed by dividing the difference between the post- and pre-evaluation by the preevaluations. Note that significant changes occurred in the organization functions of philosophy, program evaluation, employer expectations, and (use of) natural environments/supports.

Changes in Overall Organizational Functions

Function	Average evaluation		Change ratio
	Pre-	Post-	
Philosophy	2.0	2.6	0.30*
Program and resources	2.3	2.5	0.09
Program practices	2.1	2.2	0.05
Program evaluation	2.0	2.3	0.15*
Person–job match	2.4	2.6	0.08
Employer expectations	2.3	2.6	0.13*
Systems interface	2.0	2.1	0.05
Natural environments–supports	2.1	2.4	0.14*
Quality of work life	2.5	2.7	0.07
			Average = 0.12

*$p < .05$

Exhibit 8-3
Example of Longitudinal Status Comparisons Design

Purpose

The purpose of the study (Schalock & Harper, 1978) was to determine (1) the current status 9 years after deinstitutionalization of a group of 166 adults with mental retardation who had been placed into a community-based program for persons with mental retardation; and (2) the significant predictors of both successful community placement and program progression.

Outcome Variables	*Number of Persons*
Community successful	
4 = exited or remained in program (10 or fewer incident reports)	117
3 = exited or remained in program (10 or more incident reports)	23
Nonsuccessful	
2 = admitted to a mental health facility	12
1 = returned to state mental retardation facility	14
Program successful	
4 = exited (placed in independent/assistance housing and work)	55
3 = exited (placed in independent/assistance housing or work)	31
Nonsuccessful	
2 = progressed through one or more training components (did not exit)	29
1 = no training program progression (within 2 yrs.)	51

Predictor Variables

COMMUNITY SUCCESS: family involvement, work skills, institution size, visual processing, sensorimotor skills, gender, family-attended Individual Program Plan (IPP), social–emotional behavior, community size.

PROGRAM SUCCESS: Language skills, sensorimotor skills, tested intelligence, previous education, family attendance at IPP, institution size, visual processing, community.

assumptions on the evaluation's certainty, precision, comparability, and generalizability.

Matched Pairs (Cohorts)

There are two techniques that are used most frequently in equating participants in an evaluation study: randomized placement into two or more conditions, or matching participants and creating matched pairs prior to random assignment (Fairweather & Davidson, 1986). If equated on relevant variables, then the matched pairs theoretically should provide a relatively equivalent representative sample from the targeted population, who can then be randomly assigned to the two (or more) programs being compared. When this is done, the design is frequently referred to as a *matched-group design*.

Matched pairs (cohorts) is a very nice OBE design to use if (1) you have individuals in two different programs or significantly different program foci; (2) you have comparable person-referenced outcomes; and (3) you can match the individuals, groups, or programs on a number of recipient-characteristic variables that are logically and statistically related to the outcome measure(s). This third criterion is very important, because you want to be able to say that these individuals were essentially the same prior to the intervention. Common recipient-characteristic variables on which individuals are matched include age, gender, functional level, intellectual level, diagnosis, or the individual's time in the program. Examples of matching procedures are presented in Exhibit 8-5.

Experimental/Control

This is the "true" evaluation design. It is also what most OBE evaluators strive for. It is the best OBE design, because it controls for both internal and external validity. Before considering an example, let's review some of the key points about internal and external validity (referred to in Figure 8.1 as "certainty" and "generalizability").

Internal validity focuses on the certainty as to whether the intervention produced the effects, or as Rossi and Freeman (1989) state, "the extent to which the effect of the treatment variables can be disentangled from the correlated extraneous variables" (p. 98). In order to demonstrate internal validity, one must demonstrate successfully that the following "threats" to internal validity have been controlled (Cook & Campbell, 1979; Schalock & Thornton, 1988): selection bias, selection maturation, history, instrumentation, and an effect referred to as *regression toward the mean*, which involves

Exhibit 8-4
Hypothetical Comparison Group

This study (Rusch, Conley, & McCaughlin, 1993) analyzed the benefits and costs of supported employment programs in Illinois from 1987 to 1990. Benefits and costs were identified and valued from three perspectives: society's, taxpayers', and supported employees' (see Table 5.2 for a summary of these three perspectives). Calculating costs and benefits involved, in part, the use of a hypothetical comparison group as seen in each of the three analytical perspectives.

Social Perspective

Social benefits were measured by the increase in earnings of supported employees over what they would have earned in an alternate program, and the costs that would have been incurred if they had been placed in an alternate program. A key assumption was that all participants would have been placed in an alternate program if not engaged in supported-employment. One justification for this assumption was that almost all supported-employment participants were selected out of alternative programs.

Benefits and costs were measured over each of the 4 years that the 30 programs were in operation,

as well as the combined 4-year period. To estimate increased earnings, the first step was to calculate the gross earnings of participants. The second step was to estimate the earnings that participants would have had in the absence of the supported-employment program. It was assumed that participants would have had the same earnings as participants in the alternative-placement program from which the supported employment participants were selected. Average earnings currently reported by all alternative placement programs were used to estimate the probable alternative placement earnings for those few individuals who entered supported employment directly from school or without a reported previous placement. To estimate the savings in the costs of alternative placements, it was assumed that each supported-employment participant would have incurred the same average costs as current clients in their previous placement. The costs were estimated from placements to these organizations. In those few cases involving participants who entered supported employment directly from school or without a reported previous placement, the average costs of clients in all alternative placement programs combined were used to estimate what would have been experienced by these participants.

The costs of supported-employment programs were estimated by adding all reported payments by state and local agencies to the 30 providers and the tax savings to employers who made use of Target Jobs Tax Credits program for participants involved in these programs.

Taxpayer Perspective

Taxpayer benefits were measured as the total income and payroll taxes paid by supported employees, reductions in public support, and saving in expenditures for alternative programs, as calculated earlier. All supported-employment costs were borne by taxpayers. Benefits from the taxpayers' perspective included taxes withheld, reduction in government subsidies, and savings in operational expenditures for alternate programs. Taxpayers' costs were the same as those from society's perspective, because participants did not incur costs.

Supported-Employee Perspective

Total social benefits were divided between participants and taxpayers. The benefits to participants were estimated by subtracting taxes withheld and decreases in income support from public agencies from the estimated increased earnings of supported employees. Tax payments were estimated from the federal and state income taxes withheld, as well as FICA (Social Security), as reported monthly. For most of the 729 individuals, this was the first time in their lives that taxes had been withheld; no taxes had been deducted in their previous program placement.

Savings in government subsidies were estimated by summing decreases in Supplemental Security Income (SSI), Social Security Disability Insurance (SSDI), Public Aid (PA), and Aid to Dependent Children (ADC). Reductions were calculated for each individual by comparing monthly benefits received before entering supported employment with those received while in the program. These reductions may be understated because they are based on the amount participants received before entering supported employment and were not adjusted for cost-of-living increases. In addition, some participants received government subsidies only after entering supported employment.

Source: Reprinted by permission from F. R. Rusch, R. W. Conley, & W. B. McCaughlin, "Benefit-Cost Analysis of Supported Employment Programs in Illinois," *Journal of Rehabilitation*, April/May/June, pp. 31–36. Copyright 1993 National Rehabilitation Association.

Exhibit 8-5
Examples of Matching Procedures

EXAMPLE 1: "Reinforcement versus Relationship Therapy for Schizophrenics" (Marks, Sonoda, & Schalock, 1968).
Purpose: To evaluate the effects of reinforcement versus relationship therapy on a group of 22 persons with chronic schizophrenia.
Matching procedure: Before the study began, ward staff rated each person on the Hospital Adjustment Scale (HAS). On the basis of the total HAS adjustment scores, 11 matched pairs were selected. One member of each pair was placed randomly in the group which started with reinforcement therapy, and the other member of the pair was assigned to the relationship group. During the course of the study, each person received both therapies (10–13 weeks on each), and both members of the pair had equal number of interviews.

EXAMPLE 2: "Effects of Different Training Environments on the Acquisition of Community Living Skills" (Schalock, Gadwood, & Perry, 1984).
Purpose: To compare behavioral-skill acquisition rates of 10 matched pairs of persons with mental retardation who received individualized, prescriptive programming for 1 year in one of two training environments: their own apartments or a group home.

Matching Procedures: Persons were matched on age, tested intelligence, duration of community-living skills training, total skills on a standardized community-living-skills screening test, medication history, and the number of recorded negative behavior incidents.

EXAMPLE 3: "Skill Acquisition among Matched Samples of Institutionalized and Community-Based Persons with Mental Retardation" (Eastwood & Fisher, 1988).
Purpose: To test the hypothesis that community placement would have a positive effect on clients' skills acquisition among matched institutional and community samples.
Matching Procedure: Community residents were matched on seven variables (age, gender, level of mental retardation, secondary disability, self-preservation, mobility, and visual impairment) based on four criteria: (1) study appeared to be operative in the process of selecting persons for community placement; (2) study correlated significantly with outcome measures used in the evaluation of the placement program; (3) study had been shown to be related to similar outcome measures in earlier studies; and (4) study was considered to affect the relocated residents' rate of adjustment to life in the community.

extreme scores on the first test or observation, tending to shift toward the middle (mean) on subsequent tests or observations.

External validity is the extent to which generalizations can be made to other programs or conditions. Valid generalization depends on service recipients being selected randomly for program inclusion. If so, sampling theory would suggest that the randomness of the selection process should result in the groups being very similar to one another before the intervention. If that is true, then one can generalize the evaluation results to similar interventions or services.

Because of this ability to control internal and external validity, the experimental/control design has significant advantages over all other OBE designs. However, it is not without the following potential problems:

- It is feasible only when the demand for program services exceeds available resources. If this is the case, then some potential service recipients can be put on a waiting list and thereby serve as "controls."
- It is risky if the service recipients are known to the "controls." This situation might lead to what Cook and Campbell (1979) call "resentful demoralization" among control-group members, with potentially significant diminished outcomes.
- The effects of dropouts. Ideally, experimental/control group size should be equivalent; thus one is faced with how to handle the data from the dropouts. One might unknowingly suggest that "All you have to do is replace the ones who drop out with other persons." Unfortunately, this simple solution causes considerable problems regarding the effects of maturation, history, and program duration. My suggestion is that if some recipients do drop out, then one should conduct an attrition analysis (Schalock & Thornton, 1988) to determine whether those who drop out (or on whom one cannot obtain longitudinal follow-up data) are significantly different from those remaining. An example of an attrition analysis is presented in Chapter 10 (Exhibit 10-1).

Assuming that these problems are either nonexistent or can be worked out, and that the program's context allows the formation of experimental/control comparison conditions, then the experimental/control evaluation design is excellent to use in outcome-based evaluation. An example is found in Exhibit 8-6.

In summary, outcome-based analysis involves comparison conditions. One or more of the six OBE evaluation designs just summarized is used to provide these comparison conditions. Each of these evaluation designs has strengths and weaknesses. Those that are the easiest to do,

---

Exhibit 8-6
Examples of Experimental/Control Evaluation Design

Ramey and Landesman-Ramey (1992) used an experimental/control design in two separate studies to evaluate the effects of early educational-intervention programs designed to prevent mental retardation and to improve school readiness.

Study 1

Study 1 involved two experimental treatments and one control group. The study was designed to study home-based early intervention (wherein mothers learned more about how to provide good developmental stimulation for their infants and toddlers) compared to center-based early intervention (daily early-education intervention), compared to a control group. The procedure involved assigning all children randomly either to one of the two treatment conditions or to the control group. Children in the control group

received free health and social services.

Study 2

Study 2 involved one experimental and one control group. The target group was infants born prematurely and at low birth weight. The procedure involved assigning children and families randomly to receive either home or center-based early intervention (birth to age 3) or control services (additional medial and social services that the families ordinarily would not have received).

_____

Source: Reprinted by permission from Craig T. Ramey and Sharon Landesman-Ramey, "Effective Early Intervention," *Mental Retardation*, Vol. 30, No. 6, pp. 337–345. Copyright 1992 American Association on Mental Retardation.

---

such as person as own comparison or pre–postchange comparisons, are also the weakest in terms of certainty, precision, comparability, and generalizability. Those that are the hardest to form, such as matched pairs (cohorts) or experimental/ control, make the fewest assumptions about comparability and have the highest certainty, precision, and generalizability. Thus, the evaluator's dilemma is always attempting to balance the need for certainty, precision, comparability, and generalizability with the availability of valid comparison groups or conditions. This dilemma leads to our next guiding principle:

GUIDING PRINCIPLE 16: *The OBE evaluation design used depends upon the questions asked, the available data, and the type of comparison condition available.*

Table 8.1. Relationship between OBE
Analyses and Evaluation Designs

OBE analysis	Evaluation design
Effectiveness	Person as own comparison
	Pre–Postchange comparisons
	Longitudinal status comparisons
Impact	Hypothetical comparison group
	Matched pairs (cohorts)
	Experimental/control
Benefit–cost	Hypothetical comparison group
	Matched pairs (cohorts)
	Experimental/control

Additionally, as we saw in Chapters 3–5, some of these designs are more appropriate to one type of OBE analysis than another. This relationship is shown in Table 8.1.

General Principles Regarding Statistical Analyses

I am going to make an assumption here: Most of the readers have had at least one course in statistics and therefore have some understanding of statistics and their use. As you might remember, statistics are the methods evaluators use to understand their data, explain the results of their evaluations, and provide empirical evidence related to the theoretical construct underlying their services. Although I will discuss a number of statistical methods related to outcome-based evaluation, I am less concerned that you understand statistics *per se* than that you understand what data really mean. To that end, this section of the chapter begins by discussing a number of general principles that you should keep in mind when using statistics for any of their purposes—understanding data, explaining one's results, or supporting one's intervention or (re)habilitation approach. The section concludes with a discussion of "Which statistical test to use?"

Six General Principles

I've spent much of my professional life dealing with numbers and trying to make sense of them. Sometimes this has been an easy task, and sometimes a very difficult one. The difference was frequently how I did what the previous two chapters have suggested—selecting and measuring critical data sets in ways that are reliable and valid; designing the collection process in a logical, organized fashion; and managing the data so that they were accessible, accurate, and timely. During this time, I have also discovered the following six principles about data and their analysis:

1. Measuring and analyzing a small number of variables reliably is much better than measuring a large number haphazardly.

2. Statistical approaches and methods change with time. For example, social science has historically relied heavily on the experimental/control research paradigm in which the null hypothesis was tested to determine whether two or more groups are significantly different. The prevailing decision rule was that if the statistic (be it the t-ratio, F-ratio, or correlation coefficient) was sufficiently large, then one rejected the null hypothesis and stated that there was either a significant difference between or among groups, or a significant relationship between the variable(s). Although this is still the case in many evaluation studies, because of the complexity of most human service programs, we are beginning to see increased use of multivariate evaluation designs with intact groups, rather than strict experimental/control comparisons. This shift is important for you to keep in mind, for it affects the questions that you ask and the way you plan your evaluation efforts. One needs to think of multiple causes and multiple outcomes—and hence, multiple designs and analyses (see Figure 8.2).

3. Successful evaluation studies use a variety of methods (Johnston, 1987) to bound or simplify their data analysis: limiting the scope of their analysis; asking few questions; using data from other sources (e.g., published handbooks or evaluations of similar programs) to establish benchmarks against which to compare programmatic outcomes; limiting the follow-up period to 12–18 months, because this period balances sufficiently the instability of short-term change with the problems of missing data, sample attrition, and increased costs of longer term follow-up; using proxy measures whenever possible (e.g., length of hospital stay can be used as a proxy for resource consumption costs); and focusing only on valued, person-referenced outcomes.

4. Each stakeholder uses statistics for his/her respective purposes in the political process (Kirchner, 1993). As stated by Alonso and Starr (1987), "Political judgments are implicit in the choice of what to measure, how to measure it, how often to measure it, and how to present and interpret the results" (p. 3).

5. One has the option of focusing on either the environment or the individual to account for the person's condition or change. If the individual is the focus, then either blame or praise accrues to the person. If one focuses more on the environment, then one will measure more environmentally related factors and be more environmentally oriented in explaining either the person's condition or changes.

6. No single study is definitive. It is common for one's results to generate more questions than they answer. Thus one needs a long-term commitment to both outcome-based evaluation and the incorporation of evaluation data into the ongoing evolution and improvement of the program.

These six principles are undoubtedly not exhaustive, but I have found that they help me understand what one gets from a "data analysis." A brief example will be useful to show how these six principles have been reflected in our longitudinal studies of the placement outcomes of persons with mental retardation.

In our first studies (Schalock & Harper, 1978; Schalock, Harper, & Carver, 1981a) we were interested primarily in the placement success of individuals whom we had placed 5 years previously into independent living or competitive employment. The dichotomized variable used in the statistical analysis was whether the individual remained in the placement environment or returned to the (re)habilitation program. During that period, the program's primary goal and staffing patterns were directed at placing individuals with mental retardation into community environments that reflected increased independence and productivity.

Five years later (10 years after the initial placement) we (Schalock & Lilley, 1986) reevaluated the status of these individuals, expanding our data sets to include a measure of the person's quality of life (hence, using a multivariate approach). The addition of a QOL measure reflected the organization's commitment of not just placing persons into the community, but also assisting them to become better integrated and satisfied with their community placement. Although the organization's mission statement reflected an enhanced QOL for its clientele, the program structure during that 5-year period had not changed significantly in terms of the quality-enhancement techniques used. What we found essentially in the 1986 evaluation study was that the organization had fulfilled its goal of placing people into community living and employment environments, but had overlooked the multifaceted quality of their lives.

Based on that finding, a number of changes were made in the organization's structure and operation. Specifically, program structure (staffing patterns and resource allocation) were aligned with the mission statement, which now focused on enhanced QOL outcomes; quality management principles that empowered employees to find community-based opportunities and supports were implemented; and quality-enhancement techniques related to increased use of natural supports and the permanence of one's home were integrated into staff training. The net result was to change significantly the evaluation paradigm and data analyses used in the 15-year follow-up of the original group. In that study (Schalock & Genung, 1993), personal interview and observation data were used to evaluate the person's social and support networks, lifestyles and role functions, activity patterns, measured QOL, and expressed satisfaction. Procedures for obtaining these data were described in Exhibit 1-3.

I began this section on data analysis with an elaboration of these six principles for a simple reason: Too often, people view data and statistics narrowly, not realizing that the way one uses statistics to understand their data, to explain the results of their evaluation, or to provide empirical evidence of their program's effects, reflects their orientation and commitment to outcome-based evaluation. But it also says something about one's ability to use statistics correctly. It is to that issue that we now turn.

"What Statistical Test Should I Use?"

I enjoy teaching the second or third course in statistics, for after two or three exposures, statistics start to make sense. My experience has been that statistical computations are not a problem, especially with today's computer software programs. But always the most difficult question for students and practitioners is "What statistical test should I use?" Once that issue is resolved, then the related issue becomes "How do I interpret it?" I'll attempt to answer both of these questions in the following all-too-brief primer in statistics.

An absolute rule to follow in answering the "What" question is that the specific statistical test one employs depends upon four factors that are listed in our next guiding principle:

GUIDING PRINCIPLE 17: *The specific statistical test one employs depends on (1) the level of measurement, (2) the number of persons and groups involved in the analysis, (3) the type of design that one is using, and (4) one's ability to meet the respective test's assumption.*

A listing of the specific statistical tests keyed to these four variables is summarized in Table 8.2 and provides the basis for the following discussion. Any published statistics textbook will give computation procedures and interpretation guidelines for those statistical tests referenced in the table.

Level of Measurement

One frequently uses frequency data as the basis of his/her evaluation. Examples include the number of persons with posttreatment pain relief, the number of special-education students who are in integrated versus segregated classrooms, or the number of persons with different diagnoses

Table 8.2. Relationship between Statistical Analysis Designs and Specific Statistical Tests

Statistical analysis design	Specific statistical tests
Correlation	Pearson r (normally distributed variables)
	Spearman's rank order (ordinal level)
	Point biserial (1 continuous; 1 dichotomized variable)
	Multiple regression (multivariate; parametric)
	Multiple discriminant analysis (multivariate)
	Measure of strength of association (r squared)
Between groups	Two groups:
	$\quad$ t test (parametric data)
	$\quad$ Chi square (nominal; dichotomized variables)
	$\quad$ Mann–Whitney U-Test or Wilcoxon tests (Nonparametric)
	Three Or more groups:
	$\quad$ Analysis of variance (if homogeneity of variance)
	$\quad$ Kruskal–Wallis ANOVA (ranks)
	Measures of strength of association
	$\quad$ t test: Eta squared (reveals the proportion of the total variance in the samples measured that is due to the effect of the independent variable)
	$\quad$ ANOVA: Omega squared (same as eta)
	Follow-up tests (if F-ratio is significant): Multiple F, Scheffe or Tukey tests)
Within subjects	Graphs (person as own comparison)
	Correlated (direct difference) t test (interval level of measurement; parametric)
	Wilcoxon Signed Ranks or Friedman tests (ordinal)
	Analysis of covariance (if pretreatment differences among subjects are observed)
	Multivariate analysis of variance

living or working in particular environments. For this level of measurement, one would need to use a nonparametric statistical test such as chi-square to determine whether the groups are significantly different.

If, however, you rank your data, then you need to use a different statistical test. As the term *rank* implies, the statistical tests that are appropriate for ranked data compare the sum of the ranks in the groups to determine whether one group yields scores that are generally lower in ranking than the other group. These rank tests are also considered nonparametric, because they make no assumptions regarding the underlying distribution of the scores. Instead, statistical tests based on ranks simply assume that the dependent variable is at least ordinal in nature, so that scores can be ordered from lowest to highest and ranks can therefore be assigned (Russell & Buckwalter, 1992).

If the level of measurement is either interval or ratio, then one can use a more powerful parametric statistical test. Tests such as the *t* test or analysis of variance can be used if a number of assumptions (Russell & Buckwalter, 1992) can be met, including: the variables are at least interval level of measurement; scores on the dependent (outcome) variable are normally distributed; the variability of scores on the dependent variable within the groups is equal; and the observations are independent of one another, which means that persons cannot be in more than one grouping.

Number of Groups and Persons Involved

In reference to groups, the material presented in Table 8.2 should make sense by itself. For example, if one has two groups, then certain statistical tests (such as chi-square or *t* test) are appropriate. If, however, there are more than two groups, then depending upon the level of measurement and the ability to meet the test's assumptions, one needs to use a multiple-group comparison statistic, such as analysis of variance.

The number of persons included in the statistical analysis is very important, because the sample size determines both the magnitude of the statistic that is necessary for statistical significance, and the practical significance of the statistical result(s). For example, with 1000 subjects, and a correlation coefficient of .20, one could claim statistical significance. But the question that should be asked is "How much of the variance in the outcome variable can reasonably be attributed to the fluctuation in the independent variable?" Similarly, with between-groups design, one may have a t-ratio of 1.98 that is statistically significant at the .05 level of significance, but the practical significance of this can also be asked in the question: "What proportion of the total variation in the dependent (outcome) variable is due to the effect of the independent (intervention) variable?"

My purpose in making the distinction between statistical and practical significance (reflected in the measures of association listed in Table 8.2) is that in reporting the results of outcome-based evaluation, it is important to look at the actual amount of change in one's outcome variable that can actually be attributed to the intervention. Although the process of distinguishing between these two types of significance does not potentially diminish the significance of the results, it does reflect on the evaluator's credibility and honesty.

Type of Evaluation Design

Refer back to either Table 8.1 or Figure 8.1 for a moment. Note the six evaluation designs listed: (1) person as own comparison, (2) pre–postchange comparisons, (3) longitudinal status comparisons, (4) hypothetical comparison group, (5) matched pairs (cohorts), and (6) experimental/ control. In reference to potential statistical tests, some of these designs are referenced in Table 8.2 as within-subject designs and some are listed as between-group designs. The first three evaluation designs will require using one or more of the within-subjects statistical tests referenced in Table 8.2; the second three evaluation designs will require one or more between-groups statistical tests.

Meeting the Test's Assumptions

In addition to the three factors just discussed, one also needs to remember that there are a number of statistical assumptions that underlie statistical tests—and especially parametric ones. The two big assumptions relate to the normal distribution of scores on the outcome measure and homogeneity of variance. If one cannot meet these assumptions, then a nonparametric test, which does not make these assumptions, should be used.

I hope that this all-too-brief primer in statistics will bring back a number of significant points that you may have forgotten from your statistics background. By design, I did not intend to be comprehensive or exhaustive, but to share with the reader answers to two key questions that are often asked by students, program administrators, and policy makers: "What statistical tests should be used?" and "How do I interpret the results?" In addition, I hope that the primer has refamiliarized you with some of the vocabulary of statistics, which should facilitate communication in the next section on common OBE statistical analyses.

Common Outcome-Based Evaluation Statistical Analyses

Descriptive Analyses

An extremely important aspect of program evaluation is often to describe events accurately rather than to test specific hypotheses. Thus, sometimes all you want to do is to describe such things as the characteristics of your service recipients, to summarize the services or interventions that they received, or to summarize the status of service recipients on a range of outcome variables. If this is your need or purpose, then think about two terms: *matrices* and *descriptive statistics*.

We discussed in the previous chapter how data can be matriced so that they can be described and exhibited easily. The example shown in Exhibit 8-7 shows clearly how the matriced data lends themselves easily

Exhibit 8-7
Example of a Descriptive Analysis[a]

	Verified Handicap	
Variable	Specific learning disability (N = 189)	Mentally handicapped (N = 109)
Student characteristics		
Intelligence	93	63
Percentage of time in resource room	7.4	12.7
Hours in vocational program	22	15
Gender (no. females/males)	(59/130)	(34/75)
Current employment status		
Employed full time	70%	44%
Employed part time	13%	25%
Vocational school	6%	2%
Community Board Mental Retardation program	-0-	8%
Unemployed	10%	17%
Current employment outcomes		
Number of weeks employed	42	36
Hours/week	40	26
Wages/hour	$4.52	$2.93
Percent receiving current work-related benefits		
Medical	43	30
Unemployment	28	10
Sick	31	19
Vacation	40	25
Profit sharing	10	11
Retirement	18	6
Current living environment		
Independent	45	33
Semiindependent	55	67
Current primary source of income		
Personal (self, parent)	94	83
Public (SSI, SSDI)	6	17

[a]Based on the study described in Exhibits 1.1 and 6.3.

to the use of descriptive statistics, such as the mean (or average) and percentages.

The use of descriptive statistics is very important, because it defines important characteristics about the clientele with whom you work. It also allows you to quantify various aspects of the program and begin to generate or refine the specific questions to be answered by later phases of the evaluation (Rintala, 1987). This level of statistical analysis should not be interpreted as "high-level program evaluation," because the analyses are only descriptive in nature and do not permit you to make generalizations from the program to a larger population. That process involves the use of parametric statistics, such as those listed in Table 8.2.

Exploratory Correlation Analyses

This type of statistical analysis is an excellent next step in one's thinking about and doing OBE studies. Correlation determines the relationship, if any, between or among core data sets. Exploratory correlation studies or analyses can help explain relationships among the various aspects of the program while further refining and focusing on further questions to ask (and answer). For example, the correlation coefficients shown in Exhibit 8-8 are from a recent study (Schalock et al., in press) of factors related to recidivism of persons with mental illness. The significant correlation coefficients found between the major predictors of recidivism and other measured variables became the basis for the next phase of evaluation efforts, which involved doing in-depth interviews regarding the role that these other factors might play in recidivism.

Group Comparisons

Frequently, outcome-based evaluators are interested in whether two or more groups differ significantly on particular person-referenced outcomes. This was the case in the study referenced in Exhibit 1-3, wherein we (Schalock & Genung, 1993) compared the lifestyles and role functions of two groups ("nonservice" and "service") of individuals with mental retardation who had been placed 15 years prior to the longitudinal study into community living and employment environments. The group comparisons are presented in Exhibit 8-9.

Multivariate Analyses

You will get to this level of statistical analysis before you know it. Why? Very simply, because multivariate analyses allow you to probe more

Exhibit 8-8
Example of Significant Correlations between Predictors of Recidivism and Other Measured Variables

Predictors of recidivism	Other measured variables
Number of previous admissions	Axis I diagnosis ($r = -.19$)
	Age (.21)
	Educational level ($-.37$)
	Employment status/follow-up (.18)
Employment status at admission	Age ($-.18$)
	Living arrangement/follow-up (.23)
	Employment status/follow-up (.26)
	Instrumental activities of daily living (.21)
	Cognitive level (.33)
Health problems	Gender ($-.25$)
	Marital status (.22)
	Educational Level ($-.19$)
	Living arrangement/follow-up (.55)
	No. of community resources used (.67)
	Instrumental activities of daily living ($-.76$)
Instrumental activities of daily living	Age ($-.35$)
	Educational level (.27)
	Employment status/admin. (.21)
	Days hospitalized ($-.27$)
	Self-rating of change (.24)
	Living arrangement/follow-up (.42)
	Employment status/follow-up (.30)
	No. community resources used (.84)

deeply and realistically into many of the factors that lead to the obtained outcomes. In conceptualizing a multivariate analysis, it is useful to refer to the multivariate analysis model presented in Figure 8.2, showing the potential interactive nature of recipient characteristics (which are usually considered independent variables in the statistical analysis), core-service functions and contextual factors (intervening variables), and valued, person-referenced outcomes (dependent variables). The advantage of using a multivariate analysis is that you can begin to "tease out" the relative contribution of the multiple factors that influence programmatic outcomes.

An example is shown in Exhibit 8-10, summarizing the results of a

Exhibit 8-9
Example of Group Mean Score Comparisons

	Groups being compared		
Variables being compared	Nonservice	Service	*t*-value
Desired community outcomes			
Making decisions	2.8	2.4	2.4*
Contributing to community	2.0	1.8	0.7
Doing things myself	2.9	2.8	0.9
Arranging for assistance	2.7	1.8	4.3**
Visiting with others	2.6	1.9	2.7**
Using the community	2.7	2.3	2.1*
Spending time as others do	2.6	2.3	1.8
Living in a healthy & safe place	2.7	2.4	1.6
Owning things	2.7	2.3	2.0*
Being valued and accepted by others	2.5	2.4	0.5
Quality-of-life factors			
Independence	27	24	3.8**
Productivity	26	22	3.0**
Community integration	22	21	0.8
Satisfaction	25	24	0.7

*p < .05   **p < .01

recent study (R. L. Schalock et al., 1994) in which we evaluated the influence of three factors (referred to as "blocks" in the hierarchical statistical design) on the measured quality of life of 968 individuals with developmental disabilities 5 years after they moved into the community. The results of the analysis show that personal characteristics contributed the most to the person's total QOL score, followed by objective life conditions and perceptions of significant others.

Although attractive, multivariate analyses are not for the novice, for they do require considerable expertise in meeting the various assumptions of the tests, and computer resources for completing the statistical analyses. But they are currently both popular and very informative. They warrant your attention, but also reflect our next guiding principle:

GUIDING PRINCIPLE 18: *Don't confuse the four most common statistical analyses used in OBE: descriptive statistics, exploratory correlational analyses, group comparisons, and multivariate analyses.*

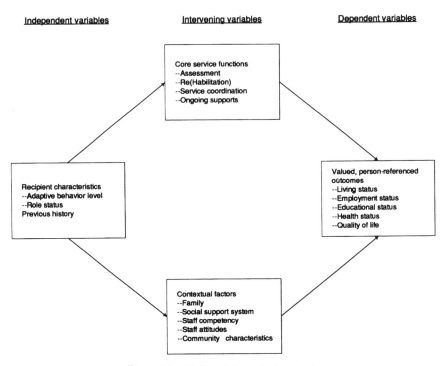

Figure 8.2   Multivariate analysis model.

Summary

In summary, this chapter has addressed three key concepts in outcome-based evaluation: evaluation designs, general principles regarding statistics, and common OBE statistical analyses. In reference to the six potential outcome-based evaluation designs (person as own comparison, pre–postchange comparison, longitudinal status comparison, hypothetical comparison group, matched pairs (cohorts), and experimental/control) that one can use, I both described these designs and discussed the relationship between the design used and decision-oriented issues, including certainty, precision, comparability, and generalizability. I also shared a number of guidelines regarding the selection of evaluation designs and statistical analyses, pointing out the importance of understanding the level of measurement, number of groups and persons involved in the analysis, the type of design that one is using, and the importance of meeting the statistical test's assumptions. I also summarized and gave examples of the common statistical tests used in OBE analyses.

Exhibit 8-10
Example of Multivariate Analysis (Hierarchical Regression) of Predictors of Total Quality-of-Life Score

Block/Predictor variable	Adjusted R squared	R Squared change	F for block	Beta coefficient
Personal Characteristics	.426	—	89.34****	
Age				−.08
Gender				.04
Adaptive behavior index				.40
Challenging behavior index				.21
Health index				−.01
Need for medication				−.06
Objective life conditions	.505	.08	53.17****	
Earnings				.17
Integrated activities				.12
Physical environment				−.03
Social presence				−.01
Living-unit size				.01
Residential supervision				−.05
Home type				.16
Employment status				.07
Perception of significant others	.519	.01	43.75****	
Client progress				.03
Environmental control				−.03
Job satisfaction				.07
Working with person				.07

****$p < .001$

As I mentioned in the overview to these three chapters, it is important to see the close relationships among the concepts discussed. For example, in Chapter 6, we discussed data collection; in Chapter 7, data management; and in Chapter 8, evaluation designs and data analysis. The relationships among these critical OBE are steps depicted in the flowchart presented as Table 8.3.

With this chapter, we have completed the "methodology of outcome-based evaluation." In Part II, we discussed the three types of outcome-based evaluation analyses—effectiveness, impact, and benefit–cost. In Part III, we discussed the "How to's" of outcome-based evaluation data—data collection, data management, evaluation designs, and data analysis.

Table 8.3. Outcome-Based Analysis Flowchart

Step	Action
1. Select questions asked	Effectiveness: extent to which program obtains its goals and objectives.
	Impact: whether program makes a difference compared to either no program or an alternative program.
	Benefit–cost: whether the program's benefits outweigh the costs.
2. Select evaluation design to answer the question (Table 8.1)	Person as own comparison
	Pre–Postchange comparisons
	Longitudinal status comparisons
	Hypothetical comparison group
	Matched pairs (cohorts)
	Experimental/control
3. Select core data sets	Recipient characteristics
	Core-service functions
	Cost estimates
	Valued, person-referenced outcomes
4. Measure core data sets (Table 6.5)	Standardized instruments
	Performance-based assessment
	Participant observation
5. Collect, organize, and store the data (Figure 7.4)	Data-collection format
	Data-based management and data entry
	Data manipulation and analysis
6. Analyze the data (Table 8.2)	Correlation analysis
	Between-groups analysis
	Within-subjects analysis

Now we turn our focus on "What do I do with OBE analyses?" Answering that question is the major focus of Part IV.

Study Questions

1. Summarize the key components of each of the six evaluation designs discussed in this chapter (person as own comparison, pre–postchange comparison, longitudinal status comparison, hypothetical comparison group, matched pairs (cohorts), and experimental/control). Give two examples of how each design might be used in outcome-based evaluation studies.

   For Questions 2–7, review journal articles containing one or more of the six evaluation designs. For each design, discuss how it was used in the evaluation and summarize the author's critique of the design's use.

8. Select one of the six designs summarized in Question 1 and critiqued in Question 2. Outline the step-by-step procedures you would develop in order to use the design in an outcome-based evaluation analysis. For example, how would you select or place your study participants; what core service functions would you select; and which valued, person-referenced outcomes would you employ? Apply the "six general principles regarding statistical analysis" to the procedures. Note the importance of data simplification, stakeholder support, and study focus (person or environment).

9. Select an outcome-based evaluation study from current evaluation literature. What statistical analyses were performed on the data? Critique these analyses in reference to the tenets of Guiding Principle 17 and the outcome-based analysis flowchart found in Table 8.3.

10. Assume that you are an evaluation producer. Under what conditions (i.e., questions asked and data used) would you use each of the following statistical analysis designs: descriptive, correlation, group comparisons, and multivariate?

Additional Readings

Campbell, J. A. (1992). Single-subject designs for treatment planning and evaluation. *Administration and Policy in Mental Health, 19*(5), 335–343.

Cook, T. D., Cooper, H., Condray, D. S. & Jones, D. F. (Eds.). (1992). *Meta-analysis for explanation: A casebook.* New York: Russell Sage Foundation.

Guba, E. S., & Lincoln, Y. S. (1989). *Fourth generation evaluation.* Newbury Park, CA: Sage.

Kazdin, A. E. (1992). *Research design in clinical psychology* (2nd ed.). Needham Heights, MA: Allyn & Bacon.

Kraemer, H. C., & Thiemann, S. (1987). *How many subjects: Statistical power analysis in research.* Newbury Park, CA: Sage.

IV

Reporting and Acting on Outcome-Based Evaluation Results

In great things it is enough to have tried.
ERASMUS

Once one completes an outcome-based evaluation analysis, the next question to ask is "What do I do with it?" And that is the focus of this section of the text.

Remember that the definition of outcome-based evaluation is that it is a type of program evaluation that uses objective, valued, person-referenced outcomes to analyze a program's effectiveness, impact, or benefit–cost. The results of one's analysis can be used for a number of purposes, such as reporting on program outcomes, data-based management, facilitating planned change, and program or policy evaluation and development.

As seen throughout this section, reporting and acting on OBE data are never done without considering the context of the program. This context is composed of a number of internal and external factors (which I refer to as *contextual variables*) that have a profound impact on determining how the program functions, and whether findings from an OBE analysis will be generalizable to—or accepted by—other constituencies. The program's context will also influence significantly whether one can use OBE data for program monitoring, planned change, or further program or policy development. In short, one cannot overlook the context (or "environment") of one's program and its effect on the OBE analysis.

Because of the tremendous impact that the program's context has on the acceptance and utilization of OBE data, I begin the fourth section of the book by discussing in Chapter 9 the importance of contextual analysis and the more important contextual variables that should be included in the implementation, interpretation, and reporting of the outcome-based analysis.

Chapter 10 focuses on reporting OBE analysis results, suggesting strongly that reporting is more than merely presenting results. Rather, it also includes establishing one's credibility, understanding the various stakeholders' perspective on—and interest in—outcome-based evaluation and using effective communication techniques.

Chapter 11 focuses on using OBE analysis results, suggesting that the specific use depends upon the type of OBE analysis completed and the major interests and concerns of the program's stakeholders. For example, effectiveness analysis is best used for formative feedback, data-based management, and program change. Impact analysis is best used for the evaluation of public policy or different programmatic approaches to the needs of individuals in education or social programs. As we saw in Chapter 5, benefit–cost analysis is used for policy evaluation in regard to equity and efficiency issues.

Throughout this section, the above statement by Erasmus will be appreciated. No analysis is definitive, as we all know. Acting on OBE analysis results is easier said than done, especially if program or system change is involved. Thus, three truisms should be kept in mind as you read these three chapters: (1) one measures what one values; (2) change comes hard; and (3) "In great things, it is enough to have tried."

9

Contextual Analysis

Overview

Education and social programs do not operate in a vacuum. The context within which these programs operate can best be described by a number of metaphors. At one level, a program's context is like an umbrella: It protects and shields programs from unwanted intrusions. It is also like a personality assessment: It explains a number of characteristics about the program, including its development and dynamics. But a program's context is also like a balloon: It surrounds the program and gives structure and dynamics to its mission, processes, and outcomes. Our task in this chapter is to analyze a program's context and attempt to understand many of the most significant contextual variables that influence outcome-based evaluation efforts.

A basic question that you might be asking as this point is "How much contextual information is really required?" Indeed, entire books and monographs are devoted to this topic. A general guideline that I use is reflected in Henry Hill's statement in *The Music Man*: One needs to "know the territory." The extent of knowing is dependent on one's role and current level of understanding. For example, if the program evaluator is external to the program being evaluated (which is not recommended), then it is crucial to spend time in the program and understand its culture, clientele, and organizational structure and operation before undertaking any analysis efforts. In contrast, if the person is a part of the program (the preferred way), then the analyst should already be familiar with most of the contextual variables discussed in this chapter. Thus, how much contextual information do you really need?

GUIDING PRINCIPLE 19: *Be able to describe the program and its contextual variables in enough detail so that it can be replicated.*

This chapter is organized into two major sections. The first summarizes a number of key contextual variables that I personally have found to affect program processes and products. In the second section, two levels of contextual analysis are presented: descriptive and inferential analysis. Throughout the chapter, I stress that one should address the critical importance of contextual analysis at both the planning and reporting stages of an outcome-based evaluation. Critical guidelines for both stages include working with important stakeholders to:

- Frame the questions on which the analysis is based.
- Determine the organization's capability regarding OBE analysis.
- Agree on the use of the analysis results.
- Select the data sets that will be used in the analysis.
- Collect and analyze the data.
- Describe how best to report the analysis results.
- Determine how best to utilize the data for data-based management and program change.

Key Contextual Variables

There are a number of key contextual variables that I have found critical in understanding how education and social programs work. These are listed in Table 9.1. Note the wide variety of contextual areas that need one's attention, including the program's history, organization, culture, capability for evaluation, time and cost restraints, and external factors. For discussion purposes, I have collapsed them into the following seven areas that provide the content of this section of the chapter: organizational

Table 9.1. Key Contextual Variables

Contextual area	Variables to understand
1. Program's history	When and why begun
	Historical strengths
	Previous evaluation efforts and experiences
	Administration and fiscal stability
	Previous program change/conversion attempts and results
2. Program's organization	Type of organization
	Governance structure
	Funding source(s) and certainty
	Control over financial incentives
	Organizational structure
3. Program's culture	Philosophy and mission
	Values, norms, and ideology
	Risk-taking attitude
	Receptivity to change
	Assumptions
	Staff turnover rates
	Commitment to person-reference outcomes
	Attitudes toward evaluation
4. Program's capability for evaluation	Resources
	Asking clear and answerable questions
	Data-management system that is accurate, timely, and available
	Time–cost constraints
5. Service system	Staff functions and competencies
	Phase of program development
	Resources
	Specific intervention components
6. External factors	Formal linkages
	Community factors
	Advocates
	Family involvement/characteristics
	Community acceptance

description, philosophy and goals, phase of program development, resources, formal linkages, relevant community factors, and family variables.

Organization Description

Education and social programs represent multifaceted organizations that vary on a continuum from reasonably simple to unbelievably complex. To help you understand this, I have developed Table 9.2 that summarizes five critical organization contextual variables, including the program's legal designation, governance structure, funding considerations, and core-service functions. As described in the table, most programs are legitimated and monitored through either a governmental or corporate structure, and their governance structure includes a board of directors. Funding sources are multiple. Funding dimensions typically focus on the certainty of funding and/or control over financial incentives. Core-service functions usually include assessment, intervention or (re)habilitation, service coordination, and ongoing supports.

Contextual analysis requires that the analyst have an understanding of each of these organizational variables, because each will affect significantly the input, process, and output from the program. Research is very clear here: Organizational design significantly affects organizational performance and one needs to understand this relationship in interpreting any program analysis (Schalock & Thornton, 1988).

Philosophy and Goals

Current programs operate from a number of philosophical concepts, such as normalization, integration, inclusion, equal opportunity, wellness, natural supports, and quality of life. The importance of a program's stating and acting on its mission and philosophy provides its purpose, direction, efforts, and expected outcomes. For example, a program with a mission statement that elaborates on the concepts of inclusion and enhanced quality

Table 9.2. Critical Organizational Description Variables

Contextual variable	Exemplary indicators
Legal designation	Governmental agency
	For-profit corporation
	Not-for-profit corporation
Governance structure	Board of directors
	Executive council
	Committee structure
Funding considerations	Funding sources (taxes, grants, client-use fees)
	Funding dimensions (certainty of funding, control over financial incentives)
Core-service functions	Evaluation or assessment
	(Re)habilitation
	Service coordination
	Ongoing supports

of life will look very different than one with a mission of self-preservation. However, as emphasized throughout the text, the mission statement cannot stand by itself. It must be reflected in all aspects of the program's service provision, including resource-allocation and staff-utilization patterns. In reference to outcome-based evaluation, again the research is very clear: A program's outcomes are positively related to its culture, including artifacts, values, norms, ideology, and assumptions (Schein, 1990).

Phase of Program Development

Not all programs are in the same stage of development. Indeed, one can probably identify at least three phases of program development: a feasibility/demonstration phase, an ongoing phase or a changing phase. OBE efforts need to be sensitive to a program's developmental phase because the program's purpose, capability, and anticipated use of analysis data are very different depending on its developmental phase (see Exhibit 3-3).

For example, if a program is established to determine the feasibility of a service or intervention, then we are dealing with a "pilot project." This is done often when policy or decision makers are interested in determining whether to invest in a new program direction or component. Probably the best example of this is the supported-employment initiative funding by the Rehabilitation Services Administration a number of years ago, in which project grants were given to a few employment programs that wanted to determine the feasibility of the concept of supported employment for persons with mental retardation. Other examples include work fairs, job retraining, inclusionary schools in special education, and clubhouse programs in mental health. From an outcome-based-evaluation perspective, it is critical to understand that a program in a feasibility phase of development is very different from one that is either ongoing or changing. Its organizational structure may well be quite different; its mission, philosophy, and goals will undoubtedly be different; and the type of data and their use will be significantly different. Here the basic question is one of cost versus outcomes, and unless the results of the analysis are favorable, then policy or decision makers are probably not going to be very supportive of further program development or expansion.

For ongoing programs, contextual analysis raises other issues. Here, the history of the organization and its "place in the community" are critical contextual variables. For example, one of the biggest barriers to community placement of individuals with special needs is the issue of what happens to the staff and the facility if all the clientele "move into the community." Additionally, the purpose for an outcome-based analysis may well be different in ongoing programs. For example, in working with both community- and facility-based programs over the years, I have found that the focus of my evaluation efforts is quite different: Community-based programs are typically more interested in placement and support evaluations, whereas facility-based programs are more interested in either change within the facility or why people return to the facility.

For programs that are in a changing phase, their contextual analysis and outcome-based-evaluation activities will look much different than either those in a feasibility or ongoing phase. Here the emphasis will be on factors such as justification for the change, barriers to the change, and/or cultural factors that will need to be developed in order to provide the ongoing support for the change.

Resources

Resources are defined broadly to mean money, experience, and time. A friend told me recently in a discussion about quality assurance that he was surprised when he visited a number of Scandinavian programs for persons with mental retardation to find that there was little emphasis given to the need for quality assurance in those programs (which is definitely not the case in the United States). In pursuing this observation within those programs, the statement was made frequently by program personnel that "with well-qualified staff, there is no real need for a formal quality assurance process, for it's done automatically by everyone in their daily activities." I mention this statement to make the point that resources are more than money: Indeed, experience and the time required to develop that experience are important contextual variables that one needs to address in either contextual analysis or outcome-based evaluation.

There is no doubt that resources will affect the program's process and outcomes, but one needs to be both critical and evaluative in reference to the assumptions one makes. For example, I was involved recently in a 30-day study that evaluated how habilitation staff spent their time. The study was initiated by a program administrator who was concerned about minimum outcomes related to skills being gained by adults with disabilities. His assumption was that the 5:1 training staff to clientele ratio was more than sufficient to permit considerable habilitation training and, hence, good skills acquisition rates. What we found was quite disturbing: Only about 15% of the staff's time was actually devoted to training. Almost 33% was spent in assisting clients, another 13% in supervising clients, and 8% supporting ("doing for") persons. Other results were equally informative: 7% of staff time was spent on "general maintenance," 7% in meetings, 3% in transportation, and only 2.5% in in-service training. The point to all of this is that there is probably no reason to assume that habiliation and training is automatically going on, based on the 5:1 staffing ratio, and that the program's person-referenced outcomes will reflect that fact. Without including reference to resources in interpreting an OBE analysis, one can overlook a critical contextual variable.

Formal Linkages

This is an era of "interagency cooperative agreements." I have been involved in such efforts for a number of years, and have written extensively about their importance in contextual analysis (Schalock, 1984, 1986). My experience suggests a simple rule of thumb in including interagency involvement in contextual analysis: Explain who does what for whom. For example, refer back to Exhibit 6-3 where you will see how the special-education and vocational-rehabilitation programs worked together to implement a job-placement process for students with special needs.

Why is a discussion of formal linkages important to include in the contextual analysis? Very simply, it helps to explain the results that were obtained. It also explains a lot about the philosophy of both programs and the combining of resources to fulfill the program's goals.

Relevant Community Factors

No education or social program exists in isolation; rather, it is part of a larger environment that has specific economic, social, and political characteristics. Again, my experience has suggested a number of community factors that exceed some threshold and thereby affect either the program's process or outcomes:

- Attitudes regarding the program, as reflected in historical funding patterns.
- Auxillary support services (mental health, community living, employee assistance programs, respite care, homemaker services, employer round tables, and so on).
- Crime rates.
- Economic indicators such as average income and employment rates.
- Public health indicators, such as life-expectancy rates.
- Mobility patterns reflected in net in-or-out migration.
- Tax structure and policies.
- Transportation availability.
- Civil rights enforcement.

Again, you might not want to analyze all of these community variables, but I can guarantee that you need to be sensitive to them when thinking about using OBE data for systems change. Communities, just like programs, resist change and, in that sense, the earlier metaphors about contextual variables make sense: Community factors can be like an umbrella or a balloon. A general guideline should help in determining how many (or which) community factors to include in the interpretation of your OBE analysis results: *Consider only those community factors with effects that exceed some threshold and thereby can reasonably be expected to affect the program and its outcomes.*

Family Variables

Families are key to understanding programmatic processes and outcomes. There is considerable empirical support for the key role that families play in person-centered outcomes. For example, in 1978, we (Schalock & Harper, 1978) evaluated the significant predictors of successful community placement for persons with mental retardation. In that analysis, we found that the best predictor was the amount of parental support, as measured by attendance at Individual Program Plan meetings and assessed agreement with the thrust of the program toward community placement. Similarly, in a 1986 study of graduates from a rural special-education program, we (Schalock et al., 1986) found that the parents' assessed level of involvement in the Individual Education Plan process was a statistically significant predictor of the postgraduation living and employment status of the students. We (Schalock & Lilley, 1986) found that the amount of family involvement was positively (and significantly) related to a service recipient's assessed quality of life.

If the family's role is so critical, then how should it be assessed or handled in a contextual analysis? My preference (as reflected in the studies referenced earlier) is to include family involvement as a variable in the multivariate analysis, so that its importance can be evaluated empirically and statistically. Once that is done, it is simply a matter of discussing family involvement in reference to the data analysis. As a side point, this is another reason why the multivariate research designs discussed in Chapter 8 are so appropriate in OBE.

In summary, I have suggested in the first part of the chapter that there are a number of critical contextual variables that need to be included in the contextual analysis that accompanies an OBE analysis. How this might be done is described in the following section that describes two approaches to contextual analysis.

Contextual Analysis Approaches

Generally, significant contextual variables are included in the method or discussion sections of a formal OBE analysis study or report. Indeed, in a number of exhibits throughout the text (e.g., Exhibits 1-1, 1-2, 1-3, 6-1, and 6-3) we have seen descriptions of service recipients, core-service functions, and organization descriptions. This approach (referred to henceforth as *descriptive level*) is by far the most common one used to date in outcome-based evaluation. However, recently, there has been an attempt to incorporate some of these potentially significant contextual variables into the analysis itself. I will refer to this approach as *inferential level*. Examples of both are described on subsequent pages.

Descriptive Level

Here, one is interested in describing as many of the significant contextual variables as possible, generally in the method or discussion section of the analysis report. Examples of such can be found in Exhibit 9-1.

Inferential Level

The advantage of incorporating potentially significant contextual variables in the planning and implementation of the actual OBE analysis is that one can determine empirically whether they are related statistically to the evaluated, person-referenced outcomes. To do so requires the use of one or more of the multivariate designs discussed in Chapter 8. An example was shown in Exhibit 8-10 that summarized the influence of a number of personal characteristics, objective life conditions, and perceptions of significant others on the assessed quality of life of 989 persons with mental retardation.

A second example is presented in Exhibit 9-2. This study (Schalock, McGaughey, & Kiernan, 1989) involved two national surveys that were conducted to document selected employment outcomes as reported by 1,500 vocational rehabilitation agencies that met one of the following criteria during the survey periods: (1) placed adults with developmental disabilities into transitional, supported, or competitive employment settings; and/or (2) provided sheltered employment for adults with developmental disabilities. The analysis involved 17 predictor variables and 8 person-referenced outcomes. The results, based on multiple regression and summarized in Exhibit 9-2, indicate the critical role that facility size and philosophy, cost per participant, hours of job support, geographical

---

Exhibit 9-1
Descriptive Level Contextual Variables

Entry, Program and Placement Description (Exhibit 8-3)

Before a client was placed from the facility into the program, the following sequential processes occurred: First the person was evaluated by receiving program staff. Second, a referral was made from the facility to the program. Third, a preliminary program plan was submitted to the facility. Fourth, there was a release evaluation made as to community-placement suitability by an interdisciplinary team at the facility. Fifth, if the team and parents agreed with the program plan, the client was placed into the program.

The sequential training components included basic skills, independent living, and competitive employment. Each training component has its own defined exit, staff, location, and training variables composed of specific behavioral skills associated with increased independence and productivity. The training sequence began with basic skills and progressed to independent living and competitive employment. The person was in only one training component at a time.

While in basic skills and independent-living training, persons were housed in 8- to 10-member group homes. The houses were renovated family homes that provided room, board, and live-in staff supervision. They were not used for systematic training. Such training occurred during the regular day. Following training in independent living, clients were placed into either a supervised apartment or a shared apartment.

School and Community Variables (Exhibit 1-1)

The program was an intermediate agency located in a rural area. The program serves 38 small rural school districts that contract for delivery of special education and related services to approximately 1,200 verified handicapped children, birth through age 21 years. Schools served by the program are located throughout a 5⅓-county area covering 3,000 square miles, and with community populations ranging from 70 to 23,000. School enrollment averaged 768 students. The average community population was 18.8 thousand, with a per capita income of $10.1 thousand. Each county had an average of 1,700 businesses with a labor force of 9.6 thousand. The average unemployment rate during the period of the analysis was 3.0%.

Exhibit 9-2
Inferential Level of Contextual Analysis: Influence of Contextual Variables on Placement into Nonsheltered Employment

Person-referenced outcome	Predictor variables
House/week	Disability level (+)*
	Facility size (+)
	Age (−)
	Wage (+)
	Receives SSI (−)
	Transititional placement (−)
	Supported placement (−)
	Hours of job support (+)
	Gender (−)
	Cost per participant (+)
Wage/hour	Disability level (+)
	Supported placement (−)
	Facility size (+)
	Transitional placement (−)
	Prior shelter employment (+)
	Percent developmentally disabled served (−)
	Hours of job support (−)
	Cost per participant (+)
SSI/SSDI benefits affected	Wage/hour (+)
Level of integration	Hours of job support (−)
	Supported placement (−)
	Transitional placement (−)
	Geographical Environment (+)
	Percent sheltered staff (−)
	Prior employment, nonsheltered (−)
	Unemployment rate (−)
Supported employment retention	Unemployment rate (+)
	Hours of job support (+)

*Denotes direction of the relationship. Specific multiple regression values can be found in Schalock et al. (1989).

environment, staff utilization patterns, and the area's unemployment rate have on placement of persons with disabilities into nonsheltered employment.

Summary

In summary, this chapter has discussed a number of critical contextual variables that need to be considered when one either does or reports on an outcome-based analysis. The more important of these include the organization's description, philosophy and goals, phase of program development, resources, formal linkages, relevant community factors, and family variables. These contextual variables need to be addressed in the OBE analysis at either the descriptive or inferential level. Contextual variables will not only affect the results of the analysis, but also how the analysis' results will be reported and acted on. It is to these topics that we now turn.

Study Questions

1. What is contextual analysis and why is it critical to include it in an outcome-based evaluation analysis?

2. Become familiar (by referring to actual experiences or examples found in the literature) with a social program. Summarize key aspects of each of the following contextual variables impacting that program: organizational description, philosophy and goals, phase of program development, resources, formal linkages, relevant community factors, and family variables.

3. For each of the seven contextual variables discussed in Question 2, discuss the potential positive and negative impacts that the variable might have on valued, person-referenced outcomes.

4. Do a literature search of three program-evaluation studies and summarize how contextual variables were dealt with either descriptively or inferentially.

5. Design an outcome-based-evaluation effectiveness analysis in which contextual variables are built inferentially into the evaluation. (*Note*: You may need to review material in Chapter 8 on multivariate analysis.)

Additional Readings

Field, S. L., & Hill, S. D. (1988). Contextual appraisal: A framework for meaningful evaluation of special education programs. *Remedial and Special Education, 9*(4), 22–30.
Goering, P. N., & Wasylenki, D. A. (1993). Promoting the utilization of outcome study results

by assuming multiple roles within an organization. *Evaluation and Program Planning, 16,* 329–334.

McDonald, R. M. (1991). Assessment of organizational context: A missing component in evaluation of training programs. *Evaluation and Program Planning, 14,* 273–279.

Schein, E. H. (1990). Organization culture. *American Psychologist, 45*(2), 109–119.

Snortum, J. R. (1988). On seeing the forest and the trees: The need for contextual analysis in evaluating drunk driving policies. *Evaluation and Program Planning, 11,* 279–294.

Reporting Outcome-Based Evaluation Results

Overview

Credibility and communication are the focus of this chapter. Just as contextual variables need to be addressed in any program evaluation, program evaluators must also deal frequently with two realities: (1) the nature of their outcome-based analysis results and (2) a skeptical audience. It would be nice if the analysis were unequivocal and the audience always friendly, but that is not the general case. Thus, evaluators must work hard to establish (and maintain) their credibility, along with communicating clearly the results of their outcome-based evaluations, which are frequently equivocal and playing to a skeptical audience.

The importance of these two realities is reflected in a recent medication study that I was asked to do by a mental health program administrator who wanted to know the effects of reducing psychotropic medication levels used on clientele. The study found that medication reduction was not associated with significant behavioral changes, increased use of restraints, or increased injuries to staff. But a skeptical audience came into play when the results were presented to the nursing and ward personnel, who were reasonably certain beforehand that medication reduction had deleterious effects. Thus, when it came time to interpret the findings, many staff were convinced that the study's results were wrong at worst, and equivocal at best.

Challenges to Reporting Outcome-Based Evaluation Results

There are two primary challenges to the successful reporting of outcome-based evaluation analyses: (1) the equivocal nature of the results and (2) a skeptical audience. There are a number of reasons why OBE results are often equivocal. Chief among these include the following:

1. We frequently know relatively little about how specific interventions produce specific outcomes. We saw in Chapter 9, for example, that numerous internal and external factors can have a significant impact on a program's results. Unless each of these contextual variables is controlled experimentally, one is often unable to attribute with certainty the person-referenced outcomes to the program's intervention. Thus, one is left frequently in the unenviable position of not knowing for sure what caused the observed changes.
2. The results might not be crystal clear or consistent. It is not unusual for some of the results to be in one direction, and others in another direction. I remember very well, for example, an evaluation that found that the assessed satisfaction of persons working in a sheltered workshop was higher than that of persons working in supported employment. This finding contradicted the evaluation's other results, which found that as the level of independence and productivity increased in both living and work environments, the assessed level of satisfaction increased. How might one explain this equivocal result and still maintain credibility?
3. The data collection may be inconsistent with the type of analysis performed. For example, if one collects data that explain only a program's effectiveness, then using that data for making impact-of-benefit–cost statements will certainly lead to both equivocal results and lack of credibility.

In addition to equivocal results, you will sometimes encounter a skeptical (if not hostile) audience for other reasons. First, people know what they want to believe. The nursing and ward personnel in the medication study mentioned earlier, for example, knew before any evaluation was done that medication reduction would have bad effects. Second, change is resisted. Despite the three "Cs" (customer, competition and change) we discussed in Chapter 1, people find change difficult. And if the analysis results are tied to proposed change, one is likely to find resistance. And third, there is frequently a conflict of interest among the program's stakeholders, some of which may want to see the analysis used for one purpose, others for another purpose. For example, in the medication study, the administration wanted to use the results to support medication reduction, but the ward staff felt that the results needed verification because "they just didn't make sense," and therefore more study was necessary before one of their supports was taken away.

Thus, the reporting of outcome-based evaluation results is sometimes not as easy as it may sound. You frequently will have results that are equivocal, and you will almost always encounter a skeptical audience. So, with these two realities clearly in mind, let's turn our attention in this chapter to the issues of establishing credibility and communicating results.

Establishing Credibility

To be credible is to offer "reasonable grounds for being believed" (Webster's Ninth New Collegiate Dictionary, 1983). Degrees, good looks, and gray hair are not enough. Rather, one needs to be viewed as both competent and honest. One is not credible unless both criteria are met. But how do outcome-based evaluators establish their credibility? I suggest four ways: (1) know the territory, (2) work with the program's stakeholders, (3) be competent, and (4) be honest.

Know the Territory

First, evaluators need to "know the territory," as described in Chapter 9 on contextual analysis. This requires that time be spent in the program before any analysis is done. One needs to understand the program's history, mission, clientele, interventions, staffing patterns, and culture before undertaking any evaluation of the program or its person-referenced outcomes. The approach that one takes, the questions that one asks, and the evaluation activities that one undertakes must be based on knowing the territory. Some of the key things to know about that territory were summarized in Table 9.1.

Work with the Program's Stakeholders

Second, outcome-based evaluators need to work with the program's stakeholders. All programs have a heterogeneous constituency that may have very different conceptions of what an outcome-based evaluation is and how the results should be used. My experience has indicated that the following are the most critical stakeholders with whom one needs to work in developing the OBE's purpose, procedures, and implementation: board of directors, administrators, staff, consumers, advocates, funders, and policy makers. Each has his/her own orientation and questions that he/ she want answered (summarized in Table 10.1).

Table 10.1. Stakeholder's Perspectives on Outcome-Based Evaluation

Perspective	Critical questions asked regarding OBE
Board of directors	Effects on cost
	Political implications
	Relation to strategic/management plan
	Consistency with policies and procedures
Administrators	Effects on cost
	Use of evaluation results
	Disruption of the ongoing program
	Personal risk
	Benefit to the program
	Acceptance by the heterogeneous constituency
	Organizational change required
	Effects on accountability
	Effects on program's perceived effectiveness, impact, or benefit–cost
Staff	Effects on job and workload
	Effects on position within the agency
	Confirmation of current beliefs/opinions
	Effects on the agency's program
Consumers	Effects on service quality and quantity
Advocates	Effects on organization's program
	Effects on service quality and quantity
	Effects on equity
Funders	Effects on cost
	Effects on efficiency
	Effects on outcomes and impacts
Policymakers	Effects on the program's impacts
	Effects on the program's equity
	Effects on the program's efficiency

Be Competent

Third, outcome-based evaluators need to be competent. Increasing the competency of OBE evaluators is obviously one of my primary purposes in writing this text. But what does being competent really mean? Again, degrees, good looks, and gray hair are not enough. Some general guidelines are worth considering. To me, competent evaluators have at least five essential characteristics:

1. They understand the basic requirements and data sets of the type of outcome-based analysis they are performing—effectiveness, impact, or benefit–cost. These requirements were summarized in Table 2.4.

2. They analyze data correctly, recognizing that different levels of measurement and analysis are based on specific data sets and on meeting the requirements of the specific statistical analysis conducted (see Table 8.2). In this regard, competent evaluators also distinguish between statistical and practical significance in regard to percent of variance explained.

3. They include the concept of *standard error* in the evaluation's report. Although this may be a new concept to the reader, it is essential to understand as either an evaluation consumer or producer. The concept of *standard error* reflects the fact that there is error involved in either measuring behavior or generalizing on the basis of the data. Thus, there is the standard error of measurement and a standard error of estimation, respectively. These two standard errors must be addressed in the evaluation's data analysis and as part of any report or implementation activities resulting from the analysis.

4. Discuss internal and external validity. External validity involves the generalizability (i.e., comparability) of the results, and is based primarily on the evaluation design used. As we saw in Chapter 8 (Figure 8.1), one has greater generalizability in using experimental/control designs than with other comparison conditions. Internal validity refers to the authenticity of treatment or intervention effects. It deals with certainty questions such as "Did your program really produce the effects?" or "Can you really support your conclusions about the program's impacts?" The degree of confidence in supporting these conclusions increases if one uses random assignment to groups, so that groups are equated initially. Then, significant postintervention effects can be attributed to the intervention received. A discussion of how well internal and external validity are controlled in the analysis needs to be an integral part of any OBE analysis report.

5. Conduct an attrition analysis to determine the influence of the loss of subjects. This is especially true of longitudinal studies wherein one is unable to contact former service recipients and therefore needs to deter-

mine whether individuals who drop out of the study are significantly different in any way from those who remain (Fitz, 1989). A simple way to complete an attrition analysis is to compare mean scores on available data sets for those who drop out with those who remain. An example is presented in Exhibit 10-1 (p. 194).

Be Honest

Fourth, OBE evaluators need to be honest. They have the following responsibilities:

1. Not to promise more than they (or the analysis) can deliver.
2. To share with the stakeholders their experience and track record.
3. To be thorough in their description of the questions asked, the type of analysis conducted, the selection and measurement of the specific person-referenced outcomes used, and the rationale and legitimate use of the data.
4. To point out the equivocal nature of the data (if such is the case) and attempt to explain why.
5. To share the "good news" and the "bad news."
6. To work with program personnel to implement the results of the analysis. This is one of the reasons I have stressed that outcome-based analysis should be an ongoing part of the service delivery program. One should not be tempted to "take the money and run."

Thus, establishing one's credibility is hard work, but essential if one is to have any impact on the analysis and its utilization. I have also found that knowing the territory, working with the program's stakeholders, being competent, and being honest (i.e., credible) are not all there is to reporting outcome-based analysis results. One must also be able to communicate. That topic is the focus of the final section of the chapter.

Effective Communication Techniques

I often think of a line in one of Shelly Berman's routines that suggests that "if people cannot communicate, the least they can do is shut up." I hope the reader has not thought this about me as we have progressed together through this OBE "odyssey." But it is important to realize that outcome-based evaluation does not end with the analysis; considerable acumen is required in communicating the results in ways that are clear, understandable, and useful. Consider the following general principles:

1. People like to know where they are and where they are going. Thus, include in the analysis report a table of contents. An example is shown in Exhibit 10-2.
2. People like to understand. Thus, one needs to use words and concepts that are familiar to the audience. Most readers of outcome-based evaluation reports are not statisticians. The audience also wants to see the practicality and utility of the results.
3. People like to read tables and look at graphs. Thus, using tabular or graphic techniques will increase both interest level and comprehension. For the reader who likes to count, there are 33 tables and 16 figures in this text.
4. People like summaries. Thus, using executive summaries, general principles, and fundamental rules will also increase one's communication. As a point of potential interest, there are 20 Guiding Principles discussed in this text.
5. People like lists. You might have come to this same conclusion about me. Lists save time. Remember that we are living in the "nanosecond nineties."
6. People like simplicity. Hence, use the Keep it Simple Stupid (KISS) principle and make words, phrases, sentences and paragraphs brief and to the point. One does not need to "dazzle people with verbiage," or overpower them with one's perceived brilliance.
7. People like examples. Thus, one needs to include numerous examples (there are 34 exhibits in this text) of the critical points that one wishes to communicate.
8. People like honesty and do not like to be misled. We spoke of this in the previous section on establishing credibility.

These are eight simple principles, but ones that I feel are absolutely necessary to follow in reporting one's evaluation results. I assume that you have seen examples of each throughout the text.

Summary

In summary, I hope this chapter has sensitized the reader to the fact that reporting outcome-based evaluation results includes more than simply writing a report. Rather, it requires establishing one's credibility so that what is said and recommended are accepted by a sometimes-skeptical audience. As discussed, credibility has a lot to do with understanding the program, its personnel, and its stakeholders; spending time with each so that one is familiar with the major contextual variables that influence the

---

Exhibit 10-1
Example of an Attrition Analysis

An attrition analysis was done as part of a study (Schalock et al., in press) to identify significant predictors of recidivism to a mental health residential facility. The study, conducted over a 5-year period, included measures on 32 predictor variables collected either on admission, on discharge, or 12–15 months following discharge or upon the person's readmission. Although the study identified health problems, instrumental activities of daily living, employment status, and number of previous admissions as significant factors in recidivism, complete data were available on only 61% of the initial sample. Specifically, the initial sample had been composed of 510 persons with mental illness; however, the eventual study sample was reduced to 309 persons due to their leaving after admission but before we could obtain discharge data ($N = 131$), or for whom we had admission and discharge data but who were not found during the follow-up contact period ($N = 70$). Thus, an attrition analysis was conducted in which these three groups ($Ns = 309$, 131, and 70, respectively) were compared on 8 "admission data sets" (age, gender, race, legal status, number of previous admissions, marital status, highest grade completed, and employment status on admission) and 13 "at-discharge data sets" (cognitive level, treatment progress, scale scores, days of hospitalization, individual psychotherapy hours, occupational therapy, industrial therapy, and recreation therapy hours, number of family visits, living arrangement at discharge, Axis I diagnosis, relationship with others, general physical health, self-image, general enjoyment of life, and average ability to cope). The only significant difference among these three groups was in reference to legal status, in which the study sample had proportionally more voluntary patients and fewer mental health board commitments than the "admission" or "at-discharge" samples (x^2 (6) $= 16.7$, $p < .05$). Exemplary data sets from the attrition analysis are presented next in tabular form.

---

program's outcomes; and using the correct analytical techniques that the evaluation questions and types of analysis require.

But credibility also involves the reasonableness of your recommendations. Reasonableness asks that you determine what is a reasonable match between certainty and applicability. That determination will depend on the level of certainty you feel is needed for a decision. Informal or easily changed program decisions require less certainty than do more important decisions (e.g., whether to continue a program or service), which will

Exhibit 10-1 (cont.)
Recidivism Study Attrition Analysis (Exemplary Data Sets)

	Attrition comparisons		
Variable	Admission data only (N = 131)	Admission and discharge data (N = 70)	Complete admission, discharge and follow-up data (N = 309)
Admission data sets			
Age	36.0	38.0	38.9
Gender (%)			
Female	34.8	42.2	43.0
Male	65.2	57.8	57.0
Legal status (%)			
Voluntary	32.6	35.0	43.1
Voluntary by guardian	8.4	2.6	8.9*
Court order	3.2	8.1	1.6
MHB/EPC	55.8	55.1	33.0*
Number of previous admissions (HRC)	2.0	1.7	2.9
Highest Grade Completed	11.7	11.8	11.7
Employment status (at admission)			
Employed	37.4	27.2	28.4
Unemployed	62.6	72.8	71.7
At-discharge data sets			
Allen cognitive level		4.9	5.0
TPS scores:			
Initial vs. discharge		7.3	7.4
Days of hospitalization		48.9	45.1
Individual psychotherapy hours		2.6	45.1
OT/IT/RT Hours		58.8	55.2
Number of family visits		2.3	2.9
Axis I diagnosis (%)			
Substance-use disorder		3.7	2.5
Schizophrenic disorder		40.3	37.6
Psychotic disorders (other)		6.9	5.3
Affective Disorders—depression		11.3	13.9
Affective disorders—other		13.8	15.9
Adjustment disorder		15.4	11.4

*$p < .05$ (denotes significant difference between groups).

Exhibit 10-2

Exemplary Table of Contents

require a closer match and more certainty. Nothing reduces a person's credibility more than his/her recommending major changes based on minimal data.

Reporting outcome-based analyses also requires good communication. Thus, the challenge to a program analyst is to do a thorough job in describing the questions asked, the type of (and rationale for) the analysis conducted, the data sets selected and how they were measured, the type of data-analytic techniques used, the practical and statistical significance of the results, the certainty of the results obtained, and the potential uses of the data.

But don't overlook how the audience views your evaluation report. The recent management literature, with its emphasis on the search for excellence, the skeptical mind, and the one-minute decision maker, suggests something about reporting evaluation results: Analysis and writing are inextricably entwined, such that analysis is thinking and writing clearly. The role that a well-written and packaged report plays in translating program-evaluation results into action cannot be emphasized too much. Decision makers are skeptical, busy, and need to be enticed to read the report and act on it. Thus, as the final list in this chapter, you might want to keep the following "product criteria" in mind as you consider reporting outcome-based evaluation results:

1. Are the findings plausible?
2. Is the report coherent?
3. Do the facts of the report correspond to known facts?
4. Is the report documented adequately?
5. Are alternative interpretations included if the data are equivocal?
6. Is the analyst straightforward about the evaluation's limitations?
7. Did the analyst use sound procedures?
8. Do the conclusions and recommendations follow logically from the information presented?

You might also want to think about how you "market" your evaluation. Some suggestions from Mangano (1992) about marketing are listed in Exhibit 10-3.

In this chapter, I shared with the reader a number of principles that I have found essential in communicating evaluation results, the most important of which may well be that people want to understand what's going on. Indeed, if program personnel are part of the evaluation effort and understand the results obtained therefrom, then they are much more likely to act on the data. The different ways by which people act on outcome-based analyses provide the focus for the next chapter.

> *Exhibit 10-3*
> ## A Marketing Approach to Outcome-Based Evaluation
>
> M.F. Mangano (1992) suggests that a marketing approach can be used in program evaluation. He also suggests that there are at least four lessons for evaluators that can be learned from his marketing experiences at Honda Motor Company:
>
> 1. Engage in sound market research.
> 2. Create top-notch production capability.
> 3. Build a better "mousetrap."
> 4. Sell your products aggressively.

Study Questions

1. Refer back to your answers to Questions 2 and 3 in Chapter 9, wherein you summarized the impact of seven contextual variables. Discuss now the impact on outcome-based evaluation of each of the stakeholder's perspectives listed in Table 10.1. To what extent should one consider these different stakeholder perspectives as additional contextual variables?

2. Obtain a copy of a corporation's annual report and compare it to one obtained from a special education, mental health, or disability program in your community. Compare and contrast these two reports in reference to format and focus, keeping the seven stakeholder's perspectives summarized in Table 10.1 clearly in mind.

3. Go back to your answers to Questions 2–4 in Chapter 3. Write up the results of one of the effectiveness analyses, following the seven general communication techniques discussed in this chapter. Use the table of contents presented in Exhibit 10-2 for necessary assistance.

4. Go back to your answers to either Questions 2–4 in Chapter 4, or Questions 2–4 in Chapter 5. Write up the results of one of the analyses, following the seven general communication techniques discussed in this chapter. Use the table of contents presented in Exhibit 10-2 for necessary assistance.

5. Study the results of the attrition analysis presented in Exhibit 10-1. How can you plan an OBE analysis so that you will have sufficient data on "dropouts" to conduct an attrition analysis comparing those who remain in your analysis with those who drop out? Suggest specific data sets in your answer.

Additional Readings

Greene, J. C. (1988). Communication of results and utilization in participatory program evaluation. *Evaluation and Program Planning, 11*, 341–351.

Hendricks, M., & Handley, E. A. (1990). Improving the recommendations from evaluation studies. *Evaluation and Program Planning, 13,* 109–117.

Lester, J. P., & Wilds, L. J. (1990). The utilization of public policy analysis: A conceptual framework. *Evaluation and Program Planning, 13,* 313–319.

Moskowitz, J. M. (1993). Why reports of outcome evaluation are often biased or uninterpretable. *Evaluation and Program Planning, 16,* 1–9.

Palumbo, D. J. (Ed.). (1987). *The politics of program evaluation.* Beverly Hills, CA: Sage.

Rapp, C. A., Gowdy, E., Sullivan, W. P., & Winterstein, R. (1988). Client outcome reporting: The status method. *Community Mental Health Journal, 24*(2), 118–133.

11

Acting on Outcome-Based Evaluation Results

Overview

Chapter 10 focused on reporting OBE analyses so that one is both credible and communicative. This is not the same as acting on the analysis. Many bookshelves (if not rooms) are filled with evaluation reports that are both credible and communicative, yet are collecting more dust than readers or action. Thus a logical question is "Why aren't more evaluation studies acted on?"

There are a number of possible reasons for not implementing OBE analyses. Part of the answer is that there is often a lag between the time when questions are asked and when the evaluation results are available. Good evaluation takes time and, as with good wine, cannot be served before its time. Part of the reason is also due to the constantly changing environment in which current education and social programs operate. What is relevant today may become secondary to a more pressing issue tomorrow, especially if different personnel are running the ship than those who originally asked the questions. And part of the reason may also be due to social–structural problems and institutional resistance to change (Moskowitz, 1993).

My strong belief is that there are two primary reasons why more OBE results are not acted on. First, many evaluations overlook the following ten key factors involved in the successful utilization of evaluation results:

1. Stakeholder participation (Greene, 1988).
2. Clear communication (Cousins & Leithwood, 1986).
3. Credibility, especially in regard to correct measurements and conclusions drawn (Newman, Hunter, & Irving, 1987).
4. A well-defined authority for decision making in the organization (Heilman, 1991).
5. Allocation of sufficient time and resources to implement the recommendations (Hendricks & Handley, 1990).
6. Consideration of the contextual factors within which the recommendations must fit (Hendricks & Handley, 1990).
7. Evaluator involvement with the evaluation's implementation (Schalock & Thornton, 1988).
8. Ongoing monitoring of implementation (Brown, 1993).
9. Effective engagement of decision makers in the evaluation (Hegarty & Sporn, 1988).
10. Reducing the extent to which evaluations create unnecessary obstructions for, or effects on, a program (Stake, 1986).

The second primary reason more OBE analyses are not acted on is the focus of this chapter: seeing the relationship between the outcome-based evaluation and its use. It's like that statement by Yogi Berra: "The problem with not knowing where you are going is that you might end up somewhere else." And this is all too true for many program-evaluation studies that have not related the type of analysis conducted to the analysis's most appropriate use.

My thesis in this chapter is very simple: The purpose of outcome-based evaluation is not just to evaluate specific programs or policies but, equally important, to provide formative feedback to program administrators, policy makers, and funding bodies. This information can be used to bring about program and system changes that will result in increased equity, efficiency, and person-referenced outcomes. Figure 11.1 summarizes this concept by depicting the relationship between outcome-based analyses, formative feedback, and change. As shown, change can come about in regard to the input (goals and objectives), throughput (core-service functions and costs), or output (person-referenced outcomes) components of a program. The model also allows one to focus on either a single program or the larger system or policy being evaluated. The cybernetic

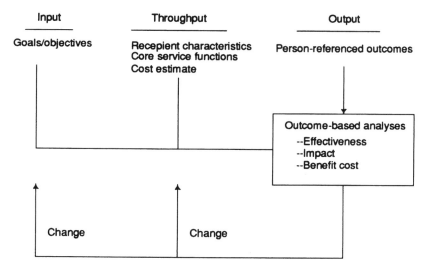

Figure 11.1   OBE formative feedback/change model.

process is the same. For a program, one is most likely to be acting on the results of an effectiveness analysis; for a system or broader policy, one would be acting on the basis of impact or benefit–cost analyses.

I have already shared a truism with you: Change is hard and comes about slowly at best. There is also no doubt that there are volumes written about organizational development and change. So, let's keep it simple: In the remainder of the chapter, I discuss four general change strategies that I have personally observed to be both productive and nonaversive. They are not definitive but reflect current literature, the outcome-based evaluation focus of the text, and the current zeitgeist. They include quality-management techniques, staff training, quality-enhancement techniques, and shared quality assurance.

Quality Management Techniques

We are living in an age of quality, and I am certain that the reader is already familiar with the vast quantity of books and "How to's." I promise not to belabor the issue, but there are two key points that I need to share. One is to summarize how human service managers have responded to the current quality revolution. For example, in a recent summary of the quality revolution in management, Albin (1992) discussed the following five ways that program administrators have responded to the current quality revolution:

1. Establishing a mission to lead quality improvement.
2. Being obsessed with quality.
3. Creating a unity of purpose.
4. Empowering employees to work to achieve the program's mission.
5. Using a systematic approach to find opportunities and to improve performance.

The second point is that program managers need to be aware of the significant paradigm shift in government that is occurring, and the components of process reengineering, which is currently impacting on both private and public management (Hammer & Champy, 1993; Osborne & Gaebler, 1993). The key concepts involved in each are summarized in Table 11.1.

Staff Training

The success of change efforts is governed by a complex network of organizational–contextual variables such as the organizational position of the change agent, the values and personal goals of dominant persons and groups inside and outside the organization, and the economic and political context in which the organization operates (Hagner & Murphy, 1989). Of one thing I am sure, however: Organizational change requires staff training—and that, too, should be evaluated.

Both public and private organizations spend billions of dollars annually on training to improve the job-skills performance of their employees (Filipczak, 1993; Lombardo, 1989). A recent review (Carnevale & Schultz, 1990) indicated that of the companies studied,

- 75% evaluated the participants' reactions to the training event.
- 25% measured learning.
- 10% determined if there is any transfer back to the job.
- 25% evaluated the training's impact on the organization.

Most training evaluations use four potential levels of outcomes (Kirkpatrick, 1967):

1. Reactive measures that indicate the participant's liking or feeling for the training.
2. Learning measures that test retention of training material and indicate the extent to which new ability or knowledge is acquired. As with effectiveness analysis, reaction and learning measures are

Table 11.1. Emerging Paradigm Shifts in Government and Components of Process Reengineering[a]

Emerging paradigm shifts in government

1. Promoting competition between service providers.
2. Empowering citizens by pushing control out of the bureaucracy into the community.
3. Measuring performance of government agencies, focusing not on inputs but on outcomes.
4. Being driven by goals, not by rules and regulations.
5. Redefining service clients as customers and offering them choices.
6. Preventing problems before they emerge, rather than simply offering services afterward.
7. Putting agencies' energies into earning money, not just spending it.
8. Decentralizing authority and embracing participatory management.
9. Preferring market mechanisms to bureaucratic mechanisms.
10. Focusing on catalyzing all sectors (public, private, voluntary) into action to solve problems.

Components of Process Reengineering

1. Work units changes: from functional departments to process teams.
2. Job changes: from simple tasks to multidimensional work.
3. People's roles change: from controlled to empowered.
4. Job preparation changes: from training to education.
5. Performaance appraisal changes: from activity to results.
6. Advancement criteria changes: from performance to ability.
7. Values changes: from protective to productive.
8. Managers' changes: from supervisors to coaches.
9. Organizational structure changes: from vertical to horizontal.
10. Executives' changes: from scorekeepers to leaders.

[a]Summarized from Hammer & Champy (1993) and Osborne & Gaebler (1993).

internal to the training program in that they are used to assess the extent to which training criteria are met.
3. Behavioral measures, such as performance evaluations, that indicate the extent to which the training transfers to the job.
4. Results measures that show whether broad organizational goals are achieved. Behavioral and results measures are analogous to impact analysis.

An example of an outcome-based evaluation of a staff-training program is presented in Exhibit 11-1 (Van Gelder et al., in press). The evaluation focused on the multiple-level evaluation of a 3-year staff-training project involving employment specialists and managers who were either providing or planning to provide integrated employment services for persons with disabilities. Note in the exhibit how all four levels of outcome were included in the evaluation.

Exhibit 11-1
Evaluation of an Outcome-Based Staff-Training Program

Reactive Measures

Each participant completed a questionnaire at the conclusion of the workshop, asking for an evaluation of the materials and techniques. The questionnaire's items addressed the issues of organization and presentation of the materials, helpfulness of ideas and information presented, usefulness of audiovisual materials and handouts, and the utility of the information presented.

Learning Measures

Each participant completed a questionnaire to assess his/her familiarity and knowledge about seven topics covered in the workshop. The questionnaire was given before and immediately after the workshop. Each of the 34 items was scored on a 4-point Likert Scale.

Behavioral Measures

This part of the evaluation involved comparing on-the-job performance of the workshop participants to matched controls who had not attended the workshop. Behaviors evaluations reflected the logical outcomes from the topics covered in the workshop.

Results Measures

Administrators of each of the participating programs completed on a pre–postbasis the Enhancing Employment Opportunities Program-Planning and Conversion Guide (Calkins et al., 1990). The nine critical agency-change functions evaluated included: philosophy, program and resources, program practices, program evaluation, person–job match, employer expectations, systems interface, natural environments–supports, and quality of work life. The "pre" evaluation was done the first day of the workshop and the "post" 5 months later. Both evaluations were done by the same person.

Results

1. Learner reactions were positive.
2. Program managers indicated a significant increase in knowledge in 26 of the 34 subareas surveyed.
3. Statistically significant impacts related to the quality of staff performance rather than the presence of specific skills.
4. Statistically significant organizational changes occurred in philosophy, program evaluation, natural environments, and employer expectations (see Exhibit 8-2).

Quality Enhancement Techniques

A number of approaches to quality enhancement are currently being used to enhance the quality-of-life experiences of persons in education and social programs. These quality-enhancement techniques focus on what program personnel and program services can do to enhance the person's real or perceived QOL. Specific programmatic changes or introduction of quality-enhancement techniques should be based on the results of one's outcome-based evaluation. Once implemented, the effect of the changes or techniques should be evaluated on an ongoing basis.

Exemplary quality-enhancement techniques related to the three areas of home and community living, school–work, and health and wellness are summarized in Table 11.2. Note that these factors are based on the QOL model shown in Figure 1.1. Techniques based on other program models can easily be substituted.

Shared Quality Assurance

The fourth general change strategy involves shared quality assurance that is based primarily on one's internal data-management system. Consumer empowerment and equity represent the essence of the paradigm shift currently impacting educational and social programs. Thus, there needs to be a reformulation of quality assurance to accommodate this change. A proposed reformulation is shown in Figure 11.2, which summarizes graphically the following key aspects of the shared process:

- There is a parallel set of activities completed by the provider (internal evaluation) and the consumer/advocate/regulatory body (external validation).
- Internal evaluation is a data-based process built around valued person-referenced outcomes that are monitored jointly by the service provider and the external evaluator(s).
- External validation involves agreeing on which quality outcomes to monitor, providing technical assistance and supports to the development and maintenance of the data system, and validating the valued person-referenced outcomes.
- Data from the quality-assurance process are used for a variety of purposes, including reevaluating program structure or process, or implementing quality-enhancement techniques.

Table 11.2. Quality-Enhancement Techniques

OOL factor	Exemplary enhancement techniques
Home and community living	Allow for choices, decision making, and environmental control. Interface with a person's social support systems. Maximize use of natural supports such as family, friends, and neighbors. Stress normalized and integrated environments, social interactions, and community activities. Emphasize family–professional partnerships. Promote positive role functions and lifestyles.
Employment–school	Facilitate employment, work status, avocational activities, or meaningful educational experience. Foster co-workers or fellow students as natural supports. Provide quality instruction and training. Promote stable, safe environments that lessen stress and increases predictability and positive behaviors.
Health and wellness	Promote wellness by emphasizing physical fitness, nutrition, healthy lifestyles, and stress management. Maximize health-care coverage. Maximize use of prosthetics that facilitate mobility, communication, and self-help. Maintain as low a psychotropic-medication level as possible.

Summary

In summary, this chapter has focused on using outcome-based evaluation data for program and systems change that will enhance equity, effectiveness, and person-referenced outcomes. Facilitating planned change is a difficult process that has been discussed in considerable detail by Forer (1987), Hagner and Murphy (1989), Howes and Quinn (1978), Keller (1989), G. Lynn and J. Lynn (1984), McDonald (1991), and Parent, Hill and Wehman (1989). In reference to acting on outcome-based evaluation results, any change involves at least the following:

- Understanding the basis and rationale for the change.
- Recognizing the benefits accruing to the change.
- Becoming involved in the change process.
- Willingness to evaluate the effects of the change.

Change also requires the realization that any system has many interrelated parts, and if one attempts to change one part, one needs also to pay attention to all parts. Also, the various components of the system (the contextual variables discussed in Chapter 9) can be viewed at any one of the system's levels depicted in Figure 11.1. And finally, change requires that

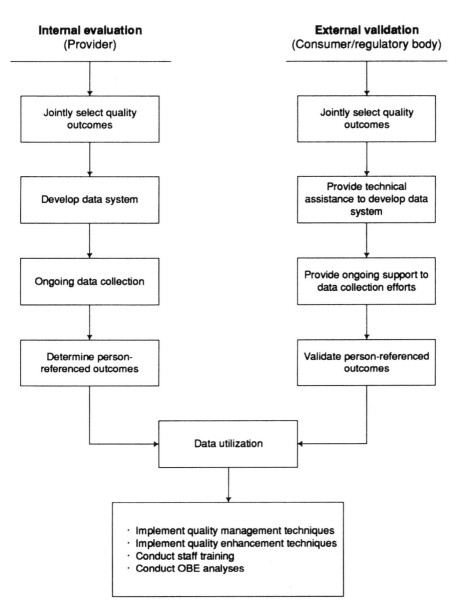

Figure 11.2   The components of a shared quality-assurance process.

one define and describe the critical activities involved in that change. Four such activities were discussed in this chapter: employing quality-management techniques, staff training, quality-enhancement techniques, and shared quality assurance.

Maybe most important, change requires that we free up programs and systems so that they can move far from their equilibrium status. However, when a system is not set free, we cannot know how the system will look after the transformation. As stated by Schalock, Alberto, Fredericks, & Dalke (1994),

> This is an uncomfortable situation because we want to know or control the outcome. We impose constraints on systems, not allowing them to reach far from equilibrium status, thus not allowing them to transform. The policies and procedures we develop attempt to restrict variability in how systems operate, thus reducing the energizing effects of contact with the environment that systems need to keep from deteriorating. ... To be efficient systems must have fields established and then self-order themselves to function best in their environment. Through laws and policies we have constrained systems from this self-order mechanism. This irony is what we must all live with in attempting to bring about systems change. (p. 209)

Outcome-based evaluation analysis will not automatically bring about change, but it won't inhibit it either. My observation has been that a key component to change is a readiness for change that results from a perceived need for relevant change. And this is where outcome-based evaluation and person-referenced outcomes come into play. In this regard, there are two key points that I hope you take from the chapter. First, change begins with formative feedback provided by outcome-based evaluation data and analyses (see Figure 11.1); and second, actual change is reflected in the consumer and organizational changes summarized in the next guiding principle:

GUIDING PRINCIPLE 20: *The major change indicators include consumer changes* (adaptive behavior and role status) *and organizational changes* (resource allocation, alignment of staff-utilization patterns with agency mission, and core-service functions.)

Study Questions

1. What is meant by formative feedback? What role does it play in outcome-based evaluation?

2. Assume that you are an administrator of an education program. What quality-enhancement techniques would you propose that would enhance the valued, person-referenced outcomes accruing to your students? Which stakeholders

(see Table 10.1) will you need to work with closely to ensure the successful implementation of these quality-enhancement techniques?

3. Assume that you are a State Program Director (you choose the program). What quality-enhancement techniques would you propose that would enhance valued, person-referenced outcomes of persons receiving mental health services? Which stakeholders (see Table 10.1) will you need to work with closely to ensure the successful implementation of these quality-enhancement techniques?

4. Characterize the emerging paradigm shift in government and management and discuss its potential impact on outcome-based evaluation.

5. Summarize the purpose, process, and intended outcomes of a quality-assurance program. Outline the specific steps and procedures that would be involved if you were to establish a shared quality-assurance process (see Figure 11.2).

Additional References

American Society for Quality Control (1992). *Malcom Baldrige 1993 award criteria*. Milwaukee, WI: ASQC Quality Press.

Deming, W. E. (1986). *Out of crisis*. Cambridge, MA: Center for Advanced Engineering Study, MIT.

Ford, D. H., & Lerner, R. M. (1992). *Developmental systems theory: An integrative approach*. Newbury Park, CA: Sage.

Howes, N. J. R., & Quinn, R. E. (1978). Implementing change: From research to prescriptive framework. *Group and Organizational Studies, 3*(1), 71–84.

Mathison, S. (1991). What do we know about internal evaluation? *Evaluation and Program Planning, 14*, 159–165.

Nagel, S. S. (1990). Bridging theory and practice in policy/program evaluation. *Evaluation and Program Planning, 13*, 275–283.

V

The Future

> *Even if you are on the right track, you*
> *will get run over if you just stand there.*
> WILL ROGERS

Well, we are about there—entering the future and completing our discussion of outcome-based evaluation. Throughout our odyssey, I have attempted to relate current and future program-evaluation needs with a practical approach to outcome-based evaluation based on valued, person-referenced outcomes. In this text, I have talked considerably about the importance of evaluation producers asking two fundamental questions: "For what purpose will I use the outcome-based evaluation data (effectiveness, impact or benefit–cost analysis)?" "What data will I need for the intended use?"

I really like the above quotation by Will Rogers, because it reflects the fact that outcome-based evaluation is a continuous process. OBE producers and consumers must be willing to meet the demands of present and future trends that will continue to impact education and social programs. As discussed in Chapter 1, the six major trends include:

- Quality revolution
- Consumer empowerment
- Accountability defined by outcomes
- Supports paradigm
- Pragmatic evaluation paradigm
- Emphasis on enhanced functioning

The Spanish philosopher Gasset is purported to have once observed that "human life is a constant preoccupation with the future." And it is to that future that we now turn. In the next chapter, I will focus on the evaluation needs of future educational and social programs, discussing six critical trends that will have a continuing profound impact on both evaluation producers and consumers. In Chapter 13, I present the final list of the book—the 20 guiding principles that I hope you will not forget, and will use in our future odyssey into the world of outcome-based evaluation.

12

Factors Influencing the Future of Outcome-Based Evaluation

Overview

The future is now. The trends that we discussed in Chapter 1, including the quality revolution, consumer empowerment, accountability defined on the basis of outcomes, the support paradigm, and the pragmatic evaluation paradigm, will continue to challenge educational and social programs, and those of us involved in outcome-based evaluation. A final truism: Education and social programs in the future will be fundamentally different than they are now. The parameters of what they will look like are summarized well in the following principles described by Osborne and Gaebler (1993), around which entrepreneurial public organizations are being built:

- Steer more than row.
- Empower communities rather than simply deliver services.

- Encourage competition rather than monopoly.
- Be driven by a mission, not rules.
- Fund outcomes rather than inputs.
- Meet the needs of the customer, not the bureaucracy.
- Concentrate on earning, not just spending.
- Invest in prevention rather than cure.
- Decentralize authority.
- Solve problems by leveraging the marketplace, rather than simply creating public programs.

These are powerful principles that many of us already see influencing education and social programs. I am convinced that they will result in profound changes in service provision, funding streams and patterns, and the locus of decision making. Obviously, they will also have a profound impact on outcome-based evaluation.

Additionally, my crystal ball forecasts other trends that will have profound impact on program evaluation. Six of these trends represent the content of this chapter. They include noncategorical approach to services and supports, accountability defined on the basis of outcomes, multiple evaluation designs, service-provider networks, consumer-oriented evaluation, and linking program evaluation and forecasting.

Noncategorical Approach to Services and Supports

Throughout the text we have discussed a number of trends that are moving social programs to a noncategorical approach to services and supports. Chief among these include:

- Emphasis in public laws on functional behavior and the major life-activity areas.
- Movement within these public laws to a functional definition of disability.
- Movement away from a focus on pathology to a focus on functional limitations.
- Consumer empowerment and inclusion.
- Supports paradigms, as reflected in supported living, employment, and education.

These trends will lessen the historical pattern of diagnostically based services, moving education and social programs quickly to a different service-delivery model: noncategorically based services and supports. This shift will have at least three significant impacts on outcome-based evaluation and analyses. First, there will continue to be an increased focus on valued, person-referenced outcomes reflecting changes in adaptive behavior and role status. Second, consumer-oriented evaluation will be paramount and characterized by less intrusiveness of interventions, increased focus on effectiveness analysis, and increased use of person as own comparison and pre–postevaluation designs. And third, we will continue to reconceptualize the relationship between the independent and dependent variables in OBE analyses. Historically, in most evaluation studies, the independent variable has been personal characteristics (e.g., IQ, adaptive behavior, mental age), with learning rates, programmatic success or failure, or community adjustment the dependent variable(s). In the future, the independent variable will be support and environmental variables, and the dependent variable will be changes in the person's adaptive behavior and role status.

Accountability Defined on the Basis of Outcomes

Over the next decade, we will continue to live in an era of accountability in which questions of equity, efficiency, and effectiveness will continue to influence the provision and evaluation of education and social programs. The continuing need to define accountability on the basis of outcomes will have at least three profound effects on outcome-based evaluation.

First, there will be an increased emphasis on—and need for—impact and benefit–cost analyses. This will challenge the field in light of consumer-oriented evaluation and the costs involved in impact and benefit–cost analyses. At the least, there will need to be heightened collaboration among programs, funding agencies, and research facilities.

Second, there will be an increased need to use OBE data for the formative feedback purposes discussed in Chapter 11 (see Figure 11.1). Chief among these include data-based decision making, shared quality assurance (see Figure 11.2), and program or systems change.

Third, all stakeholders will need to be included in the planning, implementation, and use of outcome-based analyses. In this way, internal evaluation based on valued, person-referenced outcomes becomes an integral part of the ongoing service-delivery system and its evaluation. Only then will outcome-based evaluation reach its true place in the evaluation and analysis of educational and social programs.

Multiple-Evaluation Designs

In the future, we will see new developments in OBE evaluation designs and analyses. A future reality is that singular approaches to evaluation and analysis will not answer all the questions asked by the various stakeholders, and we will need to be sensitive to the fact that different evaluation designs and OBE analyses are well suited for programs at different levels of evaluation capability and the analyst's theoretical and practical orientation and training. There is value both in multiple ways of knowing (Tharp, 1981), and in using multiple designs and analyses that allow for the integration of values, practices, policies, and science (Meyer & Evans, 1993).

In reference to outcome-based evaluation, there are a number of implications resulting from the emphasis on multiple-evaluation designs. First, we will continue to develop methodologies that are consistent with the pragmatic paradigm discussed in Chapter 1. As you will remember, in the pragmatic paradigm an intervention or program is designed to address a significant social problem in a manner that is feasible, effective, and efficient. Quantification is used to develop performance indicators of the program's functioning, and the system is monitored in terms of both baselines and changes due to identified interventions (Fishman, 1991). This movement will undoubtedly increase the types of evaluation designs that are deemed appropriate to use in outcome-based evaluation.

Second, it will be acceptable for different programs to use different outcome-based analyses. For all programs, effectiveness analysis should be a given; for others, impact analysis will be feasible; and for still others (obviously a smaller number), benefit–cost analysis will be possible. There are two points to keep in mind here. First is the need for collaboration among agencies, funding bodies, and research centers; second, one type of analysis is neither better nor worse than another. As stated so well by Meyer and Evans (1993):

> Respectable social scientists have long regarded various kinds of knowledge production as valid, and short-sighted allegiance to one or another methodology is not supported by the history of science. (p. 229)

And third, there will be continued development and use of multivariate research methods driven by hypothesis testing. These methods are particularly valuable, because they allow one to probe more deeply and realistically into the phenomena they investigate (Ittenbach, Chayer, Bruinicks, Thurlow, & Beirne-Smith, 1993). Also, they are particularly valuable in human services, wherein person-referenced outcomes have multiple origins (see Figure 8.2). And finally, they also allow one to evaluate empirically the influence of a number of contextual variables that significantly affect program outcomes.

Service-Provider Networks

Heterogeneity will continue to be alive and well in the future! This will not just be true of the consumers of service, but of those providing services as well. In thinking about service-provider networks, Osborne and Gaebler (1993) provide a useful categorization of how the public, private, and "third" sectors can fulfill the demand for quality services. For example, the public sector is probably best able to provide stability, handle issues outside the central mission (e.g., affirmative action and immunity to favoritism). The private sector, on the other hand, is probably best able to respond rapidly to changing circumstances, innovate, replicate success, abandon the obsolete or failed, take risks, generate capital, provide professional expertise, and capture economies of scale. The "third" sector, composed of religious organizations, community groups, self-help groups, and support groups, is best able to reach diverse populations, show compassion and commitment, provide a holistic approach to services, and generate trust.

These networks will definitely respond well to the issues of consumer empowerment, but how might they affect outcome-based evaluation? Probably in a number of the following ways:

1. Accountability will continue to be defined in terms of person-referenced outcomes.
2. There will be an increased need for impact and benefit–cost analyses.
3. Evaluation designs will involve more matched pairs and hypothetical control groups rather than experimental/control designs.

To overcome some of the management and evaluation problems generated by the service-provider networks, I hope there will be increasing linkages among service providers. The core catalyst for the emergence of linkages may well be the emphasis on functionality. The impact of this shift to functionality will result in the demise of diagnostically based services and the emergence of an emphasis on adaptive behavior and role status, reflected in generic services for people with special needs. Hence, all programs will begin to focus on the same things—people's living, educational and employment status, and health and wellness indicators. When this happens, it is only a matter of time until programs begin to work together in fulfilling the service and support needs of individuals. I am already beginning to see this in my own community, where personnel from various educational and social programs are working together to provide supported employment and living programs for individuals with generic needs. A number of years ago, I wrote an article (Schalock, 1984) entitled "Comprehensive Community Services: A plea for Interagency Collaboration," in which I talked about the need for a common language that would facilitate interagency cooperation and linkages. Well, I think that we now have that common language. It is composed of three basic concepts: (1) functional behavior and role status, (2) quality of life, and (3) supports. The relationship among these three concepts is shown graphically in Figure 12.1, which depicts a service array based on intensity of support, quality-of-life enhancement techniques, and person-referenced adaptive behavior and role-status changes.

The impact of this movement toward service-provider networks and functionality will also have direct influences on outcome-based evaluation. Chief among these influences are the following:

Intensity of support		Quality of life area	
Pervasive	HOME AND COMMUNITY LIVING 24-hour home care 24-hour supervision Respite care	EMPLOYMENT High-intensity supervision Prothesthetics Job accomodation	HEALTH AND WELLNESS Nutrition provided Health care availability Health care assistance Attendant care
Extensive	Homemaker services Overnight assistance/supervision Personal care assistance	Long-term assistance/ support Transportation Supervision Prothesthetics Job accomodation	Nutrition provided Meals on Wheels Home health
Limited	Community living training In-home assistance Shopping Transportation Behavioral support	Job training Job accomodation Transportation	Nutrition training and assistance Medical alert devices Recreation and leisure training and opportunities Safety training
Intermittent	Banking/financial affairs Counseling/crisis management Transitioning Legal affairs	Advocating Job counseling Transitioning Troubleshooting	Medical appointments Wellness counseling Nutrition awareness
Outcomes	Activities of daily living Intrumental activities of daily living Community integration indicators Citizenship indicators	Wages Hours worked Benefits Level of integration Job duration	Wellness indicators Physical fitness indicators Activity indicators

Figure 12.1 Service array based on intensity of support and quality-of-life outcomes.

- The need to focus on objective, measurable data sets that meet the criteria of being objective, measurable, person-referenced, logically connected to the program, and evaluated longitudinally.
- Increased accountability, defined as placement into living, educational, and employment environments that are more normalized and consistent with the society's mainstream.
- Increased emphasis on effectiveness analysis, because the various components of the network will want to determine if their goals and objectives are being met.

Consumer-Oriented Evaluation

One of the most challenging factors, which is emerging quickly, is the movement toward "consumer-oriented research," "participatory action research," and "empowerment evaluation" (Fetterman, 1994). This consumer-led movement is reflective of the paradigm shift toward consumers, empowerment, equity, and inclusion. And it is more than just consumer-oriented: it is consumer-based and focused on others helping themselves. It is designed to foster self-determination, rather than dependency. This movement will have a profound impact on the research and program-evaluation communities, because recommended approaches to research and evaluation include focus groups, in-depth interviewing, and consumer-driven quality-of-life indices.

The movement is already having a profound impact on program evaluation, including (1) a focus on both qualitative and quantitative methodologies; and (2) an emphasis on valued, person-referenced outcomes that are agreed upon by consumers, measured through interviews or surveys, and descriptive of a person's status in the areas of home and community living, school–work, and health and wellness (Oliver, 1992; Schalock, Stark, Snell, Coulter, & Polloway, 1994; and Stallard, Hudson, & Davis, 1992).

The need for consumer-oriented evaluation is also being advocated by high-profile groups such as infants, young children, families (Allen, 1987), and the homeless (Mercier, Fournier, & Peladeau, 1992). These groups, among others, are asking effectiveness and equity questions and represent stakeholders who are demanding and requiring new and expanded programs. For this reason, consumer-oriented evaluation is sometimes referred to as participatory action research (PAR). The impact on outcome-based evaluation is obvious: *Feasibility studies, policy evaluations*, and *systems change* will be common terms in the future, along with *quality evaluations* (Schwandt, 1990).

Linking Program Evaluation and Forecasting

Forecasting is not yet one of the more common uses of outcome-based evaluation, but it probably will be in the future. As discussed by Chelimsky (1987), forecasting seeks to make policy makers aware of emerging future problems, and allows them enough lead time to develop policies and programs to address these problems.

Both formal and informal forecasting exists, but not as a part of the program-evaluation literature. Makridakris et al. (1984), for example, cited four methods for obtaining forecasts: (1) purely judgmental and intuitive methods; (2) causal or explanatory methods, such as regression or econometric methods; (3) times series (extrapolative methods); and (4) a combination of all these methods.

One of the advantages of doing the type of longitudinal follow-up studies suggested in this book is that they allow one to make predictions (hence, forecasts). For example, in a recent 15-year follow-up study (Schalock & Genung, 1993), we found that about 30% of the individuals with mental retardation placed into independent living and competitive-employment programs 15 years ago had returned to the service-delivery program, with the concurrent need to plan for long-term services for this population. Similarly, a recent 5-year longitudinal placement study (Schalock et al., in press) of persons with mental illness found that over that period of time, 37% of the persons had returned to the mental health facility one or more times. And finally, a recent study (Schalock et al., 1992) of graduates from a special education program found that 67% of graduates were still living with their parents and 18% were still unemployed 5 years after graduation.

Program-need forecasting has always been a part of doing a "needs assessment." And that activity will undoubtedly remain a part of program-development activities. What I am proposing is that one think about forecasting as a result of outcome-based longitudinal evaluation studies, in which a person's role status is used to project future program needs, as well as to make program and systems change.

Summary

In summary, these six factors—noncategorical approach to services and supports, accountability defined on the basis of outcomes, multiple-evaluation designs, service-provider networks, consumer-oriented evaluation, and linkage of program evaluation and forecasting—will undoubtedly set the agenda for our future work in outcome-based evaluation. They might even determine the chapter headings for a subsequent book on outcome-based evaluation! But regardless of the role that they play, they underscore the importance of both evaluation producers and consumers remaining competent in outcome-based evaluation by knowing the territory and anticipating the future.

Conclusion

In conclusion, the role that evaluation plays in program development and policy analysis has progressed significantly since the early 1960s. Despite this progress, the future promises a number of challenges. As stated recently by Shadish, Cook, and Leviton (1992):

> We are worried about program evaluation. From the start, debates about method choices dominated the field, so much so that it is often seen as applied social science methodology. Such debates proliferate with little sense of important theoretical issues implicit in them, especially of those issues that are unique to program evaluation and help define the field. Key questions are not isolated, with little emerging synthesis, nor even a common vocabulary to use in debate. It should be no surprise, then, that program evaluation is in low academic repute, for the theoretical basis of the field seems in disarray. (p. 329)

Two major trends are emerging in the program-evaluation field that have the promise of "moving the field along" toward a more coherent approach, better use, and greater acceptability. First is the trend of moving away from a "goal-fixed" approach to a "multigoal, theory driven" approach to program evaluation. Whereas the "goal-fixed" approach typically focuses on identifying officially stated program goals, selecting a subset of measurable outcome measures, and assessing whether the program achieves the narrowly defined effects implied in the outcome measures, the "multigoal, theory driven" approach evaluates both the status of goal attainment and the effects of the program on multiple goals based on a theoretical understanding of the problem (Chen & Rossi, 1989). The second trend is to rethink program evaluation theory and to expand it to include components dealing with practice, knowledge, value, use, and social programming. As stated by Shadish et al., (1991):

> The fundamental purpose of program evaluation is to specify feasible practices that evaluators can use to construct knowledge of the value of social programs that can be used to ameliorate the social problems to which programs are relevant. (p. 36)

The approach to outcome-based evaluation presented in this text is both consistent with—and supportive of—these two trends. By focusing on valued, person-referenced outcomes within the context of quality of life, functional limitations, and noncategorical service delivery, the suggested OBE approach is value based and amelioration oriented. By employing either effectiveness, impact, or benefit–cost analyses, the approach is multifaceted and helps programs be both accountable and better able to answer policy and funding issues related to equity and efficiency. By focusing on formative feedback and internal program evaluation, the suggested approach to outcome-based evaluation addressed issues of knowledge and practice. By focusing on reporting and using outcome-based evaluation analyses, the approach addresses concerns about use and social programming.

Hopefully, this text on outcome-based evaluation will help the field of program evaluation progress to its next evolutionary stage: To provide practitioners, policymakers, funding agencies, and other critical stakeholders with the attitudes, skills, and knowledge that are required to conduct their own program evaluations, and thereby meet the true definition of an efficient program: one that uses one or more types of outcome-based evaluation analysis to increase its effectiveness and impact on the social problems that gave rise to its birth. If that is the case, the effort has been well worth it.

Study Questions

Note: Each of the following questions requires a literature search, preferably of post-1993 publications. Ideally, you will search relevant literature in your programmatic area to answer each question.

1. What evidence do you find for using a noncategorical approach to services and supports?

2. What evidence do you find for using multivariate designs to answer program evaluation/analysis questions?

3. What evidence do you find that provider networks are increasing? Is there any evidence of their effectiveness?

4. What evidence do you find regarding consumer-oriented evaluation? If found, what types of questions and outcome-based analysis designs are being employed?

5. What evidence do you find of attempts to link program evaluation to forecasting? If found, what are the major forecast areas?

Additional Readings

Alkin, M. C. (1990). *Debates on evaluation*. Newbury Park, CA: Sage.
Bickman, L. (1987). The functions of program theory. In L. Bickman (Ed.), *Using program theory in evaluation* (pp. 5–18). San Francisco: Jossey-Bass.

Brizius, J. A., & Campbell, M. D. (1991). *Getting results: A guide for government accountability.* Washington, DC: Council of Governor's Policy Advisors.

Mathison, S. (1994). Rethinking the evaluator role: Partnerships between organizations and evaluators. *Evaluation and Program Planning, 17,* 299–304.

Muraskin, L. D. (1993). *Understanding evaluation: The way to better prevention programs.* Washington, DC: U.S. Department of Education.

13

Those Guiding Principles You Should Not Forget

Throughout the text, I have presented and discussed a number of fundamental rules that, if followed, will result in credible and communicative outcome-based evaluations that will be acted on. In this short chapter, I list them for you so that you will have easy access to those points about outcome-based evaluation that you should not forget. Each is listed along with a page reference, should you need to go back and refresh your memory about its importance and use.

1. The type of OBE analysis conducted must be consistent with the program's capability. (p. 40)
2. Effectiveness analysis is an absolute requirement in the 1990s. (p. 54)
3. Impact analysis involves comparing outcomes from two comparable conditions or groups. Statistically significant differences between these outcomes represents the program's impacts. (p. 72)
4. In benefit–cost analysis, the three most important analytical perspectives are social (society), participant, and the rest of society ("taxpayer"). (p. 80)
5. In benefit–cost analysis, the comprehensive framework should include all benefits and costs, regardless of whether they can be monetized (i.e., include both tangible and intangible benefits and costs). (p. 86)
6. Choose your data sets very carefully, because data collection is neither easy nor inexpensive. (p. 100)
7. The current trend is to consider generic groups with functional limitations, rather than individuals with specific diagnostic labels. (p. 103)
8. Be sure that the services provided are consistent with the program's mission and goals, and logically affect the program's outcome. (p. 106)
9. The type of cost data collected and the complexity of the cost

analysis is dependent upon the type of outcome-based evaluation analysis planned. (p. 112)

10. Person-referenced outcomes should be valued by the individual and related demonstratively to the services provided. (p. 115)

11. Outcome-based evaluation data should be collected in four areas: recipient characteristics, core-service functions, cost estimates, and valued, person-referenced outcomes. (p. 115)

12. A good OBE data-management system is based on collecting and organizing one's data in a 2 × 2 matrix: service recipients × core data sets. (p. 128)

13. Data should be collected by individuals who are trained in either standard assessment instruments, performance-based assessment techniques, and/or participant observation techniques. (p. 129)

14. OBE data collection should be organized around a simple matrix: service recipients by core data sets. (p. 130)

15. The computerization of management data should flow from data-collection format, to database management/data entry, to data manipulation and analysis. (p. 134)

16. The OBE evaluation design used depends upon the questions asked, the available data, and the type of comparison condition available. (p. 154)

17. The specific statistical test that one employs depends on (1) the level of measurement; (2) the number of persons and groups involved in the analysis; (3) the type of design that one is using; and (4) one's ability to meet the respective test's assumptions. (p. 158)

18. Don't confuse the four most common statistical analyses used in OBE: descriptive statistics, exploratory correlational analysis, group comparison, and multivariate analyses. (p. 165)

19. Be able to describe the program and its contextual variables in enough detail so that it can be replicated. (p. 174)

20. The major change indicators include consumer changes (adaptive behavior and role status) and organizational changes (resource allocation, alignment of staff-utilization patterns with agency mission, and core-service functions). (p. 210)

References

Accrediation Council (1994). *Outcome based performance standards*, Landover, MD: Author.

Albin, J. M. (1992). *Quality improvement in employment and other human services: Managing for quality through change*. Baltimore: Brookes.

Allen, D. A. (1987). Measuring rehabilitation outcomes for infants and young children: A family approach. In M.J. Fuhrer (Ed.), *Rehabilitation outcomes: Analysis and measurement* (pp. 185–195). Baltimore: Brookes.

Alonso, W., & Starr, P. (Eds.). (1987). *The politics of numbers*, NY: Russell Sage Foundation.

American Psychiatric Association (1994). *Diagnostic and statistical manual of mental disorders*, 4th Edition. Washington, DC: Author.

Baker, E. L., O'Neil, H. F., & Linn, R. L. (1993). Policy and validity prospects for performance-based assessment. *American Psychologist, 48*(12), 1210–1218.

Baker, F., & Curbow, B. (1991). The case-control study in health program evaluation. *Evaluation and Program Planning, 14*, 263–272.

Bekke, J. S. (1987). The model-guided method of program implementation. *Evaluation Review, 11*, 281–300.

Brown, A. C. (1993). Revitalizing "handicap" for disability research: Developing tools to assess progress in quality of life for persons with disabilities. *Journal of Disability Policy Studies, 4*(2), 57–76.

Calkins, C. F., Schalock, R. L., Griggs, P. A., Kiernan, W. E., & Gibson, C. A. (1990). Program planning. In C. F. Calkins & H. M. Walker (Eds.), *Social competence for workers with developmental disabilities: A guide to enhancing employment outcomes in integrated settings* (pp. 51–64). Baltimore: Brookes.

Campbell, J. A. (1992). Single-subject designs for treatment planning and evaluation. *Administration and Policy in Mental Health, 19*(5), 335–343.

Campbell, D. T., & Stanley, J. C. (1963). *Experimental and quasi-experimental designs for research*. Chicago, IL: Rand McNally.

Commission for the Accreditation of Rehabilitation Facilities (1995). *Standards for employment and community support services*. Tucson, AZ: Author.

Carnevale, T., & Schultz, R. (1990). Best practices: What works in training and development. *Training and Development Journal, 27*(7) (Supplemental), pp. 1–75.

Chambers, F. (1994). Removing confusion about formative and summative evaluation: Purpose versus time. *Evaluation and Program Planning, 17*, 9–12.

Chelimsky, E. (1987). Retrospective and prospective analysis: Linking program evaluation and forecasting. *Evaluation Review, 11*(3) 355–370.

Chen, H., & Rossi, P. H. (1983). Evaluating with sense: The theory-driven approach. *Evaluation Review, 7*, 283–302.

Chen, H., & Rossi, P. H. (1987). The theory-driven approach to validity. *Evaluation and Program Planning, 10*, 95–103.

Chen, H., & Rossi, P. H. (1989). Issues in the theory-driven perspectives. *Evaluation and Program Planning, 12,* 299–306.

Clark, A., & Friedman, M. J. (1993). Nine standardized scales for evaluating treatment outcomes in a mental health clinic. *Journal of Clinical Psychology, 39*(6), 939–950.

Clifford, D. L. & Sherman, P. (1983). Internal evaluation: Integrating program evaluation and management. In A. J. Love (Ed.), *Developing effective internal evaluation: New directions for program evaluation* (pp. 20–34). San Francisco: Jossey-Bass.

Conley, R. W., & Noble, J. H. (1990). Benefit–cost analysis of supported employment. In F. Rusch (Ed.), *Supported employment: models, methods, and issues* (pp. 271–288). Sycamore, IL: Sycamore.

Cook, T. D., & Campbell, D. T. (1979). *Quasi-experimentation: Design and analysis issues for field settings.* Chicago, IL: Rand McNally.

Coulter, D. L. (1991). The failure of prevention. *Mental Retardation, 29,* 3–4.

Cousins, J. B., & Leithwood, K. A. (1986). Current empirical research on evaluation utilization. *Review of Educational Research, 56,* 331–364.

Crimmins, D. B. (1994). Quality of life for persons with challenging behaviors: Intervention goal, contradiction in terms or both? In D. Goode (Ed.), *Quality of life for persons with disabilities* (pp. 208–217). Boston: Brookline.

Criscione, T., Kastner, T. A., O'Brien, D., & Nathanson, R. (1994). Replication of a managed health care initiative for people with mental retardation living in the community. *Mental Retardation, 32*(1), 43–52.

Cronbach, L. J. (1963). Course improvement through evaluation. *Teachers College Record, 64,* 672–683.

Cronbach, L. J. (1982). *Designing evaluations of education and social programs.* San Francisco: Jossey-Bass.

Cronbach, L. J., & Suppes, P. (Eds.). (1969). *Research for tomorrow's schools: Discipline inquiry of education.* New York: Macmillan.

Dennis, M. L., Fetterman, D. M., & Sechrest, L. (1994). Qualitative and quantitative evaluation methods in substance abuse research. *Evaluation and Program Planning, 17,* 419–427.

Drucker, P. (1988). *Optimal performance* (video tape). Oakland, CA: Thinking Aloud Productions.

Eastwood, E. A., & Fisher, B. A. (1988). Skills acquisition among matched samples of institutionalized and community-based persons with mental retardation. *American Journal on Mental Retardation, 93*(1),75–83.

Edgerton, R. B. (1990). Quality of life from a longitudinal research perspective. In R. L. Schalock (Ed.), *Quality of life: Perspectives and issues* (pp. 149–160). Washington, DC: American Association on Mental Retardation.

Eisen, S. V., Grob, M. C., & Dill, D. L. (1991). Outcome measurement: Tapping the patient's perspective. In S. M. Mirin, J. M. Bassett, & M. C. Grob (Eds.), *Recent advances in outcome research* (pp. 150–164). Washington, DC: American Psychiatric Press.

Fairweather, G. W., & Davidson, W. S. (1986). *An introduction to community experimentation: Theory, methods, and practice.* New York: McGraw-Hill.

Fetterman, D. M. (1994). Steps of empowerment evaluation: From California to Cape Town. *Program Planning and Evaluation, 17*(3), 305–313.

Filipczak, B. (1993). Training budgets boom. *Training Magazine, 30*(10), 37–47.

Finney, J. W., & Moos, R. H. (1989). Theory and method in treatment evaluation. *Evaluation and Program Planning, 12,* 307–316.

Fishman, D. B. (1991). An introduction to the experimental versus the pragmatic paradigm in evaluation. *Evaluation and Program Planning, 14,* 353–363.

Fishman, D. B. (1992). Postmodernism comes to program evaluation. *Evaluation and Program Planning, 15*, 263–270.

Fitz, D. (1989). Attrition and augmentation biases in time series analysis: Evaluation of clinical programs. *Evaluation and Program Planning, 12*, 259–270.

Forer, S. (1987). Outcome analysis for program service management. In M. J. Fuhrer (Ed.), *Rehabilitation outcomes: Analysis and measurement* (pp. 115–136). Baltimore: Brookes.

Freedland, K. E., & Carey, R. M. (1992). Data management and accountability in behavioral and biomedical research. *American Psychologist, 47*(5), 640–645.

French, M. T., Bradley, C. J., Calingaert, B., Dennis, M. L., & Karuntzos, G. T. (1994). Cost analysis of training and employment services in methadone treatment. *Evaluation and Program Planning, 17*, 107–120.

Greene, J. C. (1988). Communication of results and utilization in participatory program evaluation. *Evaluation and Program Planning, 11*, 341–351.

Guba, E. S., & Lincoln, Y. S. (1989). *Fourth generation evaluation.* Newbury Park, CA: Sage.

Hagner, D. C., & Murphy, S. T. (1989, July/August/September). Closing the shop on sheltered work: Case studies of organizational change. *Journal of Rehabilitation*, 68–78.

Hammer, M., & Champy, J. (1993). *Reengineering the corporation: A manifesto for business revolution.* New York: HarperCollins.

Hegarty, T. W., & Sporn, D. L. (1988). Effective engagement of decision makers in program evaluation. *Evaluation and Program Planning, 11*, 335–339.

Heilman, J. G. (Ed.). (1991). *Evaluation and privatization: Cases in waste management: New Directions in Program Evaluation.* San Francisco: Jossey-Bass.

Hendricks, M., & Handley, E. A. (1990). Improving the recommendations from evaluation studies. *Evaluation and Program Planning, 13*, 109–117.

Hersen, M., & Barlow, D. H. (1984). *Single-case experimental designs.* New York: Pergamon.

Himmel, P. B. (1984). Functional assessment strategies in clinical medicine: The care of arthritic patients. In C. V. Granger & C. E. Gresham (Eds.), *Functional assessment in rehabilitative medicine* (pp. 343–363). Baltimore: Williams & Wilkins.

Howes, N. J. R., & Quinn, R. E. (1978). Implementing change: From research to a prescriptive framework. *Group and Organizational Studies 3*(1), 71–84.

Institute of Medicine (1991). *Disability in America: Toward a national agenda for prevention.* Washington, DC: National Academy Press.

Ittenbach, R. F., Chayer, D. E., Bruininks, R. H., Thurlow, M. L., & Beirne-Smith, M. (1993). Adjustment of young adults with mental retardation in community settings: Comparison of parametric and nonparametric statistical techniques. *American Journal on Mental Retardation, 97*(6), 607–615.

Jenkins, R. (1990). Towards a system of outcome indicators for mental health care. *British Journal of Psychiatry, 157*, 500–514.

Johnston, M. V. (1987). Cost–benefit methodologies in rehabilitation. In M. J. Fuhrer (Ed.), *Rehabilitation outcomes: Analysis and measurement* (pp. 99–113). Baltimore: Brookes.

Kazdin, A. E. (1993). Psychotherapy for children and adolescents: Current progress and future research directions. *American Psychologist, 48*(6), 644–657.

Kazdin, A. E., & Tuma, A. H. (Eds.). (1982). *Single case research designs.* San Francisco: Jossey-Bass.

Keller, M. (1989). *Rude awakening: The rise, fall and struggle for recovery of General Motors.* New York: Harper Perennial.

Kerachsky, S., Thornton, C., Bloomenthal, A., Maynard, R., & Stephens, S. (1985). *Impacts of transitional employment for mentally retarded young adults: Results of the STETS demonstration.* Princeton, NJ: Mathematica Policy Research.

Kirchner, C. (1993). Disability statistics: The politics and science of counting. *Journal of Disability Policy Studies*, 4(2), 1–7.

Kiresuk, T. J., & Lund, S. H. (1978). Goal attainment scaling. In C.C. Attkisson, W.A. Hargreaves, & M. J. Horowitz (Eds.), *Evaluation of human services programs* (pp. 341–369). New York: Academic Press.

Kirkpatrick, D. L. (1967). Evaluation of training. In R. L. Craig and L. R. Bittel (Eds.), *Training and development handbook* (pp. 135–160). New York: McGraw-Hill.

Lewis, D. R., Bruininks, R. H., & Thurlow, M. L. (1991). Efficiency considerations in delivering special education to persons with severe mental retardation. *Mental Retardation*, 29(3), 129–137.

Lewis, D. R., Johnson, D. R., Bruininks, R. H., Kallsen, L. A., & Guilley, R. P. (1992). Is supported employment cost-effective in Minnesota? *Journal of Disability Policy Studies*, 3(1), 67–92.

Lombardo, C. A. (1989). Do the benefits of training justify the costs? *Training and Development Journal*, 43(12), 60–64.

Luckasson, R., Coulter, D. L., Polloway, E. A., Reiss, S., Schalock, R. L., Snell, M. E., Spitalnick, D. M., & Stark, J. A. (1992). *Mental retardation: Definition, classification and systems of support*. Washington, DC: American Association on Mental Retardation.

Lynn, G., & Lynn, J. B. (1984, November). Seven keys to successful change management. *Supervisory Management*, pp. 30–37.

Makridakis, S., Andersen, A., Carbone, R., Fildes, R., Hibon, M., Lewandowski, R., Newton, J., Parzen, E., & Winkler, R. (1984). *The forecasting accuracy of major time series methods*. New York: Wiley.

Maltz, M. D. (1994). Deviating from the mean: The declining significance of significance. *Journal of Research in Crime and Delinquency*, 31(4), 434–463.

Mangano, M. F. (1992). A marketing approach to evaluation. Four lessons for evaluations from the Honda Motor Company. *Evaluation and Program Planning*, 15, 233–237.

Marks, J., Sonoda, B., & Schalock, R. (1968). Reinforcement vs. relationship therapy for schizophrenics. *Journal of Abnormal Psychology*, 73(4), 397–402.

Mathison, S. (1992). An evaluation model for inservice teacher education. *Evaluation and Program Planning*, 15, 255–261.

McDonald, R. M. (1991). Assessment of organizational context: A missing component in evaluations of training programs. *Evaluation and Program Planning*, 14, 273–279.

McKillip, J., Moirs, K., & Cervenka, C. L. (1992). Asking open-ended consumer questions to aid program planning. *Evaluation and Program Planning*, 15, 1–6.

Mercier, C., Fournier, L., & Peladeau, N. (1992). Program evaluation of services for the homeless: Challenges and strategies. *Evaluation and Program Planning*, 15, 417–426.

Meyer, L. H., & Evans, I. M. (1993). Science and practice in behavioral intervention: Meaningful outcomes, research validity, and usable knowledge. *Journal of the Association for Persons with Severe Handicaps*, 18(4), 224–234.

Morell, J. A. (1979). *Program evaluation in social research*. New York: Pergamon.

Moskowitz, J. M. (1993). Why reports of outcome evaluations are often biased or uninterpretable. *Evaluation and Program Planning*, 16, 1–9.

Mowbray, C. T., Cohen, E., & Bybee, D. (1993). The challenge of outcome evaluation in homeless services: Engagement as an intermediate outcome measure. *Evaluation and Program Planning*, 16, 333–346.

Newman, F. L., Hunter, R. H., & Irving, D. (1987). Simple measures of progress and outcome in the evaluation of mental health services. *Evaluation and Program Planning*, 10, 209–218.

Nisbet, J., & Hagner, D. (1988). Natural supports in the workplace: A reexamination of supportive employment. *Journal of the Association of Persons with Severe Handicaps, 13,* 260–267.

Noble, J. H. & Conley, R. (1987). Accumulating evidence on the benefits and costs of supported and transitional employment for persons with severe disabilities. *Journal of the Association for Persons with Severe Handicaps, 12*(3), 163–174.

Oliver, M. (1992). Changing the social relations of research production? *Disability, handicap and society, 7,* 101–114.

Osborne, D., & Gaebler, T. (1993). *Reinventing government: How the entrepreneurial spirit is transforming the public sector.* New York: Penguin.

Parent, W. S., Hill, M. L., & Wehman, P. (1989, October/November/ December). From sheltered to supported employment outcomes: Challenges for rehabilitation facilities. *Journal of Rehabilitation,* pp. 51–65.

Patton, M. Q. (1986). *Utilization-focused evaluation* (2nd ed.). Beverly Hills: Sage.

Perry, R. D., Hoff, B. H., & Gaither, D. S. (1994). The process study component of mental health evaluation. *Evaluation and Program Planning, 17,* 43–46.

Posavac, E., & Carey, R. (1980). *Program evaluation: Methods and case studies.* Englewood Cliffs, NJ: Prentice-Hall.

Ramey, C. T., & Landesman-Ramey, S. (1992). Effective early intervention. *Mental retardation, 30*(6), 337–345.

Rapp, C. A., Gowdy, E., Sullivan, W. P., & Winterstein, R. (1988). Client outcome reporting: The status method. *Community Mental Health Journal, 24*(2), 118–133.

Reichardt, C. S. & Rallis, S. F. (Eds.). (1994). *The qualitative-quantitative debate.* San Francisco: Jossey-Bass.

Rintala, D. H. (1987). Design and statistical considerations in rehabilitation outcomes analysis. In M. J. Fuhrer (Ed.), *Rehabilitation outcomes: Analysis and measurement* (pp. 87–97). Baltimore: Brookes.

Roberts, R. N., Wasik, B. H., Casto, S., & Ramey, C. T. (1991). Family support in the home: Programs, policy and social change. *American Psychologist, 46,* 131–137.

Rocheleau, B. (1993). Evaluating public sector information systems. *Evaluation and Program Planning, 16,* 119–129.

Rossi, P. H., & Freeman, H. E. (1985). *Evaluation: A systematic approach* (3rd ed.). Beverly Hills: Sage.

Rossi, P. H., & Freeman, H. E. (1989). *Evaluation: A systematic approach, 4th edition.* Newbury Park, CA: Sage.

Rusch, F. R. (1990). *Supported employment: Models, methods, and issues.* Sycamore, IL: Sycamore.

Rusch, F. R., Conley, R. W., & McCaughlin, W. B. (1993, April/May/June). Benefit–cost analysis of supported employment programs in Illinois. *Journal of Rehabilitation,* pp. 31–36.

Russell, D. W., & Buckwalter, K. C. (1992). Researching and evaluating model geriatric mental health programs Part III: Statistical analysis issues. *Archives of Psychiatric Nursing, 6*(3),151–162.

Schalock, M., Alberto, P., Fredericks, B., & Dalke, B. (1994). The house that TRACES built: A conceptual model of service delivery systems and implications for change. *Journal of Special Education, 28*(2), 203–223.

Schalock, R. L. (1984). Comprehensive community services: A plea for inter-agency collaboration. In R. H. Bruininks & K. C. Lakin (Eds.), *Living and learning in the least restrictive environment* (pp. 37–63). Baltimore: Brookes.

Schalock, R. L. (1986). Service delivery coordination. In F. R. Rusch (Ed.), *Competitive employment issues and strategies* (pp. 115–127). Baltimore: Brookes.

Schalock, R. L. (Ed.). (1990). *Quality of life: Perspectives and issues*. Washington, DC: American Association on Mental Retardation.

Schalock, R. L. (1994). Quality of life, quality enhancement and quality assurance: Implications for program planning and evaluation in the field of mental retardation and developmental disabilities. *Evaluation and Progam Planning, 17*(2), 121–131.

Schalock, R. L. (1995). The assessment of natural supports in community rehabilitation services. In D. C. Karan & S. Greenspan (Eds.), *Community rehabilitation services for people with disabilties* (pp. 184–203). Newton, MA: Butterworth-Heinemann.

Schalock, R. L., Gadwood, L. S., & Perry, P. B. (1984). Effects of different training environments on the acquisition of community living skills. *Applied Research in Mental Retardation, 5,* 425–438.

Schalock, R. L., & Genung, L. T. (1993). Placement from a cummunity-based mental retardation program: A 15-year follow-up. *American Journal on Mental Retardation, 98*(3), 400–407.

Schalock, R. L., & Harper, R. S. (1978). Placement from community-based mental retardation programs: How well do clients do? *American Journal of Mental Deficiency, 83*(2), 240–247.

Schalock, R. L., & Harper, R. S. (1982). Skill acquisition and client movement indices: Implementing cost-effective analysis in rehabilitation programs. *Evaluation and Program Planning, 5,* 223–231.

Schalock, R. L., Harper, R. S., & Carver, S. (1981a). Independent living placement: Five years later. *American Journal of Mental Deficiency, 86*(2), 170–177.

Schalock, R. L., Harper, R. S., & Genung, T. (1981b). Community integration of mentally retarded adults: Community placement and program success. *American Journal of Mental Deficiency, 85*(5), 478–488.

Schalock, R. L., Holl, C., Elliott, B., & Ross, I. (1992). A longitudinal follow-up of graduates from a rural special education program. *Learning Disability Quarterly, 15,* 29–38.

Schalock, R. L., & Keith, K. D. (1993). *The Quality of Life Questionnaire*. Worthington, Ohio: IDS.

Schalock, R. L., & Kiernan, W. E. (1990). *Habilitation planning for adults with disabilities*. New York: Springer-Verlag.

Schalock, R. L., Kiernan, W. E., McGaughey, M. J., Lynch, S. A., & McNally, L. C. (1993). State MR/DD agency information systems and available data related to day and employment programs. *Mental Retardation, 31*(1), 29–34.

Schalock, R. L., Lemanowicz, J. A., Conroy, J. W. & Feinstein, C. S. (1994a). A multivariate investigative study of the correlates of quality of life. *Journal on Developmental Disabilities, 3*(2), 59–73.

Schalock, R. L., & Lilley, M. A. (1986). Placement from community-based mental retardation programs: How well do clients do after 8–10 years? *American Journal of Mental Deficiency, 90*(6), 669–676.

Schalock, R. L., McGaughey, M. J., & Kiernan, W. E. (1989). Placement into nonsheltered employment: Findings from national employment surveys. *American Journal on Mental Retardation, 94*(1), 80–87.

Schalock, R. L., Stark, J. A., Snell, M. E., Coulter, D., & Polloway, E. (1994b). The changing conception of mental retardation: Implications for the field. *Mental Retardation, 32*(1), 25–39.

Schalock, R. L., & Thornton, C. (1988). *Program evaluation: A field guide for administrators*. New York: Plenum.

Schalock, R. L., Touchstone, F., Nelson, G., Weher, L., Sheehan, M., & Stull, C. (in press). A multivariate analysis of mental hospital recidivism. *Journal of Mental Health Administration*.

Schalock, R. L., Wolzen, B., Elliott, B., Werbel, G. & Peterson, K. (1986). Post-secondary community placement of handicapped students: A five-year follow-up. *Learning Disabilities Quarterly, 9,* 295–303.

Scheier, M. A. (1994). Designing and using process evaluation. In J. S. Wholey, H. P. Hatry, & K. E. Newcomber (Eds.), *Handbook of practical program evaluation* (pp. 40–68). San Francisco: Jossey-Bass.

Schein, E. H. (1990). Organizational culture. *American Psychologist, 45*(2), 109–119.

Schlenger, W. E., Roland, E. J., Kroutil, L. A., Dennis, M. L., Magruder, K. M., & Ray, B. A. (1994). Evaluating service demonstration programs: A multi-step approach. *Evaluation and Program Planning, 17,* 381–390.

Schwandt, T. A. (1990). Defining "quality" in evaluation. *Evaluation and Program Planning, 13,* 177–188.

Schwartz, D. B. (1992). *Crossing the river: Creating a conceptual revolution in community and disability.* Brookline, MA: Brookline.

Scriven, M. (1967). The methodology of evaluation. In R. W. Tyler, R. M. Gagne, & M.Scriven (Eds.), *Perspectives of curriculum evaluation* (pp. 39–83). Chicago: Rand McNally.

Scriven, M. (1972). The methodology of evaluation. In C. H. Weiss (Ed.), *Evaluating action programs: Readings in social action and education* (pp. 123–136). Boston: Allyn & Bacon.

Shadish, W. R., Jr., Cook, T. D., & Leviton, L. C. (1991). *Foundations of program evaluation: Theories of practice.* Newbury Park, CA: Sage.

Shadish, W. R., Jr., Cook, T. D., & Leviton, L. C. (1992). A response to Nick L. Smith and Eileen Schroeder: Thinking about theory in program evaluation—a five component approach. *Evaluation and Program Planning, 15,* 329–340.

Sherwood, C. D., Morris, J. N., & Sherwood, S. (1975). A multivariate, nonrandomized matching technique for studying the impact of social interventions. In E. L. Struning & M. Guttentag (Eds.), *Handbook of evaluation research* (Vol. 1, pp. 183–224). Beverly Hills, CA: Sage.

Snell, M. E. (Ed.). (1993). *Systematic instruction of students with severe disabilities,* 4th ed. New York: Macmillan.

Stainback, W., & Stainback, S. (1989). Using qualitative data collection procedures to investigate supported education issues. *Journal of the Association for Persons with Severe Handicaps, 14*(4), 271–277.

Stallard, P., Hudson, J., & Davis, B. (1992). Consumer evaluation in practice. *Journal of Community and Applied Psychology, 2,* 291–295.

Stake, R. E. (1978). The case study methods in social inquiry. *Educational Researcher, 7,* 5–8.

Stake, R. E. (1980). Program evaluation, particularly responsive evaluation. In W. B. Bockrell & D. Hamilton (Eds.), *Rethinking educational research* (pp. 72–87). London: Godden & Stoughton.

Stake, R. E. (1986). *Quieting reform: Social science and social action in an urban youth program.* Urbana, IL: University of Illinois Press.

Suchman, E. A. (1967). *Evaluative research: Principles and practice in public service and social action programs.* New York: Russell Sage Foundation.

Tharp, R. G. (1981). The metamethodology of research and development. *Educational Perspectives, 20,* 42–48.

Thornton, C. (1984). Benefit–cost analysis of social programs: The case of deinstitutionalization and education programs. In R. Bruininks (Ed.), *Living and learning in the least restrictive environment* (pp. 225–243). Baltimore: Brookes.

Thornton, C., & Maynard, R. (1989). The economics of transitional employment and supported employment. In M. Berkowitz & M. A. Hill (Eds.), *Disability and the labor market.* New York: ILR Press.

Toffler, A. (1990). *Powershift: Knowledge, wealth and violence at the edge of the 21st century.* New York: Bantam.

Van Gelder, M., Gold, M., & Schalock, R. L. (in press). Does training have an impact? The evaluation of a competency based staff training program in supported employment. *Journal of Rehabilitation Administration.*

Webster's Ninth New Collegiate Dictionary (1983). Springfield, MA: Merriam-Webster.

Wehman, P., & Moon, M. S. (1988). *Vocational rehabilitation and supported employment.* Baltimore: Brookes.

Weiss, C. H. (1972). *Evaluation research: Methods for assessing program effectiveness.* Englewood Cliffs, NJ: Prentice-Hall.

Weiss, C. H. (1987). Evaluating social programs: What have we learned? *Society, 25*(1), 40–45.

Wholey, J. S. (1981). Using evaluation to improve program performance. In R. A. Levine, M. A. Solomon, G. M. Hellstern, & H. Wolman (Eds.), *Evaluation research and practice: Comparative and international perspectives* (pp. 92–106). Beverly Hills: Sage.

Wholey, J. S. (1983). *Evaluation and effective public management.* Boston: Little, Brown.

Zola, I. K. (1993). Disability statistics: What we count and what it tells us. *Journal of Disability Policy Studies, 4*(2), 9–39.

Author Index

Subject Index